BIRDS OF THE SEA

150 Years of the
General Steam Navigation Company

by

Nick Robins

PREFACE

Why such a famous and fondly remembered company as GSN has never previously enjoyed a comprehensive documented history reflects the scarcity of the historical data that have survived. Spanning just short of 150 years, the company is remembered partly for the excursion ships it operated on the Thames and on day trips to France and Belgium and partly for the Continental and Mediterranean traders, the 'Navvies' as they were affectionately known, that were synonymous with the Home Trade for so long.

The story of the company includes numerous ups and downs, of constant modernisation and increased efficiency to see it through the depressed years of the late Victorian era and between the Great War and the Second World War. GSN also had a policy in its earlier years of buying out any rival company that might be heading towards a price war, it also collaborated and pooled resources with others to provide better services for the user community and more revenue for the respective owners. GSN constantly had an eye to expansion, and as opportunity arose it acquired businesses that were complementary to its own; the marriage made in heaven was, of course, the purchase of the Moss Hutchison Line of Liverpool. This then is the story of the men and women who managed, operated, maintained and supported the ships, and it is to the memory of this large family of people that this book is dedicated.

However, no book of this kind can be created without the kind support of many individuals. Andrew Davis, the Curator of Manuscripts at the Greenwich Maritime Museum was immensely constructive in directing searches into the GSN archive. Eddy Lannoo with help from Captain Louis VandeCasteele uncovered the wartime link with one of the Belgian Government ferries and Iain Hope and George Gardner, the latter at Glasgow University Archive Services, exposed the ancestry of the *Golden Eagle*. Anecdotal evidence has been given by a variety of people over a number of years and this is credited in the text where appropriate. The author is also grateful to two readers, Professor Donald Meek and author Iain Hope, who kindly checked the text for errors of fact whilst correcting the author's misplaced use of English. Above all, the author must thank P&O Historian and Archivist Stephen Rabson, for suggesting the project in the first place and latterly providing immense help in sourcing documentation and providing additional information about GSN as well as checking the manuscript for errors and omissions.

The photographs are from the author's collection unless stated otherwise, but the originator of all photographs is given wherever it is known. The author is most grateful for the wonderful work of Bristol artist Robert Blackwell which adorns the cover and advertises this book so beautifully and thanks Robert also for the discussions about the Navvies in the Bristol Channel (and the vision of the happy band of tipsy dockies springing the barrels of sherry destined for Harveys). Again thanks are due to Gil Mayes for his thorough checking of initial drafts and to Bernard McCall for taking on this project and seeing it through to the high quality product typical of all his publications.

Nick Robins, Crowmarsh, Oxfordshire   November, 2007

Published by Bernard McCall, 400 Nore Road, Portishead, Bristol, BS20 8EZ, England.
Website : www.coastalshipping.co.uk
Telephone/fax : 01275 846178. E-mail : bernard@coastalshipping.co.uk
All distribution enquiries should be addressed to the publisher.

Printed by Cromwell Press, Aintree Avenue, White Horse Business Park, Trowbridge, BA14 0XB
Telephone : 01225 711400; fax : 01225 711429
E-mail : books@cromwellpress.co.uk
Website : www.cromwellpress.co.uk

ISBN : 978-1-902953-32-8

CONTENTS

FOREWORD

Had the dreams of its founders come to fruition, the General Steam Navigation Company might have become a world-ranging shipping group like P&O or Royal Mail, or a five-star operator like Cunard or White Star. As it was, ambition outreached the available technology, and by the time P&O and Cunard were laying their foundations, the 15-year-old General Steam had settled into the trades that served it well, and which it served well, for almost a century and a half: the short-sea trades between the UK and the Continent and up and down the East Coast, and Thames excursion voyages to Margate and beyond.

General Steam was the first steamer company to carry a reigning British monarch on one of its ships, the buyer of part at least of the Navy of the Germanic Confederation, and the operator of the "husbands' special" down-Thames after lunch on a Saturday. Its ships were well-known for their bird names, French and Dutch as well as English, classical birds as well as waterfowl, finches and (especially) eagles. In its later years it pioneered roll-on/roll-off ferries across the North Sea and the English Channel. It owned well over 350 ships in its time, and yet since it disappeared in the P&O Group reorganisation begun in 1971, it has been largely forgotten.

There is no satisfactory history of General Steam. The company's own centenary volume published in 1924 is rather embarrassing, its sequel covering the years up to 1948 is much better, especially where the Second World War is concerned, but there is little else. The only academic research, one paper and one thesis separated by 24 years, deals primarily with the nineteenth century. The General Steam archive, part of the P&O collection at the National Maritime Museum, is disappointingly small for a company that lasted so long. One suspects that it only recorded what it had to, only preserved what it needed to, and even then much has been lost.

From such unpromising foundations and a wide variety of other sources, Nick Robins has fashioned a valuable history of a historic company. A company which few had bothered to write about, has turned out to be worth writing about, and at last there is a worthwhile history of General Steam.

STEPHEN RABSON - P&O Historian and Archivist, DP World

Front cover : The **Starling** (1930) in the Bristol Deep passing the English & Welsh Banks Light Vessel.

(From an oil painting by Robert Blackwell)

Back cover : The **Nautilus** (1874) lies outside the **Lapwing** (1879) at the company's Irongate Wharf in the Lower Pool, London. St Katherine's is beyond.

(DP World P&O Heritage Collection)

How the Thames was won - the GSN heyday

The paddle steamer *Royal Eagle* (1932)

Main dining saloon aboard the *Royal Eagle*.

The back of the postcard notes "322 diners can be accommodated at the same time in the saloons of the *Royal Eagle* ...... Excellent breakfasts, luncheons and teas at very moderate prices are served, the steamers being fully licensed. The large windows provide a wonderful view of the points of interest during a voyage."

The *Royal Sovereign* (1948) off Southend Pier on 21 August 1962.

[Nick Robins]

As the postcard tells us, this is the main dining saloon of the *Royal Sovereign*, looking forward.

CHAPTER 1

THE GLOBAL VISION

"In the year 1824, England for nine years had been suffering under precisely the same evils as those from which she had suffered during the six years from 1918 to 1924: heavy debt, high taxation, excessive prices, a depreciated currency, much unemployment, the failure of foreign markets, dangerous discontent and the threat of revolution. The plain, kindly old gentleman, King George III, had passed away in 1820; and George IV, a dissipated person, had proceeded from the Regency to the sovereignty of England. The real ruler was the sagacious Prime Minister, Lord Liverpool...."

From **A CENTURY OF SEA TRADING**, Cope Cornford, 1924

The year 1824 was not the most opportune time to start a shipping company with a vision of trading across the Seven Seas. The Honourable East India Company was effectively the Merchant Navy, and any idea that a set of small, cranky, wooden, steam engined paddle steamers could successfully take on the regimented might of the East India Company's sailing ships was ludicrous. Besides, Britain was just emerging from the Industrial Revolution. The poor of the nation continued to leave the land for the prospect of factory employment, whilst food was scarce and a surplus of labour held wages down. Slow lumbering sailing ships waited offshore at Gravesend - the emigrant boats - and promised a new life in the Antipodes provided that the emigrant and his family could survive the rigours of the voyage. Trade with France was impossible as that nation was still recovering from its own Revolution, and many of the other foreign markets had also failed.

But it was in 1824 that GSN (General Steam Navigation Company) was incorporated by Private Act of Parliament. The company prospectus stated a clear vision of creating steamer routes to India, North and South America, Russia (where Alexander I was busy expanding his power), dishevelled France, Spain, Portugal and Holland. Things could only improve, and improve they must.

The seed that germinated as GSN was a small consortium of shipowners trading on the London to Margate route via the so-called 'Long Ferry' to Gravesend, the traditional and protected reserve of the Thames Watermen. The leader of the consortium was Thomas Brockelbank, who had placed his paddle steamer *Eagle* on the service to Margate in 1820. It appears that the *Eagle*, traditionally considered as the first GSN steamer, was never owned by GSN, much the same as P&O never actually owned their 'first ship' the *William Fawcett*. The *Eagle* was followed by the *Hero*, *Royal Sovereign*, *Brockelbank* and *City of London*, all of which were built at Brockelbank's own yard at Deptford. The subsequent *Harlequin* and *Columbine* were built by the shipbuilder Mr Evendon in 1825 and 1826 at Brockelbank's yard. Brockelbank was originally a timber merchant, whose job was to supply the numerous shipyards that lined the Thames. The purpose of the consortium was simply to pool resources against the competitive wrath of the Watermen who saw the arrival of the steamship as a serious threat to their livelihood, and the wake of the steamers as a real danger to their lighters and other small craft.

During 1824, William John Hall, whose ships traded along the coast to Hull, joined forces with Brockelbank, and together they devised a plan to float the consortium as a new joint stock company. Their declaration for the new company read:

"...profitable to those engaged in it by affording them the means of establishing between the United Kingdom of Great Britain, and such places as may be deemed advisable, a certain expeditious intercourse for the conveyance of passenger and merchandise, which the combined powers of capital and steam at their disposal will enable them under judicious management to accomplish."

Other signatories included W J Jolliffe and Sir Edward Banks who owned the Calais steamers **Lord Melville** and **Earl of Liverpool**, Michael Shepley, John Jones, W J de Buck, Thomas Hamlet, James Lett, J H Deacon and Tory MP Thomas Attwood. The share capital of the company was set at 20,000 shares of £100 each, and these were widely advertised in the press and elsewhere. Calls on each share, however, amounted to a more modest £13 over the first four years to 1828. The company offices were established at 24 Crutched Friars. It was intriguingly minuted at one of the first Board meeting on 23 December 1824, that "a letter dated 21 December from Mr John Smith was read, and the request therein contained was directed to be complied with" – but of John Smith's request we may never know!

The original fleet of Thames steamers comprised five ships. This was the more remarkable because the first steamship on the Thames started in service only in 1814. This was the **Richmond**, which plied erratically between

Hammersmith and Richmond and was seen off within a year by a combination of the Great Frost, when the river froze over, and the defiant stand of the Watermen against the dangerous, smoky, and generally unreliable, paddle boat. The **Richmond** was followed in 1815, some three years after Henry Bell's successful trials with the **Comet** on the Clyde, by a down river steamer called the **Marjory**. She ran under Captain Cortis between Wapping Old Stairs and Milton just below Gravesend – so as not to offend the Watermen's right to operate the Long Ferry, with their sails and oars, to Gravesend itself. The **Marjory** was scheduled to carry out three return trips per week, each with a single outward or return leg per day at a princely return fare of 8/- in the main cabin and 4/- in the fore cabin. In actual fact she missed numerous trips while her engineer tinkered with valves and adjusted levers and rods to ensure that the vessel would actually complete her next trip up or down river without mishap.

The wooden-hulled paddle steamer had become slightly more reliable by the mid-1820s but the engines remained temperamental, and their paddles liable to damage in contact with all but the meanest flotsam. Their funnels were as tall as the mast and favourable winds would see a full set of sail unfurled to assist the passage. Whilst the river steamers struggled on with their war with the Watermen, the GSN Board decided almost immediately to widen its remit from London and East Coast services onwards to Leith, and to develop the London to Calais via Margate and London to Ostend routes. It also inaugurated a new service between the new Chain Pier at Brighton to Dieppe. The Dieppe service maintained a departure from Brighton on Tuesdays and Saturdays, summer only for the first few years, but later all year round. However, the exposed nature of the Chain Pier did little to promote the schedule. Prior to this the Continental services had all been operated by naval ships, and the commercial venture was ambitious in the least.

Three new passenger ships were ordered for the Dieppe and Ostend routes, the third destined for a new service between London and Great Yarmouth. New tonnage also appeared when the **Lord Melville** and **Earl of Liverpool** were bought from Messrs Jolliffe and Banks and the **Royal Sovereign** and **City of London** from Thomas Brockelbank to help pioneer the new routes. The steamer **Rapid** was chartered from W Busby and W & G Peters of London for the Calais service before being transferred to work between Brighton and Dieppe. She was bought outright at the end of March 1825. The **Rapid** had been built in 1820 at Greenock for the Clyde Shipping Company, was sold in 1822 to David Napier of Glasgow, then came to London in 1824. She was equipped with a main cabin, ladies cabin and a 'handsome dining room', but by all accounts was slow. While on the Clyde her owners attributed the tardiness of the **Rapid** to foreign bodies in the engine, and managed to demonstrate their theory by exhibiting pieces of foreign material at a hotel in Greenock. She was re-engined before moving to the Brighton to Dieppe route, and was later involved with a new London to Rotterdam service.

The **Earl of Liverpool** (1824)
at the entrance to Ostend Harbour

[DP World P&O Heritage Collection]

Although the coastal services were quickly profitable, as there were no railways and few passable roads in the UK at that time, the Continental routes were slower to mature, a reflection of the depressed state of the Continental markets. Nevertheless, at the end of the company's first year of trading GSN was the owner of 15 wooden paddle steamers and its Board determined to pay the shareholders a dividend of 16%. GSN was not only (almost certainly) the first steamship company to trade on a regular schedule to foreign ports, but it was also up and running and in profit.

During 1825 additional routes were opened including services to Dunkirk and a passenger service between Portsmouth and Le Havre. Now with sanction from the Government to carry cargo on its vessels, GSN sought to optimise its revenue by carrying manufactured goods to the continent, returning with cereals and other foods to feed the factory workers. In 1825, the company also entered the live animal trade carrying sheep and cattle into London from Rotterdam and other ports in the Lowlands and northern France. This was to become one of the more profitable activities for the company as the nineteenth century progressed and it proved to be a great revenue earner. Meanwhile, the Thames services were booming and it is recorded that over a million passengers used the Margate boats each year by the late 1820s. Finally, additional land was bought from the East India Company at Deptford Creek adjacent to Brockelbank's yard in order to consolidate the shipbuilding and repair works for the company.

By April 1825 GSN owned:

Lord Melville	**Earl of Liverpool**	**Royal Sovereign**
City of London	**Belfast**	**Superb**
Eclipse	**Talbot**	**Rapid**
Hylton Jolliffe	**Attwood**	**Brockelbank**
Nottingham	**Mountaineer**	

By February 1826 it had acquired in addition:

Columbine	**Duke of York**	**George IV**
Harlequin	**Sir Edward Banks**	**Waterloo**
William Jolliffe		

Palmer (1982) in her paper 'The most indefatigable activity' - the General Steam Navigation Company 1824-50' reported:

"*In 1826 the GSN faced a severe financial crisis. The lag between contracting for vessels to be built and their completion necessarily delayed the introduction of new ships and hence return on investment, but only half the company's fleet was actually employed, and not all these vessels on a regular basis. Some of the vessels bought from other owners required extensive and costly repair before they could be put into service: a result of poor investment decisions. Even the ships built specially for the company represented problems. Twenty engines had been ordered from a Derby company but, as was normal practice, no attempt had been made to co-ordinate hull and engines in advance, with the result that 'defects in steam engines and in vessels themselves when set to work together were discovered'. Delivery delays further compounded these difficulties. Frustrated by dependence on outside firms, the Directors decided to develop workshop facilities at Deptford, a decision which was to prove of great significance in later years.*"

As the economy slowly mended, France got back on its feet and the near Continent determined to trade with industrial Britain, so business began to improve. The London to Hamburg service was opened in 1826. Disposition of vessels - 'First Class and Powerful Steam Packets' - according to a passenger sailing schedule dated 1826 (see Table 1), included a new service to Lisbon, Vigo or Oporto and Gibraltar by the **George IV** and **Duke of York**. The service to Bordeaux, initially based at Portsmouth, was not destined to start until 1828. Sailings were advertised from an anchorage off the Custom House or Tower, except the prestigious Gibraltar service which left from Deptford, although it would call off Brighton or at Portsmouth given three days notice in the office at London for passengers unable to travel from Deptford. The Schedule advised also that 'refreshments may be had on board, and that all the packets have elegant state cabins for the ladies and female attendants'. Wigram & Green closed their Rotterdam service in 1830 when GSN, in expansive mood, purchased their steamer **Queen of the Netherlands**. However, none of the longer routes were initially profitable.

Palmer (1982) again:

"*In March 1827 a group of shareholders, no doubt worried about regular calls for additional finance, and mindful of their unlimited liability, attempted to dissolve the company. Although the Directors successfully resisted this attack, it must have been clear that criticisms of the company's management were not unfounded and that continued support from shareholders could not be taken for granted. In the autumn of that year the three Executive Directors, who had effectively run the company from 1824, were replaced by three committees for finance, stores and purchases, and general purposes – on the grounds that 'a concern such as this in the hands of a small number possesses none of the advantages peculiar to a public or private management; but is subject to disadvantages incident to both'. A general tightening up of procedures followed, noticeable to the present-day researcher in the more systematic presentation of accounts. The following year saw the company move into a state of profit, which permitted steps to be taken to alter its legal status... The improved condition of the GSN's finances after 1828 cannot be attributed solely to reform of its internal organisation, but this marks the transition from an essentially amateur concern, dominated by a few men, to a broader based enterprise capable of developing professional standards of management.*"

The company quickly required more office space and moved into a large house at 71 Lombard Street in 1829. GSN had no wharfage on the Thames and was dependent on availability and the whims of wharf owners, with much of the human traffic loaded and unloaded by tender. The Margate steamers used Fresh Wharf immediately below London Bridge, although occasionally they were also dependent on tenders to embark or disembark passengers. The Margate route connected with coaches for Dover, Deal and Sandwich from 1832 onwards, providing one of the first examples of integrated sea and land transport. Meanwhile the Bordeaux service transferred from Portsmouth to Southampton with an additional call at Plymouth.

One small set-back was the publicity gained by the dismissal of the officers and crew of the *Belfast*. During 1831 they were found guilty of smuggling between England and France, and the story attained banner headlines in the newspapers. The *Belfast* was bought from George Langtree in 1824, for whom she had inaugurated the Belfast to Liverpool service which then passed to the newly-formed Belfast Steam Packet Company that same year. The *Belfast* was the first substantial steamer to be built in Ireland and had been launched, appropriately, on St Patrick's Day 1820. Her 35 horse power side lever engine was manufactured by Coates & Young, also of Belfast.

But best of all, in 1834, the tenth year of trading, an Act of Incorporation was granted extending the privileges of GSN and allowing it to tender successfully for the carriage of His Majesty's Mail, initially on the services from London to Boulogne, Ostend, Rotterdam and Hamburg. By all accounts the Hamburg contract was secured from the Saint George Steam Packet Company, who won it in 1831, by secret payments from GSN alleged to be £2,000 per year, but worthwhile for a grant of £17,000 from the Post Office which was to last until 1849. The Rotterdam contract involved the expensive purchase of the rival steamer *London Merchant* for £12,000, amidst a sustained press campaign against GSN ostensibly fed by the rival company.

The master of the *Tourist* was taken to task by the Post Office for delaying the mails when he put back to Harwich with a broken paddle wheel in November 1834. The Royal Mail services were shortly extended to include London to Calais and Antwerp, and Brighton to Dieppe, the latter occasionally diverting to Shoreham when the weather made landing at the Chain Pier at Brighton an uncertainty. The Dieppe service was variously served by the smaller steamers *Eclipse*, *Talbot*, *Harlequin*, *Lord Melville* and *Attwood*. Their arrivals and departures at the French port were regularly adjusted to suit the tide, although the *Talbot* went aground off Shoreham in 1830, and was later rescued by the *Hyperion*, which was employed on some form of blockade duty in the area.

In 1835 GSN bought 500 shares in the Lower & Middle Rhine Steamship Company to facilitate inland continental connections. Thereafter GSN took a portion of the revenue in the Rhine traffic 'in return for promoting a through service'. From 1836 to 1841 GSN colluded with the Antwerp Company, taking a quarter of its passenger receipts in return for conceding the Sunday night service to Antwerp to that company.

Mindful of the dangers of competition and price cutting, GSN approached its rivals on the Edinburgh route with a view to co-ordinating resources and schedules. Receiving an unsatisfactory response, GSN made a generous offer to the Scots, for the London & Edinburgh Steam Packet Company, its goodwill, nine steamers, offices and warehouse facilities which were absorbed into the larger company during 1836[1]. The steamers included the *Monarch* which had been commissioned from her Blackwall builders in 1833 under the command of Captain Bain, when the Press enthusiastically described the new vessel as:

"Larger than any of His Majesty's frigates, and longer than our 84 gun ships . . . the accommodation below is so extensive that she will make up 140 beds, and 100 persons may conveniently dine in her saloons."

A few years later, the *Monarch*, as a GSN ship, was featured in the London press:

"Descending a few steps by a commodious companion you reach the entrance to various cabins, a pair of folding mahogany doors opening into the saloon, which for light, dryness and comfort is superior to all we have seen... light pours in at a number of large windows of plate glass, and the traveller may, whilst sitting at a table or lounging upon a sofa, gaze out over the clear expanse of ocean or survey the splendid scenery of the coast, as she 'flies' past it. The panelling around is of satin wood and the ceiling white and gold. The floor is entirely covered (as are all the chief cabins) with Brussels carpet, the pattern of which is the crest, a globe surrounded by a garter with the initials [GSN] and the date of their institution, 1824. The centre is occupied by a noble stove of brass, extremely elegant and chaste in design and shining in spotless brilliancy of polish, partially concealing the mizen mast."

---

[1] The London & Edinburgh Steam Packet Company is not to be confused with the London & Edinburgh Shipping Company which at this time was still using sailing vessels. Some years later, however, it too would become a competitor of GSN.

Other Edinburgh vessels acquired along with the **Monarch** were the **Mountaineer**, built in 1821,which had also seen service on the Irish Sea, the **James Watt** built in 1822 for David McIver on the Clyde, the **City of Edinburgh**, built at Blackwall in 1821 and pioneer on the Leith to London route, and the brand new **Clarence**, **Caledonia**, **Ocean**, **Giraffe** and **Countess of Lonsdale**. They were joined on the Edinburgh service in 1837 by the **Leith**, the largest vessel in the fleet to date and built appropriately at Leith 'for the purpose of conciliating the feelings and opinions of those among whom to a considerable extent the influence of the company was comparatively unknown'. The launch of this large ship of 907 gross tons attracted several tens of thousands of onlookers.

In this watercolour by William John Huggins, the *Clarence* (1836) leaving for Leith, the *Leith* (1837) arriving from Leith, and the *Columbine* (1826) arriving with Her Majesty's mails from Rotterdam, are seen off Brunswick Wharf, London.

[DP World P&O Heritage Collection]

The *Caledonia* (1836) and *Neptune* (1837) at the entrance to the River Elbe

[DP World P&O Heritage Collection]

In a move to reduce the competition on the Kent services GSN bought the Margate & Gravesend Steam Packet Company in 1836 along with the steamers **William IV**, **Royal George**, **Royal William** and **Royal Adelaide**. This fleet retained its separate identity until the vessels were sold.

Purchase of rival companies and consolidation of the resulting assets and goodwill, first seen in 1836, became a recurrent theme of the company for the rest of its existence. GSN was fortunate in having sufficient reserves to be able do this, as the company was always reluctant to embark on price wars and over-commitment to routes which would consequently become only economically marginal.

The next new steamer to be commissioned was the **John Bull** with engines built at the company's Deptford yard. As always the company had an eye for opportune charters, and it was the **John Bull** which was temporarily taken away from its running mate on the Hamburg run, the **City of Hamburg**, to take the British Legion to San Sebastian in 1836. Further new builds were completed, notably the **Neptune** which was built for the company at Blackwall by the famous shipbuilders Wigram & Green.

From 1829 onwards all new vessels were fitted with engines built at Deptford and many second hand ships were likewise re-engined. There was also an extensive programme of refurbishment and ship lengthening, the latter, for example, allowing the **Harlequin** to be promoted from Thames duties to the Hamburg service.

At the close of the reign of William IV and the accession of his niece Victoria in 1837, GSN owned 40 wooden steamers. The key foreign destinations were Antwerp, Le Havre, Boulogne, Calais, Dieppe, Ostend, Hamburg, Rotterdam and Bordeaux, all of which had dedicated agents acting on behalf of the company. The East Coast service operated between London and Leith, and included calls at Berwick, Newcastle, Sunderland and Ipswich whilst the Kent steamers served Margate, Ramsgate and Herne Bay. There was also a regular service between Leith and Hamburg. Against all this activity the annual coal bill averaged some £50,000 throughout the 1830s. To put the achievement of GSN into perspective, 1837 was also the year that the Peninsular Company, the forerunner of P&O, won the first of many mail contracts[2], and another three years were to elapse before the British & North American Steam Packet Company would evolve into the Cunard Line.

GSN experienced its fair share of casualties, not surprising when the small size of the vessels is considered. One of these was the loss of the *Talbot*. The *Talbot* had been acquired in 1825 having previously been one of the Dover-Calais Post Office Packets, although the steamer was originally built for, and inaugurated steamer services between Holyhead and Howth near Dublin in 1819. But with nearly ten years of Continental trading under her belt this little stalwart was lost in a storm off Ostend in 1833. In October 1834 the newly re-engined *Superb* was lost off the German coast with all hands. Several other mishaps are documented, but the company was undeterred by these setbacks.

Whether GSN was the oldest and longest lived steamship company is open for debate. The Scots will tell of the Clyde Shipping Company dating from 1815, and the Irish of the Saint George Steam Packet Company which was founded in 1821. But only one company started with global aspirations, and from the outset the GSN flag became the globe in red on a white ground with the Indian Ocean foremost.

The Saint George Steam Packet Company must have been a cause of frustration to the GSN Board. It had become hugely successful with a wide network of passenger and cargo routes, both on the Irish Sea and to the Continent and Baltic. It also hosted the inaugural cross-Atlantic voyage of the steamer *Sirius*, which in 1838, completed an 18 day voyage from Queenstown (Cork) to New York during which not one sail was unfurled. Her $8\frac{1}{2}$ knots was sustained by the consumption of 24 tons of coal each day. The voyage was undertaken for the newly formed British and American Steam Navigation Company who segregated the 40 passengers on board into three classes: the 25 Guinea' class, the intermediate 20 Guinea' class and the steerage at a mere 8 Guineas for the trip. It seems that outright purchase of the Irish upstarts was out of budget, even for GSN; otherwise, expansion of the London-based company could have been even more majestic. Nevertheless, GSN, like the young Queen Victoria who was sitting nervously on her unfamiliar throne, was set to blossom.

**A CENTURY OF SEA TRADING -
book cover featuring the
Halcyon (1921) by J Spurling.**

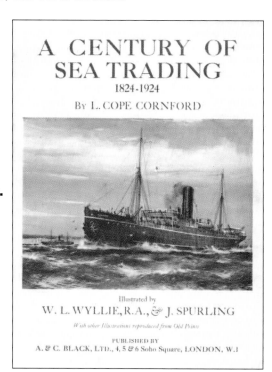

A CENTURY OF
SEA TRADING
1824-1924

By L. COPE CORNFORD

Illustrated by
W. L. WYLLIE, R.A., & J. SPURLING

With other Illustrations reproduced from Old Prints

PUBLISHED BY
A. & C. BLACK, LTD., 4, 5 & 6 Soho Square, LONDON, W.1

---

[2] 1837 is the traditional date of the founding of the Peninsula Steam Navigation Company, but it never had any corporate existence and P&O's Charter dates only from 1840.

A COMPANY WITH ALMOST NO HISTORY

The General Steam Navigation Company conducted its business in such a way that it rarely achieved the headlines, but routinely satisfied the requirements of its clients. Not being at the glamour end of the shipping industry with dignitaries and politicians to carry across the Atlantic or to and from India in first class luxury, the comings and goings of the 'Navvies' have received scant attention from authors over the last two centuries. And worse, precious few of the company papers have survived, other than a near complete set of the Minutes of the Board, lodged with the National Maritime Museum Archive in Greenwich by parent company the P&O Group in 1975. The GSN Minute Books provide summaries of the financial status of the company, and record that the minutes of the various committees have been heard. It is the Committee Minutes that would have contained the fabric of the company history, but these have not survived.

There are also some timetables, sailing bills and descriptions of vessels as well as the plans for a number of ships, along with several certificates of registry. Very little correspondence has survived. There is a similar dearth of material retained for some of the major subsidiary companies such as the Moss Hutchison Line, the records of which amount to just 6 feet of shelf space held at the Mersey Maritime Museum. The whole GSN collection at Greenwich, which includes a small amount of information on the Great Yarmouth, Grand Union and New Medway companies, amounts to 24 feet of shelf space with an additional 6 feet of material currently held by Dubai Ports World in London. By way of contrast the more glamorous deep sea brethren are better represented, there being over 500 feet of shelf space devoted to P&O company records at Greenwich. The archives of Coast Lines, the only other company at all similar to GSN and which also became part of the P&O Group, offer some 40 feet of records distributed between centres in Liverpool, Belfast, Glasgow, Newcastle, Aberdeen, Cork and Greenwich.

Thank goodness the company had the wit to commission a celebratory book on its first hundred years, *A CENTURY OF SEA TRADING* by Leslie Cope Cornford. This book was published by A&C Black of London and contains a number of that publisher's characteristically high quality colour prints taken from paintings by the renowned marine artists, W L Wyllie and J Spurling. The book is now very much a collector's item because of the prints alone, but if its objective was to narrate the history of GSN from its inception in 1824 up and until 1924, then it fails. What it does do, however, is describe the trading conditions prevailing through that period with occasional references to the activities of the ships and their crews, and the staff onshore and in the Board Room. The story of the development of the company and its routes, the evolution of its ships, the change from shipper to through freight agent in the early 1900s, the first voyages to the Mediterranean, and trips to North and South America as well as West Africa remains barely told.

P&O's centenary historian 'Boyd Cable' (Colonel E A Ewart, the company's Public Relations Manager) also produced a manuscript on General Steam, but it was not published. Maritime historian H E Hancock produced a useful narrative in 1949. This was published by GSN under the title *SEMPER FIDELIS, THE SAGA OF THE NAVVIES 1924-1948*. Hancock described how the Navvies were indeed ever faithful throughout the depressed years between the wars, how heroic was their Second World War and how austere was their emergence after the Armistice. This is a very readable story, which does provide a valuable history of this 25 year period of the company history. Thereafter, there has been little published on the company, leading up to its demise in 1973, although a later in-house manuscript by Smeeton and Morris was left unpublished by changes within the P&O Group. The monthly shipping magazine *SEA BREEZES* sponsored histories of most of the leading shipping company in its pages since post-war publication was recommenced in 1946. Although these included many short sea and coastal operators, GSN was not one of them, and mention of the company is made in passing, and only rarely. The Moss Hutchison Line did receive such attention, however, in a brief article published in April 1949, and even the Bennett Steamship Company was highlighted in the October 1968 edition of the magazine.

The *GSN NEWS LETTER*, which was published between World War II and 1971, offers little insight into the company. Its pages are almost entirely devoted to the staff and their families with little reported on the activities of the company itself. The Editorial characteristically began, Dear GSN...'.

Recently, there have been two very useful academic papers on the early company history and Norman Middlemiss attempted to bring the fleet lists up to date (see reference section). Otherwise, it is as though GSN almost never existed. The company is, of course, fondly remembered by an ageing population who once enjoyed the 'Eagle Steamers' excursions on the Thames, 'weather and other circumstances permitting'. This small area of the company history has been well documented, in for example, the seminal work of Frank Burtt (but which also contains some errors of fact) which was published in 1949.

That so little is written about the coastal, continental and Mediterranean services of GSN to this day is surprising for such a well known, long-lasting and famous company. Indeed, this was a company that ran the early cross-Channel service from the Chain Pier at Brighton to Dieppe and later had the largest and fastest packet steamers on the North Sea running between Harwich Parkeston Quay and Hamburg. There were also the attractive looking passenger and cargo steamers employed on the London to Bordeaux service, the Edinburgh steamers and the Mediterranean steamers as well as the countless little vessels that maintained cargo services to northern France and the Low Countries. Indeed, the Navvies had an important role in maintaining trade with the Empire and the Americas by providing feeder services to the main liner companies that sailed from the Port of London, and in due course becoming the preferred carrier for British India and P&O. Clearly, the scarce volume of company papers that has survived, coupled with the documented history published on the first hundred years, and several cases of apparent mistaken identity published thereafter, have almost defied historians to describe the trials and tribulations of the company. GSN is the company with almost no history.

TABLE 1 Fleet disposition in 1826

Route	Vessels	Masters	Departures	Fare chief cabin/fore cabin	Four/two wheeled carriages	Horses and dogs
London to Lisbon, Vigo, Oporto and Gibraltar	George IV, Duke of York	P Black, Commander J Mowle, Commander	To be advised	£31-10s and £26 Gibraltar £25 and £20 other ports*	By agreement	By agreement
London to Boulogne (15 hours)	Rapid	Captain Jennings	Out: Tues and Fri Return: Sun and Wed	£1-16-0 and £1-6-0	£4-10-0 and £3	£4 and 5/-
London to Calais (12 hours)	Attwood, Lord Melville	Captain Stranack Captain Middleton	Mon, Wed, Thur, Sat	£1-13-0 and £1-2-6	£4-4-0 and £2-2-0	£3-3-0 and 5/-
London to Ostend (16 hours)	Earl of Liverpool, Mountaineer	Captain Peake Captain Mate	Wed and Sat	£2 and £1-10-0	£4-4-0 and £2-2--0	£4-4-0 and 5/-
London to Rotterdam (26 hours)	Belfast	Captain Roberts	Out: Sat 0900 h. Return: Tues 1000 h.	£2-10-0 and £1-15-0	£6-6-0 and £3-3-0	£6-6-0 and 10/-
London to Hamburg (54 hours)	Sir Edward Banks, Hylton Jolliffe	Captain Howlett Captain Mowll	Out: Sat 0700 h. Return: Sat early	£9 and £7	£10 and £6-6-0	£8-8-0 and £1
Brighton to Dieppe (8 hours)	Eclipse, Talbot, Quentin Durwood	Captain Cheeseman Captain Norwood [Brighton Company]	Mon, Tues, Wed, Thur, Fri	£2 and £1-50-0	£4-4-0 and £2-2-0	£3-3-0 and 5/-
London to Margate and Ramsgate	Harlequin, City of London, Columbine, Royal Sovereign	Captain Corbin Captain Martin Captain Grant Captain Major	Margate - Mon to Sat 0900 h. Ramsgate - Wed and Sat 0800 h.	12/- and 10/- children and servants 6/-	Not carried	Not carried

* Fare includes 'provisions and attendance'

CHAPTER 2

AN EXPANDING ECONOMY: STEAM, IRON AND SCREWS

"Steamboats have been found to require in a very great degree the exertion of the most indefatigable activity and rigid economy in order to obtain from them any returns."

MINUTES OF THE BOARD OF GSN 1839

The early 1840s is characterised both by royal and famed patronage of GSN and by buoyant and increasing demand for its services and expansion of its fleet. The 'English' steamer *City of Edinburgh* was chartered at London by Prince Louis Napoléon for his historic landing at Wimereaux near Boulogne on 6 August 1840 when he staged his second attempted coup. As a member of the Bonaparte family he had been exiled as a child in 1815 when the Bourbon Monarchy was restored. Jailed for his attempted coup, Louis Napoléon subsequently escaped, disguised as a mason, and returned to England, later to became Emperor of the French.

The reign of Victoria had an auspicious start when the young Queen opted to travel aboard one of GSN's newest fleet members, the paddle steamer *Trident*, rather than her own royal yacht. GSN offered to make the steamer available to the Monarch for her visit to Scotland in September 1842, the *Trident* being a superior vessel to the royal sailing yacht HMY *Royal George*, which was manned by a scratch crew from the Reserve whenever it was in service. Although the Queen and Prince Albert sailed north on the royal yacht, they opted to return courtesy of GSN. The royal party was delighted with the accommodation provided and enjoyed a fast 48 hour passage back to the Thames. It appears that the *Trident*, in company with the GSN steamer *Monarch*, which conveyed the royal baggage, set off from the Forth at the same time as the royal yacht and other official vessels. By dusk on the first day, only the two GSN vessels were in convoy, the Government ships having been left far astern. Within a year, of course, by Royal insistence, the new HMY *Victoria and Albert* had been designed, built at Pembroke Dockyard and delivered in time for an inaugural summer coastal cruise. But at the same time, despite the royal accolade at one end of the North Sea, the steamer *Caledonia*, while on passage from Hamburg, was caught with illegal tobacco on board!

Trident (1841)
at Woolwich with the Royal Party returning from Scotland on 13 September 1842

[DP World P&O Heritage Collection]

The company was also conveying author Charlotte Brontë on a regular basis between London and Antwerp en route to her school in Brussels. Brontë later used these experiences in her novel Villette, which was published in 1853, in which she described summoning a boatman one dark evening to take her out to join the steamer *Vivid* whilst it was moored off Deptford awaiting the embarkation of passengers.

But one of GSN's pioneer routes was lost at an early stage, and lost to a railway company at that. Throughout the 1830s various wooden paddle steamers had supported the Brighton to Dieppe service (see Chapter 1). The ships carried passengers as well as the horses and coachmen of the well-to-do, who preferred not to suffer the discomfort of the 'diligences' then available between Rouen and Dieppe. There had been only one casualty, which considering the tidal problems at Dieppe and the exposed Chain Pier at Brighton, was remarkable in itself, when the *Attwood* was wrecked at Shoreham in 1838.

In 1841 the London to Brighton railway was opened incorporating an existing connection to Shoreham. The Paris to Rouen line opened in 1843 and the London & Brighton Railway Company started to take a keen interest in the activities of the GSN steamers, whilst promoting the railway and steamer route via Brighton as the shortest (by some 30½ miles) and fastest between London and Paris. Complaints from the railway company about the inadequate size of the GSN steamers were answered in 1844 by deploying the larger and faster steamers *Menai*, sailing on Tuesdays and Fridays to Havre, and the *Fame* on the Dieppe route which now featured two sailings per week from Shoreham as well as two from Brighton. The third steamer was the *Magnet*. However, GSN did not take kindly to the prying interests of the railway company, and in particular to that of Rowland Hill, one of the London & Brighton Railway directors and, of course, champion of the 'penny post'. B E O'Mahoney takes up the story in an article which first appeared in SEA BREEZES, September 1979:

"Difficulties between the two companies were building up mainly due to continuing complaints about the size of the vessels, the tonnage of which was disputed by the railway company, who suffered a rebuff when they sent a representative to question the manager of a shipyard engaged in building a vessel for the GSN. In June [1844], when the two companies were co-operating in an endeavour to improve the service, a further sign of trouble appeared when, in response to a request by the railway company, the GSN refused to give a weekly traffic return to the railway company, causing the directors to minute that such behaviour was 'vexatious and ungentlemanly".

GSN increased the service during August from four to six sailings a week coinciding with a three day visit to Dieppe by King Louis Phillippe and his entourage. But as time went on the rift between the shipping company and the railway company encouraged the latter to consider running its own steamers. But as it was not empowered by Parliament to run the steamer service itself, it created the Brighton and Continental Steam Packet Company which commissioned three new steamers, the *Brighton*, *Newhaven* and *Dieppe*, to inaugurate an alternative route between a new port to be built at Newhaven, and Dieppe. The GSN Chairman, John Wilkin, responded with a total withdrawal of the Dieppe service from 30 November 1846, the end of the summer season. The cessation brought immediate complaints from both the railway company and the Mayor of Dieppe, but to no avail.

The new steamers were on station in the spring of 1847, and in July 1848 the railway between Rouen and Dieppe was completed by a workforce of over 2,000 largely British men. Now with the rail and steamer link in place between London and Paris, the rival company from the Folkestone to Boulogne crossing, the South Eastern Railway, jealously cried foul and the ferries were tied up in Newhaven Harbour for the rest of the summer. The argument was that whereas the South Eastern Railway ran steamers as a joint venture with a private company, the Newhaven steamers were wholly-owned through a subsidiary of the railway company and were thus being operated illegally.

GSN was asked to come back and reinstate the missing link. Following a protracted ten month delay whilst the channel at Newhaven was deepened, the iron-hulled GSN steamer *Magician* resumed the Newhaven crossing in May 1849. However, the relationship with the railway company remained uneasy, and in April 1851 the London, Brighton & South Coast Railway, as it had become, informed Wilkin that GSN's services were to be terminated. A collaborative venture with the local shipowner Henry Maples was planned to become the railway's sole provider for the crossing. Thus ended GSN's involvement in packet services across the English Channel.

GSN had also helped establish the early routes for the South Eastern Railway at Folkestone. On 24 June 1843, four days before a new rail service to Folkestone was opened to the public, the GSN steamer *Waterwitch*, originally built for the Humber Steamship Company in 1835[1], was chartered to run a demonstration day trip. Leaving London Bridge at 6.00 am, a special train reached Folkestone at 8.40 with Directors, Members of Parliament and other

---

[1] The Humber Steamship Company (sometimes referred to as the Humber Union) was forced out of business in a price war with GSN in 1841. GSN then bought the company and its three ships: the *Vivid*, *Waterwitch* and *Wilberforce*.

invitees aboard. The **Waterwitch** cast off about 9.15 am, and by 12.30 pm all passengers were ashore at Boulogne. The passengers partook of a 'delectable collation' served in a saloon at the Baths, and toasts were given and speeches made. After luncheon visitors returned to the steamer, *"escorted by a gazing and cheering multitude"* to quote from the newspaper report. Leaving Boulogne at 2.40 pm, the **Waterwitch** made Folkestone Harbour by 6.30 pm, and by 10.05 pm the train was back in London. The **Waterwitch** and the **Sir William Wallace** (acquired with the Dundee, Perth & London Shipping Company in 1829) were chartered for some time by the newly formed New Commercial Steam Packet Company. This was the joint venture company that was acceptable for the South Eastern Railway even if the subsidiary company of the London, Brighton & South Coast Railway at Shoreham was not.

The **Waterwitch** (1835)

[DP World
P&O Heritage Collection]

But technology had moved on while all this wrestling with the railway companies was taking place. The first iron-hulled vessel in the GSN fleet was the **Rainbow**, commissioned in 1837 and used by the company to investigate the performance of the new technology. The pioneer vessel was also the centre of Admiralty attention, while their Lordships oversaw experiments to validate the magnetic compass aboard an otherwise magnetic ship. The **Rainbow** was then placed on the Antwerp and Rotterdam services. The next iron-hulled ship was the **Magician** in 1844 and later to be deployed at Newhaven, followed in 1845 by the **Triton**. Thereafter, only iron-hulled vessels were ordered, although a number of wooden-hulled paddlers subsequently joined the company as second hand purchases.

The **Rainbow** (1837) off Antwerp

[DP World P&O Heritage Collection]

Another significant advance was the acquisition of the leasehold for a Thames river wharf following the redevelopment of the St Katharine's Hospital site (on the north bank just below Tower Bridge). For the first time, intending passengers could board ship by walking up a gangway rather than summoning the boatman as Brönte had described. The Thames packet steamers, though, had always enjoyed wharfage in the city, the GSN boats started from Hungerford Market Pier in the vicinity of what is now Charing Cross Station, with calls at Old Swan Pier, and Greenwich. Nevertheless, congestion around the river piers often required passengers to embark and disembark by tender.

Casualties were inevitable given the size of the early vessels, the vagaries of the weather and the confined seaways frequented by the ships. The Hull steamer *Vivid* collided with another paddler, the *Era*, on the Thames in 1842. Although the *Era* quickly sank to the river bed, the master of the *Vivid* was able to run his leaking vessel hard on to the mud. In December 1845 the *John Bull* was inbound from Hamburg when she struck the Diamond Steam Packet Company's *Emerald* on the 'long ferry', from London to Gravesend. It was reported at the time that 'the *Emerald* was struck on the 'larboard quarter just before the paddle box...the paddle box was stove in and the funnel was cast down with a tremendous crash'. The passengers and crew were almost entirely saved by the *John Bull*, which was helped in this task by the little Blackwall Railway ferry *Railway*. The *Emerald* was later repaired and put back in service. Throughout this period GSN carried no sea risk insurance as it considered itself to be large enough to stand its own losses. In a similar way depreciation was not yet shown on the books as a cash drain.

The first generation Thames steamers were slowly replaced from 1844 onwards. The *Little Western* was bought for the Margate run, while the purpose-built *Albion* and the second hand *Prince of Wales* prepared the fleet for inevitable popularity during the Great Exhibition in 1851. In addition, the *Mercury* and *Star* were bought from the Star Steam Packet Company in 1841 and 1846 respectively. The *Magician* was occasionally relegated from the Continental services to Ramsgate duties, until in 1856 the magnificent *Eagle* was bought into the company at the age of three. Her 16 feet diameter paddle wheels carried 12 floats, which by now were fully feathering to enable maximum thrust, and which pushed the ship forward at just over 14 knots. Burtt (see references) waxed enthusiastically:

*"The **Eagle** remained on the service for some thirty years and was indeed a real picture; her funnel painted all black, her lifeboats a deep blue, white paddle boxes and red wheels, while the figurehead of an eagle and name surrounded by gold filigree work adorned the bow. She had no main deck saloon, being open from stem to stern. Prior to about 1887 the Thanet boats made only a single trip, running down to Ramsgate one day, staying there for the night, and returning to London on the following."*

By the late 1840s GSN had nearly 40 steamers in service. These were broadly deployed as follows:

From London to
Antwerp: *Giraffe, Ocean, Rainbow*
Boulogne: *Harlequin, Star, William Jolliffe*
Calais: *Belfast, Earl of Liverpool, Tourist*
Hamburg: *Caledonia, Countess of Lonsdale,*
        John Bull, Princess Royal, Wilberforce
Havre: *Columbine, James Watt*
Hull: *Vivid, Waterwitch*
Leith: *Clarence, Leith, Trident*
Newcastle: *City of Hamburg, London Merchant*
Ostend: *Sir Edward Banks, Triton, Venezuela*

From Southampton to
Bordeaux: *Lion*

From Brighton to
Dieppe: *Menai, Fame*

From Dover to
Boulogne: *City of London, Magician*

**The *Leith* (1837) off Granton
with Edinburgh Castle in the distance**

[DP World P&O Heritage Collection]

In addition there were the steamers *Attwood*, *Eagle*, *Little Western*, *Magnet*, *Mercury* and *Ramona* on the seasonal Thames passenger and excursion services most of which terminated at Ramsgate or Margate. Excursion trips round the Nore were introduced as early as 1830, despite the upper river being an open cess pit for the city until the 'Great Stink' of 1858 set parliament thinking about an engineered solution to the disposal of the capital's sewage.

Palmer (1982) reported:

"In 1838 the GSN withdrew from Margate as a regular operator, though it continued to provide a service to Ramsgate, leaving the service to the New Margate Company in return for a payment of 9d per passenger in the summer season. In 1841 the GSN threatened 'to resume the position of the Company at Margate' if the agreement was not maintained, and it seems probable that the arrangement was continued until 1849, when the GSN purchased the New Margate Company's vessels."

he would receive a lump sum of five times his annual salary should he be replaced by a railway manager, the implication being that Mr Cattarns would put the offer in a favourable light before the Board and the shareholders. At that stage in the discussion Mr Cattarns intimated that his annual salary was £2,000 and not, as was the case, nearer £1,000. Negotiations continued by letter and meeting for nearly a year until Mr Cattarns little scam was rumbled by the Consortium agent. The agent then wrote openly to both the champions of the Consortium and the GSN Chairman accusing Cattarns of incompetence and declaring that he was unfit for his job, that he knew little about the shipping business and was unsuited for the role anyway as he spoke no foreign languages. Cattarns, of course, responded with accusations of bribery on the part of the Consortium.

Records of the attempted take-over and the deceit apparent on both sides of the negotiations are archived at Greenwich. The letters between the two parties do not reveal the outcome, but Cattarns survived in post, as did Tritton, their reputations somewhat tarnished. But as both GSN and the London Steamboat Company carried on much as before, the Consortium was presumably abandoned and denials of wrongdoing issued by all concerned. Cattarns and Tritton were to enjoy a further 16 years in power before they were forced to resign (Chapter 3), a period in which GSN stagnated and was plagued with decisions that would lead it into trouble - as will be seen.

From January 1875 an incentive was given to masters and mates whose fees were increased by 'substantial gratuities for every successful voyage'. The GSN Copy Act of 1877 then allowed the company to raise yet more capital with another new share issue whilst extending its ability to take out mortgages against selected assets. Cope Cornford eloquently summarises the story of the 1870s without any mention of take over or malpractice (and why should he allude to it in a celebratory centennial history of such a respected company?):

"And in 1870, the northern ports of the Continent were blocked with ice, and the Franco-German War had begun. In 1872 the Company's profits were decreased. The price of coal and stores and the rates of wages had risen. In the following year, the Company increased their capital, and in 1874, they obtained a further Act of Parliament extending their powers and consolidating previous Acts. Then in 1876 two new routes were opened: to Harlingen and to Amsterdam; and the service to Bordeaux was reopened. In 1881 it became evident that the extension of the railways had diminished the number of passengers carried by the Company. But in the meantime, the increased efficiency obtained by the use of the screw propeller and compound engines had enabled the Company to extend its cargo trade. In 1881 the fleet of the company numbered 59 vessels, of 41,102 tons, gross registered."

The new services to Holland in 1876 were precipitated by the collapse of the Malcomson Brothers network based at Waterford, when GSN was able to acquire their London to Holland interests and Palgrave Murphy of Dublin their Portuguese interests. The Malcomson empire was the largest shipowner in the world in its day, but its impressive expansion only preceded it being declared impressively bankrupt in 1877. The new GSN services to Harlingen and Amsterdam came with Malcomson's two iron screw steamers *Nora* and *Era* dating from 1861, the veteran paddler *Lion* of 1847 and the more modern paddle steamer *Hollandia*, built in 1867. These were the last paddle steamers to enter the GSN Continental trades. The *Lion* had been built at Govan for Malcomson in 1847 with an old-style steeple engine of some 250 horse power. She was a veritable museum piece, but she served her time as a 'Navvy' until sold for demolition in 1884. The *Hollandia* briefly returned to the Irish Sea to the newly formed Waterford Steamship Company in 1878 under charter from GSN, and was eventually scrapped in 1888. The *Nora*, sadly, was wrecked on passage from Amsterdam to the Thames in the Goeree Roads in November 1879, whilst the *Era* survived in the GSN fleet until 1890.

The 'GSN' archive at Greenwich records that a Thos Buckley, stowaway aboard the steamer *Pilot*, was fined 20/-, or in default 14 days, at a Magistrates hearing in November 1878. Buckley opted for jail. Also in 1878, the company ships *Ostrich* and *Benbow* collided with each other in Woolwich Reach, fortunately with little damage and no loss of life, but with considerable embarrassment all round. And as if in preparation for a new period of efficiency, a contract was let to Mr W Jennings to rid the entire fleet of rats for a fee of 35/- per vessel.

Technological improvements and the efficiencies that went with them had enabled the company to remain in profit. A period of rationalisation and redirection was essential if the brand leader was to remain in front. This realisation was not unique to GSN, but was paralleled in David MacBrayne's West Highland Kingdom in Scotland and in the Irish Sea services operated by G&J Burns, the Laird Line, the Belfast Steamship Company and others during the 1880s. All sought to offer through services from door to door to keep up with the railways and their steamers, whilst MacBrayne and GSN both tried unsuccessfully to expand their sphere of operation into a global arena. The vision and inventiveness of the late-Victorian managers was about to be tested to the limit.

The *Redstart* (1880)
was one of the last iron-hulled ships to be built for GSN.
[National Maritime Museum]

BY ROYAL APPOINTMENT

Surviving documents, quoted in part by Cope Cornford, describe the voyage from Leith to London by Queen Victoria in September 1842 aboard the GSN steamer ***Trident*** as follows:

"On Her Majesty Queen Victoria's intention to proceed to Scotland by sea being publicly announced, the Directors [of GSN] immediately made a tender of any of the steamers of the company to convey Her Majesty there, or to perform any other service that might be agreeable to Her Majesty.

*The Directors were informed in reply to their proposition, that it had been submitted to Her Majesty, who had been graciously pleased to decline the offer, as arrangements had been made that Her Majesty and Prince Albert should proceed in the Royal Yacht [HMY **Royal George**] attended by several Government steamers.*

*The brand new **Trident** was, however, appointed by the Directors to accompany Her Majesty on her voyage, and instructions given to the Captain to hold himself in readiness at all times and pay every attention to Her Majesty's royal wishes and commands should any such be expressed.*

*When the Queen was about to leave the North, it was intimated to the Directors that Her Majesty had expressed her royal pleasure to return to England by the Company's splendid vessel the **Trident**, which had been fitted up in every way suited to Her Majesty and Her Royal Consort, and the Company had the honour to convey the royal visitors in safety to London, and the high gratification of learning that Her Majesty had expressed her full and entire appreciation of the performance of the vessel on her voyage and of her general arrangements that had been made aboard the **Trident** for Her Majesty's accommodation."*

Queen Victoria wrote and spoke enthusiastically of the qualities of the ***Trident***, so providing GSN with an advertisement of its excellence that lasted well into the next century: 'There is no doubt that GSN's best steamers are by far the finest on the coast, easily able to outpace the warships provided as escort.' That the old royal yacht had been towed down the Thames and during part of the North Sea journey at a stately 6 knots can only have added insult to Royal injury.

CHAPTER 3

VICTORIAN COMPETITION AND UNHAPPY SHAREHOLDERS

"Whereas the company was well managed and profitable up to 1870 under a Board which still included connections with the original directors, over investment following substantial capital increases in 1874 and 1877 presented problems in the more challenging business environment of the late nineteenth century, leading to shareholder unrest and the near collapse of the company. Financial restructuring in 1902, disadvantageous to shareholders, and a revision of the company's operating policy under Chairman White would lead to slow recovery prior to the First World War, in still difficult trading conditions."

Forrester, UNPUBLISHED PHD THESIS, 2006

The 1881 timetable of services is a landmark document for GSN. The services themselves were much as before and the tariffs unchanged. What was new was the offer of through Bills of Lading to India and other destinations in conjunction with the British India Steam Navigation Company. This marked the beginning of an important link with the liner company that would ultimately be the saviour of GSN.

GSN was able to initiate a new service through the Mediterranean to Sicily and the west coast of Italy in 1882, partly in response to a contract with the Italian Government to export livestock to Britain. It had also started a new service to Oporto in 1878, and taken over the local freight agency in Bordeaux only the previous year amid rumours of staff misconduct within the old independent agency. Some valuable Government charters were obtained to supply British forces in Egypt following the invasion of Alexandria, a move aimed at protecting a £4 million British investment in the Suez Canal - the *Osprey*, *Libra* and *Nautilus* were the mainstay of this activity.

American chilled beef and live imports hit the continental live cattle trade, but as Forrester reported:

"Ever pragmatic, in 1879 GSN arranged with the Corporation of the City of London to transport the large number of American cattle arriving in the docks to the Deptford Market. The fact that the transatlantic imports had lessened the importance of the Continental cattle trade was acknowledged."

Larger ships were required for the Mediterranean service and the company's first steel-hulled vessel, the two year old *Deak*, was bought specifically for the new trade and in due course given the name *Swan*. Experience with the *Deak* persuaded GSN to place an order with Gourlay Brothers of Dundee in 1883 for its first purpose built steel-hulled ship. There had been a long association with Gourlay Brothers and there was an established trust between shipowner and shipbuilder. The new ship was the *Cygnet*, the largest yet to fly the GSN house flag with a gross tonnage of 2,012. Although the concept of the steel hull was still new it had been successfully introduced on Clyde passenger services in the late 1870s, but the advantages of the new material were yet to be proven and the corrosion resistance of some early mild steel was poor and maintenance high. Vessels such as David MacBrayne's magnificent paddle steamer *Columba* were the pioneers. The integrity of her long slender steel hull was adequately demonstrated in 1900 when the original set of four Navy-type boilers was replaced by lighter haystack boilers, so reducing the draught of the *Columba* by five inches.

The *Cygnet* was followed by another large steel ship, the *Albatross*, in 1884 and the pair championed the Mediterranean route with some shorter voyages as far as Bordeaux only and occasional trips to support the Hamburg service. The two ships sported red-clothed saloon tables with attendant aspidistras, typical for the day. Their invasion of the Mediterranean soon included a whole range of ports, of which one or two were calls by inducement only, but which included Catania, Genoa, Livorno, Messina, Naples, Palermo, Pozzuoli, Rome (Civitavecchia), Savona, Spezia and Syracuse. It was not long before the Greek port of Patras and the Turkish ports of Smyrna (Izmir) and Istanbul were added to the schedules. At each port, as at each port in France and northern Europe, a company agent was installed in a GSN office, there to promote the company business and to look after the visit of each vessel: its pilotage, bunkering, loading and unioading. The GSN port network acted on behalf of other companies as well and was very much a profit making concern. Besides, its marketing activities promoting GSN cargo traffic must have reaped huge rewards for the company.

The Mediterranean service was interesting in that it loaded at Newcastle, Middlesbrough, London and finally Newlyn for passengers. It only catered for a small number of passengers and most ships offered berths for just twelve in first class. Despite an outbreak of cholera in France, Spain and Italy in 1883, the company pressed on to try and consolidate its new territory. This it did with vengeance and was to stay with the Mediterranean trade for the next eight decades. And in 1885 it again chartered supply ships to the Government, this time in support of the march from Alexandria into Sudan which failed to relieve General Gordon and his men besieged in Khartoum. However, profits were halved that year to £38,007 and no dividend was paid. Shareholder unrest was now apparent and there was mounting pressure on Chairman Tritton. The underlying cause was poor freight rates and rising operational costs, but Tritton continued to spend what money he had, including what would otherwise have been paid as a dividend, on new ships.

The Hamburg Dalmann Quay passenger service was transferred from London to Harwich Parkeston Quay in 1886[1]. The first sailing from Harwich was taken by the **Hawk** on 29 March, and the shorter passage time of 30 hours, with train connection to London, proved a great success with the travelling public. Elsewhere, the notable event in 1887 was the delivery of the cargo steamer **Grebe**, which had been designed specifically for use on the Tonnay-Charente brandy run.

**The *Grebe* (1887)
was delivered by Gourlay Brothers
at Dundee for use on the brandy run
from Tonnay-Charente.**

But the level of business fell away from the company as the shorter links became barely profitable. In September 1884 Chairman Herbert Tritton wrote to the captains of the GSN fleet 'inviting their suggestions as to how they might decrease permanently the expenditure incurred in working the vessels.' Although the London day service to Ostend by the paddle steamers **Swallow** and **Swift** remained popular, and the longer run to Hamburg also remained buoyant, passenger berths to Holland, Belgium and the nearer French ports were reduced to twelve and the services thereafter relied almost entirely on cargo tariffs. The sorry tale is described by Cope Cornford almost dismissively within a single paragraph, but in truth the company was on the line:

"In 1886, so bad was the trade, that the Directors remitted a part of their fees, and some of the principal officials accepted a temporary reduction in their salaries. The company, however, continued to extend its business as opportunity served, until 1889, when there befell the memorable strike of dock labourers. In the following year the costs of working were considerably increased; the cattle trade diminished; in 1892 the Continental cattle trade was closed altogether; and from 1892 to 1895 were the worst years known to the company."

Despite the depressed conditions for the cargo ships, GSN found itself obliged to re-equip its Thames excursion fleet in the late 1880s on learning of the intention that a rival company was being created to provide an excursion service to Clacton and possibly other destinations. This was the embryo Belle Steamers which had the steamer **Clacton** in service in time for the 1888 season. The Thames excursion trade was still recovering from the knock-on effects of the **Princess Alice** disaster, which had occurred in 1878 when over 200 passengers and crew lost their lives after the **Princess Alice** sank in collision with a collier off Beckton. The fall out from the accident put the River Thames Steamboat Company out of business in 1886, so bringing to an end their sailings to Clacton, but this in turn opened the door to the new Clacton-based syndicate and also offered GSN an opportunity.

The business syndicate in Clacton-on-Sea wanted to introduce a new company to try and recover the steamer trade to their town. There was then a spate of new orders by GSN which acted in response to rumours that the new operator would be equipped with modern, fast and luxurious ships, and who now, in any event, saw an opportunity to enter the Essex coast trade. GSN was also conscious of increasing competition on its traditional Thanet and cross-channel services and was seeking new trade - what better than a service to Southend and on to Clacton-on-Sea and Great Yarmouth?

---

[1] Parkeston Quay was opened in 1883 by, and named after, the Great Eastern Railway chairman Charles Parkes. The first railway service to Hook of Holland, which survives to this day under the Stena Line banner, was in 1893.

GSN embarked on its new building programme with orders for five new saloon steamers placed with J Scott of Kinghorn in Fife. These were the famous 'classical bird' class of steamers, the first of which, the **Halcyon**, was delivered in 1887 and the last, the **Philomel**, at a cost of £13,230 in 1889. The other three ships were given the names **Mavis**, **Oriole** and **Laverock**, the latter built at a cost of £12,150. They were all of broadly similar dimensions, although the **Oriole** and **Philomel** were 20 feet or so longer than their sisters and had more powerful engines, the **Philomel** significantly so with a nominal horse power of 327 compared with 240 to 260 in the other vessels. The engines were of the compound, two crank, diagonal type, lubricated by grease delivered by 'walking tubes', as used on some naval ships of the day. Their service speed was a comfortable 17 knots.

The *Philomel* (1889), one of the classical bird quintet of paddle steamers built for the Thames excursion trade, is seen leaving Great Yarmouth.

The five 'classical birds' offered saloon accommodation forward of the single funnel, with the rounded fore end of the saloon just short of the foremast. Their distinguishing features were the full width saloon and the Upper Deck carried forward to the foremast. They all had two masts. In recognition of their role as pleasure steamers, they were given cream coloured funnels and white deckhouses instead of the more utilitarian darker colours that were then standard. The ships took over the Thanet and continental trips from London Bridge, and inaugurated a two day return to Great Yarmouth, with intermediate calls including Gravesend, Southend and Clacton. The **Laverock** was also used in 1889 for excursions to Boulogne, the popularity of which was boosted by visitors to the Paris Exhibition. The older ships, **Sir Walter Raleigh** and **Hoboken**, which had joined the GSN fleet in 1862 and 1877 respectively, were retained largely for relief work, but the new quintet sent the **Eagle** to the breakers in 1886, with the now outdated **Hilda** following three years later.

This investment in the Thames services inevitably put GSN back in the frame during a period when the trade again began to boom whilst the late Victorian zeal for fresh air and a stiff sea breeze developed into a seasonal exodus from the city. But its success was a case of the tail wagging the dog, as the overall income spread throughout the year, to include the winter months of idle paddle steamers lying at the buoys off Deptford, was small and the overall return to the company would not help bail it out of the late Victorian depression. As time went on, competition on the excursion services intensified and fares came down (to the benefit of the passengers) reducing the economic margins of the ships even more. Fortunately for GSN, this did not happen until the turn of the century.

Throughout this period of depressed business in the 1880s, the Hamburg passenger and cargo service remained the jewel in the crown, whilst Edinburgh was paying its way, and Bordeaux was self-sustaining. As a result these three main passenger routes each received new ships in quick succession. Whether the investment was wise given the prevailing trading conditions is questionable. In hindsight the decision of the Board, led by Chairman Tritton and no doubt also by Manager Cattarns, to rebuild at that time unnecessarily placed GSN at risk of bankruptcy. The 1889 Dock Labour Strike did little for shippers' confidence, and at the same time import of sheep and cattle from Germany and sheep from Holland was banned - Tritton's resignation was now an inevitability. In 1890 Chairman Tritton prepared a plan to sell off its vital wharves on the Thames, which it had struggled so hard to acquire, in order to raise yet more cash for new ships. This bizarre plan was never put to the shareholders, and in so doing, Tritton bought himself a little extra time.

The London to Leith service received the **Seamew** in 1888, a fast vessel which put GSN a cut above the competition with a slightly shorter voyage time. The **Seamew** had three classes of accommodation and was able to carry about 100 passengers, first and second class were amidships with the third class accommodated in the foc'sle. She was advertised as 'illuminated throughout by electric light'. The **Rainbow** and **Osprey** were also fitted with experimental low voltage electric lighting systems.

The next new passenger vessel was the magnificent **Hirondelle**, which was built for the Bordeaux service. The **Hirondelle** and the **Seamew** were the first vessels to be routinely insured, in recognition of rising costs and increasingly sophisticated vessels. Previously steamers only carried insurance whilst chartered to a third party. The **Hirondelle** was delivered in May 1890 from Gourlay Brothers at Dundee and in June was able to carry a party of invitees in celebratory fashion to Gravesend, having picked them up on her voyage south at Parkeston Quay. Her triple expansion engines gave her a service speed of 14 knots although she attained 15.5 knots on trial. Lord Greenway described her in his book A CENTURY OF NORTH SEA PASSENGER STEAMERS (she was transferred to the Hamburg service in 1905):

**The *Hirondelle* (1890)
set a new standard for fast long distance ferries when
she started on the run to Bordeaux.
She is seen in her original form complete with flat-topped funnel
and steam deck cranes characteristic of the GSN steamers**

[Picture by the Nautical Photo Agency]

"She was a two deck steel ship with iron plating, and her hull was subdivided into five watertight compartments with a full length double bottom. Her hull gave the appearance of being flush decked but high bulwarks containing outward-swinging doors concealed a 30 feet long well deck between a foc'sle and long combined bridge and poop. A large deckhouse amidships contained a music room, smoke room and some special staterooms, whilst above these was the bridge, lifeboats and a raking horizontal topped funnel.

She was designed to carry 70 first, 50 second, and 25 third class passengers with the majority of the first class staterooms and main saloon being placed aft of the machinery on the Main Deck. Second class accommodation was forward of the engines and third class under the foc'sle, with electric lighting fitted throughout. She had a deadweight cargo capacity of some 2,500 tons, and handling equipment included four steam cranes."

The third new passenger ship was the even grander **Peregrine**, delivered by W B Thomson & Company at Dundee in 1891, and designed for the Parkeston Quay to Hamburg service. She undertook trials at the end of August and was ready for service in September. She had called at Granton on her delivery voyage, where she had been open to the public and much admired. Ambrose Greenway described the new ship:

"She was an iron ship and her hull was subdivided by five watertight bulkheads from keel to Upper Deck whilst a cellular double bottom was provided for ballast. Above the Upper or Promenade Deck was a Boat Deck and above this the bridge.

She could carry in all about 200 passengers in two classes, first and third, with some 60 berths being provided for the former under the main saloon. Electric lighting and steam heating were provided for passenger comfort and safety measures included the provision of six lifeboats."

At that time the Australian shipping company Howard Smith was urgently looking for new and upgraded tonnage with which to face competition from the rival AUSN Company on the Australian coastal routes. A representative of Howard Smith was invited along with other guests to inspect the ship during the pre-delivery speed trials, in which the **Peregrine** attained 15.5 knots. The idea was to demonstrate the state-of-the-art design that Howard Smith could modify and order for itself. Howard Smith had other ideas, and with a generous price offered to GSN, the **Peregrine** completed her maiden round voyage to Hamburg and returned to her builders to be made ready for a long sea voyage. She arrived in Melbourne on 26 November, where her accommodation was described as luxurious. Her Australian career was very successful, even coping with the Western Australian gold rush in 1893. She was never renamed. However, she was lengthened in 1906 to accommodate increasing demand and to give her more resistance to rolling, for which she had developed a poor reputation. In 1915 she opened a new East Coast mail service to Cairns but was sold in 1916 when mechanical problems started to arise.

This profit taking action on the part of GSN required an urgent repeat order to be placed. The Thompson yard was able to put another almost identical *Peregrine* into the water in May 1892 ready to take up service in July. The modified design included a full width dining saloon with seats for 70 passengers and an increased passenger capacity of 250. Her design speed was an improved 16 knots which reduced the 30 hour crossing to Hamburg to just 24 hours. The *Peregrine* was advertised as the express service vice her partner's standard service; partners varied from time to time but the *Gannet*, *Lapwing* and *Seamew* were commonly used. The single saloon fare in those days was a mere £1-10-0.

The *Peregrine* (1892)
succeeded the *Peregrine* built in 1891 on the Parkeston Quay to Hamburg service. The earlier ship,
a near identical sister, was sold, after just one round trip, for use in Australia.

Despite the new passenger ships the overall economics of a predominantly cargo carrying company remained grave and £½ million had been wiped from the value of the company shares. To make matters worse, the *Kestrel* was run down and sunk at anchor in the Elbe in 1893, the *Rainbow* collided with the German steamer *Elbe* and again two company ships, the *Petrel* and *Cormorant*, collided with each other. In the twelve months through 1889/90 there had been fifteen collisions, three involving the *Kestrel*, three groundings and five fires. The outcome of all this, with many ships still uninsured, was significant losses. In fact, in 1893 as little as £1,000 was left for the company to carry over after dividends and taxes had been paid and the remaining surplus ploughed back to cover insurance losses.

There was extensive criticism from shareholders about the poor trade with Edinburgh, compared with the evident success of GSN's competitors. The very suitability of the ships was questioned and a recommendation made to the Board that temporary passenger accommodation be provided in the summer months to satisfy seasonal customer demand. This had been the practice in the past notably when the *Triton* was on the service in the mid-1800s. There was also a demand to the Board that advertising would help, as also would the appointment of a designated manager of the Edinburgh service.

Matters finally came to a head when Chairman Herbert Tritton and his sidekick Manager Cattarns suddenly resigned and walked away from the company. Tritton turned out to be a better judge of banking than of shipping and returned to the family business at the age of 49 to become a highly respected City banker. A new Chairman was appointed from the Board, Sir Stuart Hogg. An open letter was addressed to fellow shareholders by Charles H Robins, a letter which included the following censure:

"Mr Tritton assumed the Chair about 18 years ago, and for the first time in the annals of the company, appointed a general manager, and from that day to this the company has been going from bad to worse. He found it a flourishing and dividend paying concern and he left us without a word of explanation as to the condition we are in today. The shareholders of this company have a right to judge by results, and I ask are they satisfactory?

Lamentable as it must appear, we are now plainly told by the present Directors that they intend to follow in the lines of their predecessors, notwithstanding that the results have proved so disastrous."

Perhaps armed with the success of the Mediterranean service from London, and conscious of the declining trades nearer to home and the rising costs of operating them, GSN strove to widen its empire to global proportions. Bizarrely, a number of other shipowners had realised that they too needed to widen their horizons to regain lost business nearer to home in this same difficult period. David MacBrayne looked out from the Western Isles and attempted to trade with Iceland in 1887 but had given up by the early 1890s a poorer man. The Wilson Line at Hull was more successful in expanding its Scandinavian and Baltic services to the Mediterranean and even to North America but had its fingers severely burnt when it first tried to expand its services to India in the 1880s. So too did GSN when the company directors took an almost terminal turn, which now seems almost crazy – they moved on Liverpool, picking on the West African trade.

For some obscure reason, the new company Chairman, Sir Stuart Hogg, thought he could move into Liverpool in competition with the established African Steamship Company and the British & African Steam Navigation Company, which together divided the sailings to West Africa between them. This was the established might that would eventually join forces and merge as Elder Dempster Lines. But even then the two existing operators had a comprehensive understanding of just what was on offer along with their own shared network of local agents who no doubt had a full grasp of West African business etiquette and the role of backsheesh.

The **Raven** and **Cygnet**, both of which had been enlarged in 1892 with the addition of new midships sections which extended their lengths by 32 feet, along with the **Guillemot** and **Linnet**, made a total of eighteen round voyages to West Africa. The new GSN service from Liverpool called at Freetown, Lagos and Accra, but lasted only for the brief period from February 1894 to August 1895. Somewhat hurt, the economics of the new route forced GSN to retrench its four ships to Mediterranean duties and Chairman Hogg was succeeded that same summer by Sir James Lyle Mackay, later Lord Inchcape. The mighty Liverpool companies would live to see another day!

This short episode was the subject of intense criticism by some Board members, shareholders and even the Press. A letter to the **FINANCIAL NEWS** dated 23 February 1895 read:

"Dear Sir

…Year after year the same story is told, with the same results, no dividend… But as if in burlesque, the report goes on to say that the company is meeting with increased encouragement and support on the West African trade, but owing to the keen competition, freights, at present, are unremunerative. Of course, if the company obliges certain people by running its vessels for nothing, or at a loss, it will not be surprising if it gets 'increased encouragement and support'.

Yours truly disgusted"

Stuart Hogg's retirement from the Chair came to many of the shareholders as a relief. He had been in post just two years.

Although Sir James Lyle Mackay was to remain Chairman for only a brief two year period, his tenure as the new Chairman was critical to the wellbeing of the company in later years. Mackay was an implant from the British India Steam Navigation Company, relationships now being such that British India needed to safeguard its Continental feeder network provided by GSN. It was Mackay who arrested the rot that had set within GSN through the previous twenty years of indifferent leadership by Tritton and Hogg, aided and abetted, it seems, by Tritton's Manager Cattarns. Mackay, by then Lord Inchcape, went on to become Chairman of the merged P&O and British India companies in 1914.

In the meantime, the profit and loss account for the year 1896 was rather telling: the London to Ostend service lost £2,031 and Southampton to Bordeaux lost £2,235. The most profitable were the Mediterranean and Hamburg routes which returned a profit of £17,774 and £16,345 respectively.

The West African safari of the mid-1890s had been a costly mistake, but even Mackay found it difficult to help the company out of the doldrums. If its place in the sun was to be denied in Africa, GSN was to try its luck across the Atlantic. Although it could not afford to build any new ships after 1895, it could afford to buy second hand tonnage. GSN set about buying a tramp fleet primarily for the charter market. Eight second hand vessels came into the fleet, and these were variously employed on charters principally to North and South America, although the ships also augmented expansion on the Mediterranean routes which now included calls in Algeria, Corsica and occasional forays into the Black Sea.

In 1894, the large steamer **Adjutant**, 2,392 tons gross, sailed to Uruguay with coal, returning to Rotterdam in April with grain. Eighteen months later she repeated the trip, this time returning to Sharpness Docks near Gloucester. She was on her travels again in 1898 when she sailed from Sunderland to Philadelphia, returning to Dublin, then to resume her Mediterranean sailings. The **Kelvinside** made several trips to the Eastern Seaboard of the United States with calls in Mexico and Nova Scotia returning variously to Antwerp, London and even Bordeaux. On her final initiation to the Home Trade in 1899, she was renamed **Sheldrake**, but the following year she was back on the coal run this time to Galveston, and her final transatlantic voyage was to Nova Scotia, before she settled for the more mundane destinations of the Mediterranean. So at the close of the reign of Victoria, GSN once and for all withdrew from the transatlantic charter market and again focused on its core business.

A variety of non-standard names had entered the fleet during this expeditionary period and vessels included the one time Ben Line vessel **Vesuvio**, the Glasgow tramp steamer **Merannio**, Ropner's **Preston**, and the Grampian Steamship Company's **Balgownie**, amongst others. This buying spree ended in 1902. Whether the tramping market had actually paid its way is hard to judge but it did provide the company with additional tonnage of relatively large capacity which it could also deploy on the longer routes to the Mediterranean ports and to Hamburg as business required.

GSN built one more new vessel for the Thames excursion fleet, another **Eagle**, a thoroughly modern steamer which was completed by Gourlay Brothers of Dundee in 1898 for £23,000. She was designed and built to combat the perceived threat of superiority in the rival New Palace Steamers and Belle Steamers fleets. The saloons and dining room occupied the full width of the ship, and with low voltage electric lighting she presented a modern and comfortable image. As the London terminal had now moved to Fresh Wharf below London Bridge, her funnel was not telescopic, as had previously been necessary. The navigation bridge, however, was in the traditional position across the paddle boxes and aft of the funnel.

The excursion steamer _Eagle_ (1898) brought new standards to the London to Margate day trip.

[Picture by the Nautical Photo Agency]

The **Eagle** was good for one knot more than the 17 knot **Halcyon** classical bird-class of steamer. This was a useful asset on the now highly competitive London to Margate and Ramsgate service. The **Halcyon** and **Philomel** were both reboilered in 1899. The elderly, and now thoroughly outclassed, reserve steamer **Hoboken** had been dispatched to the breakers at the end of the 1897 season.

In 1899 GSN was forced to tighten its belt further with the withdrawal of the London to Boulogne service. The long-standing rivalry on the direct London to Boulogne route between the Bennett Steamship Company of Goole and GSN, for once, ended in defeat. This was a bitter blow to GSN, as the company had traded regularly with Boulogne ever since the **Rob Roy**, as one of the forebears of the company, had been the first steamship to enter the port in April 1822. All said and done, the London to Boulogne route was well served by rail and sea via Folkestone whereas Bennett was better placed with his direct onward connection along the east coast to Goole.

Any ambition that GSN may have harboured to develop a regular service between London and Paris was thwarted also in 1899, when the Compagnie Maritime de la Seine established the London-Paris Line with five steamers especially designed for the route. This new service ran in competition with the London based company J Burnett & Sons and even bought one of Burnett's purpose-built Paris vessels, the **Mabel**, for the new French service. W H Muller later used British flag vessels on the route in the 1920s but the French company thrived. All the ships were designed with shallow draught, along with low air draught and hinged masts and funnels. The helmsman was occasionally bidden to duck as bridges approached when the Seine was in flood.

GSN was still struggling to maintain its market position in the Home Trade at the dawn of the twentieth century. The cargo and passenger routes to the Continent and Mediterranean ports were stagnant, whilst the UK and near Continental trades had never recovered from competition with the railways. Conversely, the Thames excursion routes were at their peak, but the trade on offer would no longer increase and the competition for business would become more intense.

As the engineering development and inventiveness that characterised the Victorian age finally came to an end, the Edwardian sense of achievement and grandeur set in. GSN urgently needed to find a way of boosting its market share and had yet to draw on the last of its Victorian inventiveness before it was too late. Happily it was not alone in tackling its declining economic margins, and was able to take heed from others in the same position, including various operators in the Irish Sea. All soon realised the benefits of offering a through cargo handling package from factory to wholesaler or distributor, and all to a greater or lesser degree either signed agreements with the railways, took over or partnered land-based distributors, both at home and abroad, or set up new distribution companies.

The popular *Fingal* (1894) provided keen competition on the east coast when she was first commissioned for the London & Edinburgh Shipping Company.

[Picture by the Nautical Photo Agency]

THE EARL OF INCHCAPE GCSI, GCMG, KCIE (1852-1932)

James Lyle Mackay was made a peer in 1911 for services to the nation. He was also the man that was instrumental in bringing GSN into the mighty P&O empire in 1920, and as such, he is critical to the GSN story. George Blake, in his book **BI CENTENARY 1856-1956**, describes James Lyle Mackay's childhood:

*"James Mackay was born in Arbroath, Angus, in 1852, the fourth child of a shipmaster and small shipowner: his mother being a Nova Scotian lady with the pleasing name of Deborah Lyle his father had met on one of his voyages. The family enjoyed a voyage to Archangel in one of his father's ships. He was only 12, however, when Captain James Mackay was lost overboard from the full rigged ship **Seafield** on a voyage home from Australia, probably in the Bay of Bengal, and his mother died in the same year, 1864. He had already had some schooling at Arbroath Academy, and his guardian then chose to send the orphan, presumably as some sort of boarder, to Elgin Academy, still one of the most distinguished of Scottish secondary schools. The future Lord Inchcape was thus educated up to the highest standards of Scottish teaching in his period, short of university training."*

James was entirely a self-made man and an ambitious visionary. After working with a ropemaker in his hometown for four years he went to London to join Gellatly, Hankin, Sewell & Company as a clerk. This job introduced him to the affairs of the British India Steam Navigation Company and their managing agents in India, Mackinnon Mackenzie & Company. At the age of 22, he joined Mackinnon Mackenzie & Company in Calcutta, as a general assistant. He rose rapidly through the ranks. In due course the important role of Mackinnon Mackenzie & Company in Indian commercial affairs was reflected in Mackay's appointment as Sheriff of Calcutta, election to President of the Bengal Chamber of Commerce in 1890 and finally his becoming a Member of the Viceroy's Council.

In 1893 James Lyle Mackay was recalled to London to take up an appointment as a Director of British India and within a year of his return he was given a knighthood. In February 1895 Sir James was offered the Chairmanship of GSN, a company that was in desperate need of a strategy that would put it back into profitability. The appointment reflected the increasing bond between the provider of the feeder routes with that of the liner services. Sir James gave GSN two sound ideas: the one that second hand tramp steamers could be obtained cheaply and set to work on the charter market as well as bolster the company's Mediterranean services, and the other that GSN should start to offer a door-to-door cargo-handling network in the style that the railways had already initiated. The first was acted upon with vigour, but the second was not to be instigated for several years. Sir James Mackay stood down from the Chair in May 1897, faced with an increasing workload for his prime interest, that of the British India Steam Navigation Company, although he was retained as a financial advisor to GSN for several years and later became a trustee of the company's Debenture Fund. Although not easy to decipher from company records, it is likely that the British India Steam Navigation Company began to purchase a stake in GSN as a minority but secret shareholder at about this time, whilst treating GSN as the preferred carrier for onward shipments to the Continent.

In 1901 James Lyle Mackay was sent to China to negotiate a commercial treaty following the Boxer Rebellion. Although he was successful and the treaty was duly signed, it was never acted upon due to further disagreement between Britain and China. He was rewarded in 1911 with a peerage, adopting the title Earl of Inchcape. He was appointed Chairman of the Board of British India in March 1913 following the retirement of Duncan Mackinnon. The following year Baron Inchcape colluded with fellow Scot Sir Thomas Sutherland, the 78 year old Chairman of P&O, to create a merger of P&O and British India, in which Sutherland would retire and Lord Inchcape would take over the merged group. Whilst the spin was of a P&O take over, the reality was in effect a British India take over. The respective boards were gathered together, and the vote was wholeheartedly in favour of a merger with just two abstentions. The merged capital amounted to a massive £15 million.

Lord Inchcape never forgot his years at the helm of GSN. GSN continued to provide feeder routes for the network of long-haul British India services, whilst from 1914 onwards, GSN formally became the preferred feeder service for both P&O and British India. It was common to find GSN vessels in the docks alongside one of the cargo liners loading or unloading goods for transhipment to France, the Low Countries or Germany. This was a comfortable arrangement for GSN which provided useful bread and butter income and which eventually saw P&O taking over GSN, so providing it with a valuable financial buffer. Indeed, Lord Inchcape's acquisitions during the Great War speak for themselves: New Zealand Shipping Company, Union Steamship Company, Hain, Nourse, and interests in Cory and Silley Weir; and after the war: Orient Line in 1918, the (Egyptian) Khedivial Mail Line in 1919 (resold in 1924), GSN in 1920, and the Strick Line in 1923.

George Blake illustrates Inchcape's character in the following passage:

"This was the man who could hold his own against a host of rivals and yet found time, when travelling in one of his own ships, deliberately to drop a cigarette end or burnt match on the deck and watch to see if it was duly swept up... This was the man often enough cursed by his colleagues and officers for apparent unreasonableness, who wrote to his wife twice a day when they were apart and loved to sing with his children round the domestic piano, his favourite ditty 'John Peel', who enjoyed rather schoolboyish jokes and used to startle the staff of the Bombay office by riding his pony upstairs and so among the desks."

In due course Lord Inchcape did his best to safeguard the future of the P&O empire as the world headed slowly towards the depressed years of the 1930s. He even turned a monarchy down, politely declining the proffered throne of King of Albania as 'not in my line'! However, he did accept a well-deserved viscountcy and an earldom. He died aboard his yacht whilst at Monte Carlo in 1932, having caught a chill during the trials of the new P&O liner **Carthage**. He had earlier sent a message to the P&O Board which included the sentiment 'It has been heart-rending to see the steamers leaving London, week after week... with thousands of tons of unoccupied space – so different from the old days'. That same year, in the height of the Depression, the P&O Board was unable to recommend payment of a dividend on its deferred stock.

CHAPTER 4

REFOCUSING THE BUSINESS – EDWARDIAN RECOVERY

This was a period of consolidation and stability. From the prestigious packet steamers down to the near-Continental cargo ships, good service, and prompt and regular arrivals were the key. Throughout this whole period, for example, the little steamer *Virgo* sailed without fail for Hamburg every Saturday night regardless of season, weather or tide.

The reign of Edward VII was heralded by the purchase of the little passenger and cargo steamer *Calvados* from the South Eastern Railway. Built by Denny for the London, Brighton and South Coast Railway in 1894, the *Calvados* and sister *Trouville* maintained the Newhaven to Caen passenger service with quasi-sister *Prince Arthur*. In 1901 the three ships were swapped for two elderly cargo ships from the South Eastern & Chatham Railway, the 'new' vessels which dated from 1878, were quickly given the familiar names *Calvados* and *Trouville* and life carried on much as before. Why such a deal was struck with a rival railway company and whether money also changed hands, is unclear. The *Trouville*, of the original pair, was renamed *Walmer* and served her new owners into the 1930s, whilst the *Calvados* was immediately sold to GSN and given the name *Alouette*.

The little steamer was taken in hand at Deptford and converted into a day passenger and cargo ship for use on the Ostend service. And what a lovely sight emerged from the yard. Although the French children's song was clearly not composed with the steamer in mind, as our lovely lark could not be plucked and eaten, the opening line of the song nevertheless comes to mind:

> *Alouette*, gentille *Alouette*,
> *Alouette*, je te plumerai,
> Je te plumerai la tête…

But could she roll? Ambrose Greenway (see references) described the *Calvados* and her later guise as the pretty little *Alouette*:

*"She was a steel ship with raised foc'sle and Bridge Deck and a rather unusual stern. Two steel pole masts surrounded a thin looking funnel which was painted white with a black top. Passenger accommodation was provided amidships for 44 first class travellers, whilst that of the later **Prince Arthur** catered for 66 with space for a number of third class passengers under the foc'sle. Like her sisters, **Calvados** was a twin screw ship, power being derived from two triple expansion engines; these gave her a trials speed of just under 16 knots at 1,480 indicated horse power. Her bunkers could hold about 50 tons of coal.*

*Following her transfer (sic) to GSN she was renamed **Alouette**, and wearing her new owner's all black funnel colours was placed in a thrice weekly service between London and Ostend, replacing the old paddle steamers **Swallow** and **Swift**. Apart from passengers, of which she could carry 233 in first class and 92 in second class, her cargo included a large amount of rabbits earning her the name 'Ostend Rabbit Boat' and she became a well known sight in the Thames in the years leading up to World War I. She had the reputation of being quite a roller and on one occasion is believed to have lost her funnel during a particularly bad roll in a Channel gale."*

The *Swift* (1884) in Hull & Netherlands Steamship colours was bought in 1902 and served GSN without change of name until resold in 1911.

Dutch lop-eared pet rabbits might have enjoyed sitting on the laps of their Edwardian mistresses a plenty, but GSN was still enduring a cash crisis. The dock workers and lightermen's strikes of 1900 did little to help the company, still suffering from the loss of the live cattle trade nearly ten years previously. Clearly some form of rationalisation or refocusing was in order. 1902 was the turning point for the company. Firstly, 39 year old Mr Richard White, undoubtedly the most visionary Chairman GSN was ever to enjoy[1], was appointed head of the Board, and secondly the company was rapidly reconstructed under White's supervision as a limited liability company. The latter provided a degree of protection to the shareholders, whilst the full title of the company now became General Steam Navigation Company Limited. The restructuring required the old company to elect for voluntary liquidation whilst a new company was established. This freed the ties to the various Parliamentary Acts which were now incompatible with modern operating conditions. The capital value of the fleet was also greatly reduced and dividends were once again payable to shareholders, whilst the Board was pruned to just four full time members.

Hancock, in SEMPER FIDELIS, described White:

"Conditions called for a man of courage, energy and ability to put things right. Subsequent events proved that Mr White was the man. In the ten years he had spent as a director, he had acquired experience and knowledge which in 1902, when he took the helm, enabled him to commence the reorganisation of the Company. He had seen that owning ships without controlling cargo was an unprofitable business, and he had, therefore, proceeded to obtain control of the handling and forwarding of cargoes – operations which in the past had been entirely in the hands of brokers and other middlemen. Through this policy, the Company, from being one that merely owned and managed ships, became a transport company controlling the cargo from origin to destination, with offices of its own at all the principal Continental ports."

Although the idea of door-to-door cargo handling had first been mooted by Sir James Mackay, the company had not been in a strong enough financial position to implement the policy. It was White who secured the capital within the company through careful housekeeping and the reconstruction that took place in 1902, which then allowed new investment in the appropriate infrastructure. He also created a Tourist Department at London with the objective of attracting more passengers to the company's services.

During the realignment of the company a number of new and second hand vessels arrived in the fleet. The new ships tended to be designed with large hold space relative to the ship's deadweight, as the general cargoes normal to the company were bulky, typically 100 cubic feet or more to the ton. The **Groningen** and **Leeuwarden** were delivered by Sir Raylton Dixon & Company at Middlesbrough as intermediate-sized steamers for the Dutch routes with just a handful of passenger berths.

The *Leeuwarden* (1903)
maintained services to Dutch ports for which little passenger
accommodation was required. Note the steam deck cranes.

[1] Forrester (2006) suggests that Robert White may even have been a protegé of James Mackay.

Their Dutch names reflected the pooling agreement on the Rotterdam service between GSN, Hollandsche Stoomboot Maatschappij and Wm H Muller & Company's General Steamship Company of Rotterdam from 1900 onwards.

The **Ortolan** was delivered by the Caledon Shipbuilding & Engineering Company at Dundee to serve the Bordeaux route. Two smaller vessels, the **Bullfinch** and **Goldfinch** were commissioned for the constricted waterways of the Low Countries, the German cargo routes and the East Coast UK cargo services. A number of the new ships, as well as the **Widgeon** and **Teal**, were equipped with cool chambers for the carriage of dairy products from the Netherlands.

For the Bordeaux service, the Caledon Shipbuilding & Engineering Company at Dundee built the **Ortolan** and a quasi-sister the **Grive**, which came from the same builders in 1906, both magnificent vessels with substantial passenger accommodation. They were broadly similar in design to the **Hirondelle**, which had maintained the Bordeaux passenger service since her delivery in 1890, latterly supported by the former Mediterranean trader **Albatross**. The arrival of the two new ships displaced the **Hirondelle** to Parkeston Quay, where she took up the Hamburg route alongside the **Peregrine**. This allowed the **Peregrine** to take occasional extra sailings for Det Forenede Dampskibs-Selskab A/S (better known today as DFDS) to Esbjerg in Denmark alongside their crack steamer **J C La Cour**.

The **Ortolan** (1902)
was built for the Bordeaux
passenger and cargo service

[A GSN postcard]

The **Grive** (1905)
was designed on similar lines to
the **Ortolan** of 1902 and was also
built for the Bordeaux service.

The ultimate development of the **Hirondelle**-class of vessel was the **Fauvette**, which completed the new building for the Bordeaux service in 1912. The **Fauvette** was equipped to carry 106 passengers in one class, with the cabins and saloon on the Shelter Deck and the music room, smoking room and ladies room above on the Bridge Deck. The three ships each carried general cargo which included the traditional import of wine and brandy, but they also had small thermally insulated compartments for the carriage of meat. Inward voyages were typically heavily booked whereas many outward sailings could sail only lightly loaded with exports.

The **Fauvette** (1912)
was a one-class passenger
and cargo steamer
designed for the Bordeaux service.

An important lesson in stowage of mixed chemical and flammable cargoes was learned by all with the loss of the **Cygnet** on passage to the Mediterranean in 1903. Cope Cornford reported:

*"In December 1903, the steamship **Cygnet** was lost by fire in the Atlantic. She carried a mixed cargo of coal, 57 casks of binoxide of barium [barium oxide], old rope, 380 bags of ammonia, 80 casks of tallow, 81 casks of seed oil, 15 barrels of oil, 700 bags of manure, some scrap iron nails, and other goods making in all about 2000 tons of general cargo. One of the questions before the court held to investigate the matter, was whether the barrels of binoxide of barium were properly packed and stowed, because it was suggested that under certain conditions binoxide of barium might ignite."*

Despite the inability of the court to determine how the fire started, the incident highlighted the dangers of mixed chemical and flammable cargoes to all shipowners and the practise all but ceased thereafter.

The **Cygnet** was succeeded by two new steamers, the **Stork** and **Crane** which were delivered from their builders on Teesside in 1904. Essentially cargo ships, they could accommodate 12 passengers as required, usually only during the summer months. The Edinburgh route received a new ship two years later when the **Woodcock** was delivered from her builders at Dundee with substantial passenger accommodation in two classes.

**The *Stork* (1904)
was designed for the Mediterranean
trade and offered only limited
passenger accommodation.**

[Picture by A Duncan]

In a space of only four years Richard White oversaw a substantial rebuilding programme of a fleet that had hitherto relied for some time on second hand purchases. In addition, White had promoted the purchase of existing companies and the placement of new structures to support his policy of door to door cargo handling. In 1905 he had agreed to membership of the Greek Conference with GSN in the fore. In 1906 he was able to buy the assets and goodwill of John Crisp & Son which included their London to Lowestoft and Norwich cargo business along with a number of Norfolk wherries, but more importantly the wharves, warehouses and associated agencies that Crisp owned and operated. Three years later the freehold of Brewers, Chesters and Galley Quay, long used by GSN on the Thames, was finally purchased, and in 1909 the company celebrated its new-found strength by moving into its prestigious and purpose-built head office at 15 Trinity Square, almost overlooking the Tower of London. It had occupied number 55 across the square since the 1880s, earlier known as 55 Great Tower. The huge cargo hall on the ground floor of the new building had a pseudo stucco ceiling, was decorated in marble and featured marble pillars altogether reminiscent of the main bank branch offices once to be found in any major city. GSN appointed its first Commodore in 1910 – Captain C Joslin, who had joined the company in 1857 and who now received an honorarium of £25 per year and the privilege of flying a pennant-shaped house flag. Edwardian grandeur at its best - the company was indeed back on its feet.

As if to celebrate the great Edwardian feeling of arrival, the company made one of its rare livery changes, and so provided a striking and modern appearance to its ships. Black from top of funnel to water line apart from the dark brown deck houses, the ships of the GSN fleet looked fit for purpose, but also a bit forbidding. The simple addition of a thin white strake to the ships' hulls not only modernised their appearance but also gave them a distinctive brand. The strake did not wrap around the stern of the ship but stopped short beneath the poop in a rounded arrow device, so allowing the ship's name and port of registry full access to either the stern or the quarter stern areas of the hull. At the bow the ships name usually appeared above the strake, but not universally so. Even more radical, some of the passenger units had the outer deck supports painted white, picking out the detail of the ship and highlighting their role as passenger carriers.

With an eye to expansion, GSN tried its luck at Liverpool once again, and more particularly at Manchester, now that the Manchester Ship Canal was open for business. From Liverpool, a short-lived service was offered to Oporto, and from Manchester an even briefer service was operated to Rotterdam. The former fell against established competition with the Moss Steamship Company, the latter with the Hollandsche Stoomboot Maatschappij and the Cork Steamship Company, the forebear of the British & Continental Steamship Company. There was also a new weekly service inaugurated in 1906 by the *Falcon* between Hull and Great Yarmouth and London with calls as required at Grimsby, King's Lynn and Lowestoft.

The Thames excursion trade was enjoying its halcyon years as every Edwardian city dweller strove to retreat to the seaside during summer weekends. The famous 'Husband's boat' was timed to leave London or Gravesend with a train connection, allowing the husbands to finish work at midday on Saturday and arrive at Margate by steamer in time to join their families for tea. Although competition was fierce with the magnificent Belle Steamers fleet and the New Palace Steamers' *Koh-i-Noor* and *Royal Sovereign* all vying for trade, the pickings remained plentiful for all. GSN's passenger receipts for 1902, however, indicate how marginal an operation the summer excursion ships were with their extensive winter retirement and spring refurbishment:

	Overseas routes	Excursion ships
Gross takings	£14,558	£22,200
Expenses	£3,640	£22,680
Profit	£10,918	£2,520

The direct-drive turbine steamer *Kingfisher* (1906) was an innovative day excursion steamer used on the seasonal Tilbury to Margate and cross-Channel routes. Although a popular vessel she was too expensive to operate for summer only use and was sold in 1912.

Nevertheless, GSN was sufficiently confident in the excursion trade to order a new vessel for the Continental day trips, the large and fast state of the art direct-drive steam turbine *Kingfisher*, the only turbine steamer ever to be owned by GSN. The *Kingfisher* arrived on the Thames from William Denny's shipyard at Dumbarton ready for the 1906 season. But she was initially dogged with mechanical problems which took a while to iron out. Nevertheless, the luxuriously appointed *Kingfisher* was good for just over 21 knots, and with her speed and bulk it made sense to base her at Tilbury rather than London. The *Kingfisher* ran daily from Tilbury, to Southend, Margate, Ramsgate and Deal followed by either a trip across the Channel to Boulogne or a coastal cruise, which from 1907 included a call at Dover.

Halcyon, the first of the 'classical birds' class was sold the previous year but non-payment of instalments saw her repossession and resale for use on the River Elbe. The remaining vessels were fast becoming inadequate for the grander Edwardian expectations, and the *Philomel* was sold in 1907, followed by the *Laverock* in 1908, the *Mavis* in 1909 and the *Oriole*, having been retained as spare ship, in 1912.

Their collective replacement was the magnificent *Golden Eagle*. The *Golden Eagle* was manoeuvrable at the exposed piers of the estuary, she could get up to speed and slow down rapidly and above all, with a speed of 19 knots driven by triple expansion engines, she was economical. Her overall size was broadly similar to that of the *Kingfisher*, although she was 25 feet shorter in length than the rival *Royal Sovereign*.

The *Golden Eagle* (1909) was everything that the *Kingfisher* was not, and was probably the most successful steamer ever to serve the Thames excursion trades.

The **Golden Eagle** retained the traditional bridge across the paddles behind the single large funnel, whilst the Promenade Deck led from the bows almost to the stern. The design of the **Golden Eagle** was based on a former rival company's vessel, Planet Steamers' **Mercury**, which was ordered but never delivered to the Thames. The **Mercury** was slightly smaller than the **Golden Eagle** with twin cylinder engines. Unable to pay the shipbuilders for the vessel, the Clydebank Engineering & Shipbuilding Company, which, as John Brown & Company, also built the **Golden Eagle**, sold the **Mercury** on the slipway to the Glasgow & South Western Railway in 1898 and they named her the **Juno**. The similar appearance of the **Juno**, long serving Ayr excursion ship, and her larger triple expansion engined sister the **Golden Eagle** is uncanny. The **Golden Eagle** was placed on the Fresh Wharf to Margate and Ramsgate run, displacing the **Eagle** which now took up service from Tilbury to Southend, Margate, Ramsgate, Deal and Dover. The **Golden Eagle** hit the news in 1911 when the ship's carpenter, Richard Bell, jumped overboard off Margate to rescue a passenger in the sea. Bell subsequently received the Bronze Medal of the Royal Humane Society. The **Kingfisher**, perhaps too big for the excursion trade but too small for cross-channel work, was sold to Italian owners in 1911.

The company still only insured selected units in its fleet which it considered to be more valuable than others. In 1907 just 15 vessels were insured. The insurance on the other vessels was deemed to be carried by the company, the size of which is reflected in its workforce which in 1907 stood at just under 2,000 comprising 1,200 afloat, 250 at 'the Factory' at Deptford, 450 on the wharves, 150 London staff, and 42 staff at outports.

Concern was expressed by Robert Kelso (see Chapter 7) about inadequate accommodation for the stewards aboard certain ships in 1908. He ordered that No. 14 cabin aboard the **Ortolan**, a dark and dingy affair that passengers avoided at all costs, be given over to the stewardess, and that additional accommodation be designated for the stewards aboard the **Grive**. There was also a problem aboard the **Woodcock** with passengers perpetually complaining of lack of sleep because of the repeated noise from the ash chute throughout the night. Kelso's remedy to this problem is not recorded, but the vision of the firemen tip-toeing around in the dead of night is not an easy one!

The *Woodcock* (1906)
was designed specifically for the London to Leith
service with luxury accommodation amidships,
and third class in the poop.

The new Mediterranean steamer **Drake** became quite a celebrity after being in service for only a few months. Lying alongside at Messina in Sicily over Christmas in 1908, the **Drake**, under Captain Frederick Carter, was able to survive the earthquake and tidal waves that all but destroyed the town just before dawn on Monday 28 December. Chief Officer F Etherington takes up the story as quoted by Cope Cornford:

"There was a fearful rumbling and shaking of the ship, which was evidently thrown up broadside on the quay, for we heeled over to an angle of about 45°. After a space of time which could not be counted, and I suppose was only a matter of seconds, we began to right again, and then all was a deathly silence, broken every now and again by the crash of falling masonry and a cry for help. We could see nothing, and we did not know what had happened to the ship. There was a horrible earthy smell in the air and the air was full of powder, and we could hardly breathe...At last daybreak came, and what a scene of devastation it showed! Our ship was covered inches thick in a fine white dust, while we ourselves could hardly recognise one another, while onshore it was devastation."

Two other merchantmen and one warship were also in port, and the respective ships' companies set about rescue, and with the help of those few survivors with medical skills, tended the injured once they had been brought on board. The work of nurse MacDonald, who had been working in Messina, greatly helped the crew of the **Drake** in tending to the wounded. By nightfall, and with the fear of a repeat tidal wave, the overcrowded **Drake** set off with 317 souls aboard including 63 nuns and orphans from the local convent school. The **Drake,** looking as though she had been through a mud bath, arrived off Syracuse the following morning, the ship's ensign flying at half mast, there to tell the world of what had befallen Messina the previous day.

The crew was subsequently fêted and Captain Carter received various accolades and awards on their behalf. These included a letter of appreciation from the rescued citizens of Messina which translates broadly as 'we... feel acutely the duty of thanking with all the emotion of our grateful hearts, Captain Carter and all the crew of the steamer **Drake** of the English flag...'. The master was subsequently presented with the Order of the Crown of Italy by King Victor Emmanuel and received by Pope Pius X, who bestowed upon him the "Bene Merenti" Gold Medal.

The _Drake_ (1908) was a Mediterranean vessel equipped with deck cranes rather than conventional derricks.

The _Drake_ herself survived the ordeal. It was perhaps fortunate that it was the _Drake_ that happened to be alongside that awful morning, as the shell of an older ship might not have been quite so resilient to the initial pounding against the quayside.

The company was also able to provide humanitarian relief a few years later when the _Balgownie_ was lying at Oporto in January 1913. Lamport & Holt's eight year old liner, the _Veronese_, left Vigo on passage from Liverpool to South America, and hours later, just before dawn, had run hard aground in mountainous seas on the Boa Nova Rocks off Leixoes just to the north of Oporto. Aboard was a crew of 98 and 117 passengers. The local volunteer life-saving crew failed to get a line to the vessel, even though the seas had abated, as they apparently knew little of communication between the shore and the wrecked vessel.

Fortunately J R Dicks, Second Mate of the _Balgownie_ and steward Mr A Tingey had set out from Oporto to observe the rescue of passengers and crew. Realising the impotence of the existing shore crew they summoned additional help from the _Balgownie_. Chief Officer F Steffano, and Boatswain A Danielson were quickly brought on site. Steffano had taken the ship's signal flags and morse lamp and quickly engaged in conversation with the _Veronese_. By evening a rocket-fired line had successfully been retrieved and a hawser passed across to the wreck - eight women were brought ashore. Three times the line parted, and three times it was replaced, eventually with a 2½ inch manila hawser. Working almost continuously for 48 hours the four men were responsible for saving over one hundred of the passengers and crew. The last man ashore was the master, Captain Charles Turner, who first went to thank the signalman from the _Balgownie_, without whom the rescue could not have been successful. Sadly, 43 people lost their lives, the balance of the survivors being rescued by Portuguese gunboats.

The fleet replenishment programme continued and several more vessels were completed for the near Continental cargo trades. Between 1909 and 1911, the novel engines-aft steamers _Corncrake_ and _Laverock_ were built at Troon, and the more traditional sisters _Lapwing_ and _Swift_ came from the Clyde and Forth respectively. The latter pair was capable of 13 knots, and were excellent sea boats with accommodation for six passengers. The _Swift_ started life on the Leith run from London. The Ailsa yard at Troon then delivered a quartet of vessels in 1914 and 1915, the _Oriole_, _Raven_, _Seamew_ and _Halcyon_, all designed for the coasting and near continental routes but also capable of deputising on the longer routes to Bordeaux, Portugal and the Mediterranean. Of this quartet, the _Oriole_ and the _Halcyon_ gave less than a year of service before they became war losses. The _Corncrake_ and _Laverock_ not only had their engines aft, but the main accommodation was aft as well. The master's rooms were amidships beneath the bridge, where there was also a small 'owner's cabin' with two berths for passengers. In later years the _Laverock_ was used on the Bordeaux service, as A W Younghusband recalled in an article which first appeared in SEA BREEZES July 1954:

"In bad weather, particularly if light, she used to pile drive, and it was practically impossible even for experienced seamen to get aft to the saloon. It was in the **Laverock** passing through the Bay of Biscay one November ... that I was initiated into the degrees of sea-sickness, 'I think I'm going to die' passed to the second 'I'm sure I'm going to die' and finally 'I hope I am going to die'. For two days I had been obliged to remain in my cabin amidships, and being the only passenger, had nothing better to do than commiserate with myself and hope for a speedy relief, until, when very nearly at the end of my endurance, the ship met the father and mother of all waves head on with a particularly heavy slam. The captain chose this moment to visit the passenger quarters to see how his passenger was getting along, only to find him on his knees..."

**The *Corncrake* (1910)
was one of a pair of prototype
engines-aft steamers built for GSN
by the Ailsa yard at Troon.**

**The *Swift* (1911)
was typical of the cargo steamers designed for
the near Continental services.**

While numerous new vessels had been commissioned under the leadership of Richard White, older vessels were sold for scrap or further service. Overall costs had mirrored expenses leading to profitable years until 1911, from which time outgoings virtually equalled income and little profit was made. Not all the replacement ships were planned as this was still an age when travel by sea was hazardous given both the vagaries of the weather and the confined seaways the company ships frequented. The *Osprey* had been lost to collision in 1904, and in May 1906 the *Preston*, one of the second hand ships acquired in the late 1890s, was wrecked at Point Bay near Camarinas on passage from London to Genoa. Three elderly ships were lost in quick succession: the *Merlin* wrecked in 1911, and the *Widgeon* and the *Petrel* sunk in collisions in 1911 and 1912 respectively. The younger *Guillemot* had also foundered at sea in December 1911. In October 1914 the *Adjutant* sank on collision with a Prince Line vessel off Deal, on passage from Naples to London. In addition, the *Cygnet* had been lost to a cargo fire in 1903 in the Bay of Biscay.

Such high losses, excessive though they may seem, were typical for shipowners during this era. They were not, however, to be tolerated in peacetime thereafter, as safety measures were greatly improved with the experience and technical advancements that were shortly to be funded through Lord Kitchener in his new role as Minister of War. The dramatic events that took place in Europe during the early summer of 1914 led Britain to declare war on Germany on 4 August. The dark days of the Great War commenced with little warning, while the company's ships were on their normal business distributed between northern Germany and North Africa.   The fleet was at its zenith and comprised over 50 ships, with an aggregate 60,000 gross tons.

THE MAIN ROUTES SERVED IN 1914

From London:

Thames excursions, summer only
To UK ports: Leith (passenger service), Hull, Grimsby, Great Yarmouth, Lowestoft (for Norwich) and Southampton.
To Germany, Hamburg only, also passenger service from Harwich.
To Dutch ports: Amsterdam, Rotterdam and Harlingen.
To Belgian ports: Antwerp, Ostend – passenger and cargo service, Ghent and Terneuzen.
To French ports: Dunkirk and Havre, and to Bordeaux (passenger and cargo service) and Tonnay Charente (for wine and brandy imports).
To Portugal, Oporto only – provision for some passengers.

From Newcastle, Middlesbrough, London, Cardiff, Newport, and Newlyn:
To Genoa, Leghorn, Naples, Messina, Palermo, Syracuse, Patras and Smyrna – provision for some passengers.

Continental excursions ranged from 5 days to Dutch or Belgian ports for £2-12-6 to seven weeks in the Mediterranean for £25. On the Bordeaux service, coupons were issued for hotel accommodation and rail excursions.

CHAPTER 5

HEAVY LOSSES

"The national services rendered during the war by the GSN as a whole, together with the individual deeds and sufferings of their indomitable officers and men, are embodied in the histories of the Great War, there to remain on record so long as the English tongue and the English nation shall endure. Throughout the war, the Company maintained and enhanced the traditions of the British Merchant Marine, and what more can be said?"

Cope Cornford, 1924

Within days of the declaration of war on Germany, Lord Kitchener's famous pointing hand was asking for 100,000 men to join the Army. Although the First World War was the last great infantry war, it was also fought at sea. Britain lost 9 million tons of shipping during the four year conflict, and several new and deadly weapons were deployed, including the submarine and various types of mine. Cope Cornford introduces the story:

*"The war service of the Company (GSN) began at 6.59 pm on 31 July 1914, when the Company received, from the Lords Commissioners of the Board of Admiralty requesting information concerning the last movements and expected movements of all the steamships of the Company. The Admiralty then requested twenty one vessels, subsequently releasing two ships, the **Balgownie** and **Mallard**. The remaining nineteen ships requisitioned by the Admiralty were employed upon the various duties of mine-laying, mine-sweeping, flotilla and squadron supply, carrying munitions and stores, Fleet messengers and troop transports."*

One of the first duties of the war was the dispatch of officers and crew aboard the **Alouette** to Antwerp, there to bring 32 German vessels that had been interned in the port to Britain. The first batch of eight vessels were crewed and ready to sail on 5 September when, to the disappointment of all, the General in command of Antwerp ordered the ships to stay put. The **Alouette** returned with the men to London, and, of course, when Antwerp was later occupied, the Germans took back the interned ships to use against the Allies.

Had the interned ships been allowed to sail, it would have been fine retribution for the loss of the **Auk**, **Virgo** and **Iris**, which had been illegally interned by the Germans. All three had been cleared from Hamburg, but were intercepted at the mouth of the Elbe off Cuxhaven and sent back up river to Brünsbuttel on the eve of war. Having made several abortive attempts to leave, they were ordered further up river back to Hamburg. This was on the morning before war was declared. The crews along with the Hamburg agent, Robert Kelso, were transferred to the prison ship **Seigfried** and later transferred to Ruhleben as prisoners of war. Robert Kelso was to become a Director of the company after the war, and was subsequently elected Chairman of the Board in succession to William McAllister. Indeed it was Kelso who would see the company through the horrors of the Second World War.

The **Lapwing** was sent to Southampton on cross channel trooping duties during the autumn, followed for a brief period by the **Fauvette** and in February 1915 by the Thames pleasure steamer **Golden Eagle**. The **Golden Eagle** and the **Eagle** had kept up the Thames excursion services to the end of September, many thinking that hostilities would be over by Christmas and normality would resume. Thereafter, they lay in the docks awaiting orders, one destined to be a trooper alongside the big excursion steamer **La Marguerite**, the other a minesweeper working alongside the former excursion fleet of Belle Steamers.

The troopers sailed with men and stores, and returned on some trips with prisoners. Under Captain F J Adams, the **Golden Eagle** was used to ferry aeroplanes across to the continent along with their crew and support staff. But her trooping duties were unequalled, with over half a million men carried aboard the paddle steamer during the war years.

The ships that were requisitioned fared better than those left to carry the precious supplies under the Red Ensign. Cope Cornford again:

"Taking the number of ships sailing on cargo voyages, and the number of ships requisitioned or flying the White Ensign, the proportion of ships lost on cargo voyages was the greater. They were practically defenceless; the small guns mounted astern being useless, because the ships were almost invariably attacked from forward or from off the beam. The officers and men whose ships were put down immediately applied to go afloat again. Those for whom there was no employment in the rapidly diminishing Merchant Marine joined the Royal Navy."

Three ships were lost to the difficulties of navigation in blackout conditions. The **Adjutant** was the first ship to be lost in collision. She was returning from Naples, and had got to a position off Deal, when she collided with another vessel in The Downs and sank. There was no loss of life, but her largely perishable mixed cargo was unsalvageable, as indeed was the ship itself. The **Starling** was also lost to collision, but much later on in the war, during March 1918. The saddest loss of all was the grounding and subsequent abandonment of the **Peregrine** on 29 December 1917.

The **Peregrine** had thus far an interesting war, being occupied as a Flotilla Supply Ship until November 1915, then returning to civilian duties to maintain the service between Harwich and neutral Rotterdam. In one brush with a submarine, the **Peregrine** was able to outrun the enemy with engines at 'full ahead and a bit', so leaving the enemy in her wake. The **Peregrine** was not so lucky in December. Aboard were 59 passengers, including a large contingent of French women and children on their way from Rotterdam to Harwich. It was a dark night and the familiar lights such as the nearby Sunk Light Vessel, were, of course, extinguished. Having passed the Shipwash Light Vessel, Captain W G Braithwaite altered course in order to clear the wreck of the steamer **Isis** which lay near the Sunk Light Vessel. Cope Cornford reports:

*"Shortly afterwards the **Peregrine** ran aground. The Captain hoisted two red lights, and hailed the vessels astern, warning them. He kept his engines going astern. The vessel slid off the sand, then turned broadside on to the breakers, and began to bump heavily, and to ship heavy seas which washed away the starboard lifeboats and all the moveable deck fittings. Captain Braithwaite sent a wireless call for help.*

*...At half past eleven the **Peregrine** was driven across the bows of the sunken wreck with a dreadful grinding. Huge seas swept the deck.... The captain knowing that at any moment the ship might break in half, persuaded the paralysed and weeping passengers to move to the Boat Deck, where the crew lashed them to the engine room skylight and funnel, and covered them with blankets and tarpaulins. Then a tremendous sea washed right over the Boat Deck and passengers, and made a clean sweep of the port lifeboats. The starboard boats had already gone, and but one was left for 59 passengers and 33 officers and men."*

The Walton-on-the-Naze lifeboat was able to come alongside at daybreak, by all accounts a display of very accomplished seamanship, and take the passengers and two of the crew to safety, returning a couple of hours later for the balance of the crew. In the meantime, the **Peregrine** broke her back on the falling tide, an unfitting end to a fine ship.

Coincidentally, her former sister, the **Peregrine**, which had been sold for use on the Australian coastal routes and whose name had never been changed, was returned to Europe in 1915, but was wrecked near Portland Bill just six months before her younger namesake. She was salved, and ended her days as a storage hulk before being sold to a scrapyard in 1922.

But the enemy was responsible for the rest of the carnage (Table 2). Reports on the conduct of GSN officers and men, describe without exception, well disciplined and orderly crews who acted with great courage despite the awfulness of the conditions. Four ships were lost in 1915. The first was the brand-new **Oriole**, which was torpedoed in the Channel with considerable loss of life. The other three, the **Leeuwarden**, **Ptarmigan** and **Groningen**, were also lost to submarine activity, either directly or from mines laid by submarine. Captain J Salmon, master of the Groningen, had earlier been praised for quick action in his use of helm and engines, as he managed to avoid eight or nine bombs dropped by air. The company Directors voted extra pay amounting to one week for all hands.

The *Leeuwarden* (1903) is seen leaving the Pool of London. She became an early war loss, the victim of a German 'U Boat'.

[Picture by Judges of Hastings]

But worse was to come as the German 'U Boats' got to grips with their prey and even started to hunt in packs. Seven company vessels were lost during 1916, fortunately with relatively small loss of life, although a number of men were taken prisoner. One of the losses was HMS **Fauvette**. At the beginning of the war the **Fauvette** was placed at the behest of the French Government, the seat of power having been dispatched from the capital to Bordeaux. From there she was used to transport and lay a boom defence in the Mediterranean, and after being requisitioned, and, as HMS **Fauvette**, she was equipped as an armed escort and placed in the attack. Her subsequent exploits included the bombardment of the Dardanelles, trooping to Suvla Bay and Helles, Salonica, Bulgaria and carrying refugee soldiers from Serbia to Corfu. She was mined off the North Foreland on 9 March 1916 on her way home from Girgenti to London.

In 1916 mines were also to blame for the loss of the **Balgownie**, **Vesuvio**, **Halcyon**, and **Gannet**. Nobody survived the blast on the bridge of the **Vesuvio**, including the master Captain Elgar. Eight men lost their lives when the **Gannet** was cut in two by a mine off the Shipwash Light Vessel. Her master Captain F G Cole was the last to leave. Choked with fumes, he leaped into the water hitting debris, and was fortunate to survive his fall and be plucked into the starboard lifeboat by his second officer. And like the new **Oriole** lost the previous year, the **Halcyon** hardly had time for the builder's paint to dry on her plates before she too was lost to a mine.

Losses continued throughout 1917, including the stranding of the **Peregrine**. The **Hirondelle** was one of these, as Ambrose Greenway reports, sinking with no loss of life:

"Immediately following the outbreak of war she was taken up as a Squadron supply ship, pennant number Y9.17, and continued this until 7 June 1915 when she became a water carrier. She later returned to commercial service and was presumably back on the Bordeaux run when she was torpedoed and sunk 13 miles south by east of Belle Ile."

One of the major passenger units to be lost was the *Hirondelle* (1890) seen as she was configured for service to Hamburg from 1905 onwards complete with a new conventional shaped funnel and additional lifeboats aft.

Yet another of the big passenger carriers was lost shortly afterwards, as Cope Cornford noted:

*"The steamship **Ortolan**, Captain Acors, was torpedoed in the North Atlantic on 14 June 1917 nearly 200 miles west of the Isles of Scilly. Three men were killed. The ship sank inside five minutes. The officers and the rest of the men got away in the boats."*

In December, not only was the **Peregrine** lost but so too was the **Grive**. As if by design the major passenger units of the company had been singled out and destroyed. Not that it was of concern at the time, but this was to have a major influence on the reconstruction of GSN once hostilities ceased and peaceful commercial operations could once again resume.

The **Heron** and, two hours later, the **Drake** were lost to submarine attack in the same convoy in September some three days out from Falmouth. The Chief Engineer of the **Drake**, Mr J Peters, not only survived the sinking of the **Hirondelle**, but that of the **Drake** as well.

Losses continued into 1918 with the **Starling**, the second ship of the war to be lost by collision, and in September the **Philomel**, hardly old enough for the master to have found his cabin. GSN had a bad war, its surviving men and ships battered by four long years of hardship and terror. But although twenty three ships had been lost, others had come through unscathed, some with remarkable stories.

The Ostend rabbit boat **Alouette**, for example, became a fleet messenger in September 1914, and with one 12-pound gun fitted at Deptford, became the armed boarding steamer HMS **Alouette**, number N.54. She was deployed around Scapa Flow and acted as relief on the all-important Scrabster to Stromness ferry for the *St Ninian*, and later replaced the Edinburgh steamer *Fiona* which had been wrecked on the Pentland Skerries whilst deputising for the Great Eastern Railway steamer *Vienna* on the ferry run. The *Alouette* remained in the north until November 1919 when she was returned to her owners. Other survivors led more mundane lives. The elderly *Nautilus*, which had adopted the name *Nautpur*, along with the *Redstart*, barely left sight of Felixstowe pier, having spent the entire war on duty as the Harwich guardships.

Whilst the big Thames paddle steamer *Golden Eagle* had been ploughing back and forth with troops across the channel her smaller and older consort the *Eagle* had been equipped as a minesweeper in December 1915, and was released from these duties only in July 1920. As *HMS Aiglon* and later *HMPMS 938* the former *Eagle* worked the 'Dover Patrol' alongside her former excursion rivals: *Clacton Belle*, *Yarmouth Belle*, *Walton Belle*, *London Belle* and *Southend Belle*. Admiral Sir Reginald Bacon later commented on the role of the paddle steamer in maintaining the Dover Patrol:

"The paddle minesweepers were the safest vessels for sweeping owing to their small draught and to their great speed – some ten to eleven knots – which enabled the moorings of the German mines to be immediately cut. These then floated to the surface and did not remain entangled in the sweep, and were, therefore, less dangerous to the sweeping vessel. The only defect of the paddle minesweepers was their inability to keep at sea or to sweep efficiently in bad weather."

None of these gallant little ships from the Thames was lost.

The renaming of the *Swift* to *Dean Swift* in 1914 occurred when she was commissioned as a flotilla supply ship. This avoided confusion with the flotilla leader, also named *Swift*. The *Dean Swift* served both the Navy and the Army until she was returned to GSN in 1916 to take up the London to Rotterdam service, later transferring to the London to Bordeaux route. Wartime rules prevented her name reverting to *Swift* until after the war had ended.

With the war ended, the commercial world was left to pick up the pieces. GSN had lost almost its entire Home Trade passenger carrying capacity and a good deal of its cargo carriers. Like other companies, it had lost a large part of its assets and many of its staff but it had been amply compensated as Forrester describes:

"The wartime years were highly profitable for the company, as they were for most British ship-owners. High freight rates and large insurance payments for tonnage lost pushed receipts to in excess of £1 million in 1916, and vast sums were set aside to reserves. In 1917 a further reorganisation increased nominal capital to £1 million and doubled the nominal value of ordinary shareholdings."

As GSN faced the future, it would need to put its hand deep into its pockets and at the same time make some hard decisions as to where its future lay. Others were less well placed, and on the Thames neither Belle Steamers nor New Palace Steamers were ever able to recover from this four year hostile period, starved of passenger receipts.

The saviour of GSN was to be its time-honoured philosophy that merger or purchase of the opposition was preferable to price wars. Besides, Lord Inchcape was watching over his 'preferred feeder carrier' for his mighty P&O/British India empire and he clearly retained a very soft spot for the 'Navvies'.

But there were yet to be two more war losses. Whilst the Treaty of Versailles dealt with interned German vessels and their becoming the properties of the Allied Countries, the three GSN vessels laid up at Hamburg following their illegal internment, which had occurred before war had even been declared, were again available to the company. Of the three, the *Virgo* was a relatively young vessel and she duly sailed to London to await her turn for refurbishment and gave many more years service to her owners. However, the *Auk* and the *Iris* caught the eye of the Admiralty – World War One might have ended but the Estonian Liberation War had begun during 1918 almost as the new state had been created. In 1919 the two elderly steamers were towed through the Kiel Canal into the Baltic and then sunk as blockships at Pärnu, a deterrent to any renewed Russian attempt at retaking Estonia.

TABLE 2   Losses to Enemy Action 1914 to 1918

Ship and year built	Date	Incident[1]	Location
Auk (1877)	4 August 1914	Interned at Hamburg[2], sunk as blockship in 1919.	Pärnu
Iris (1872)	4 August 1914	Interned at Hamburg, sunk as blockship in 1919.	Pärnu
Oriole (1914)	30 January 1915	Torpedoed on passage London to Havre. 21 crew lost.	English Channel
Leeuwarden (1903)	17 March 1915	Captured by submarine and shelled. On passage London to Harlingen.	Off Maas Light Vessel
Ptarmigan (1891)	15 April 1915	Torpedoed on passage Rotterdam to London. 8 crew lost.	Off North Hinder Light Vessel
Groningen (1902)	23 September 1915	Mined on passage Harlingen to London. 1 crew member lost.	Off Sunk Head Buoy
Balgownie (1880)	6 February 1916	Mined on passage London to Leith. 1 crew member lost.	Off Sunk Head Buoy
Fauvette[3] (1912)	9 March 1916	Mined on passage Girgenti to London.	Off North Foreland
Vesuvio (1879)	6 April 1916	Mined on passage Messina to London. 7 crew lost.	Off Owers Light Vessel
Halcyon (1915)	7 April 1916	Mined on passage Bordeaux to London.	Off Folkestone
Teal (1876)	29 April 1916	Captured by submarine and torpedoed on passage Leith to London.	Off Seaham Harbour
Gannet (1879)	7 July 1916	Mined on passage Rotterdam to London. 8 crew lost.	Off Shipwash Light Vessel
Sheldrake (1894)	8 November 1916	Captured by submarine and shelled on passage Naples to London.	Off Marittimo Island, Italy
Hirondelle (1890)	25 April 1917	Torpedoed on passage London to Bordeaux.	Bay of Biscay, off Belle Ile
Ortolan (1902)	14 June 1917	Torpedoed on passage Genoa to London. 3 crew lost.	Off Bishop Rock
Heron (1889)	30 September 1917	Torpedoed on passage Newcastle to Oporto. 22 crew lost.	Bay of Biscay, off Belle Ile
Drake (1908)	30 September 1917	Captured by submarine and shelled on passage London to Genoa.	Off Ushant
Lapwing (1911)	11 November 1917	Mined on passage Rotterdam to London.	Off Southwold
Grive[3] (1905)	8 December 1917	On active service. Torpedoed - sank two weeks later.	Off Lerwick
Philomel (1916)	16 September 1917	Torpedoed on passage London to Brest.	Bay of Biscay, off Lorient

[1] In addition, the **Adjutant** and **Starling** were lost on commercial service in collisions due to the blackout, and the **Peregrine** was wrecked on passage from Rotterdam to Harwich.

[2] The **Virgo** was also interned at Hamburg during the war, but was returned to GSN in 1919.

[3] **Fauvette** and **Grive** were lost on active service as Armed Boarding Steamers.

CHAPTER 6

PICKING UP THE PIECES

"Bordeaux itself lies some 50 miles up river on the Garonne, and was reached in the early afternoon. Customs formalities were soon completed – a tin of cigarettes with a tot of rum were accepted in full and final settlement of all fees and duties – and 72 hours after leaving London I took my first steps on French soil."

From 'TO FRANCE IN GSN SHIPS', an article by A W Younghusband,
which first appeared in SEA BREEZES, July 1954.

The Merchant Navy had paid a terrible toll during the war, but GSN had paid more than its fair share. The company emerged from war with half its fleet gone, and with none of the major passenger units it had taken to war four years earlier. The Hamburg steamers **Hirondelle** and **Peregrine** were gone, the Bordeaux steamers **Ortolan**, **Grive**, **Fauvette** and **Drake** were gone. It was almost as though the enemy had targeted the larger passenger-carrying members of the fleet to put an end to any post-war prospect of running the Hamburg packet and the big passenger ships down to Bordeaux. The first decision that GSN had to make was what type of ship should replace these losses. Clearly services, albeit at a reduced frequency, could resume using the cargo steamers that had survived, but that would mean the end of the passenger services at least to Hamburg and possibly also Bordeaux and Edinburgh.

Not only was it hard for GSN to resume trading after the war because of lack of tonnage, but it had also suffered grave losses both of officers and men, whilst other seagoing staff had taken up commissions in the Royal Navy. Many of the Continental and Mediterranean shore agencies had disappeared although others had been detailed to look after the interests of the Government in various ports, where they had undertaken a magnificent support role under difficult conditions. Reinstatement of the offices was undertaken as a priority task, and this was done either directly from London or through subsidiary companies. By mid-1919 offices were available in Italy, four in France, three in Holland and three in Germany. The Edinburgh office was relocated at the seaward end of Leith Walk, not far from the main dock gate.

Just as the seagoing men had been put under immense pressure during the war years, so too had the company managers and shore staff. The Deptford yard had been placed at the disposal of Government and had carried out an almost non-stop programme of repair and make do on a variety of vessel types, only occasionally working on one of the company's own ships. Management had been given a variety of important roles in addition to their day to day duty of running a major shipping company at war. Members of the Board served, amongst other appointments, on the National Maritime Board, the Home Trade Transport Control Committee, which apportioned cargoes by sea and rail, and Richard White sat on the Committee of Shipowners, whose job it was to control trade to southern Europe. After the war GSN personnel were appointed as agents in various ports to oversee and secure those German vessels which had to be given to the Allies under the terms of the Treaty of Versailles.

So, from the war emerged a tired and greatly depleted fleet of ships, without exception in desperate need of refurbishment and repair, charged with weary crews and managed by a Board that had been overworked for four long years. Of course, once the war was over, Europe and Britain in particular had the Bird Flu epidemic to contend with, a disease that killed both the young and the old.

On a lighter note, a brief record in the DAILY MAIL, 17 September 1919, observes:

"The most beautiful view in the city is claimed for the Board Room of the GSN at the corner of Trinity Square. The windows command an enchanting prospect - the green Trinity Square garden, the Tower of London and the great bridge behind, the panorama of the river at its foot, and away in the distance the hills of Kent."

But casualties could still occur even in peacetime. The **Swift**, newly renamed from her wartime **Dean Swift**, suffered serious collision damage in Limehouse Reach, outward bound for Amsterdam in 1919 and was out of service for several weeks. On her return, she became a most reliable unit on the Amsterdam route.

The Harwich to Hamburg packet service was abandoned, but cargo services to Hamburg resumed from London in September 1919 under the protection of Article 327 of the Treaty of Versailles:

"The nationals of any of the Allied and Associated Powers as well as their vessels and property shall enjoy in all German ports and on the inland navigation routes of Germany the same treatment in all respects as German nationals, vessels and property."

The inaugural voyage to Hamburg was taken by the **Falcon**. The day passenger steamer **Alouette** was released from official duties only in November 1919, and after a brief refurbishment and refit went back to her return roster from London to Ostend. At the time, the Ostend passenger service seemed assured, a useful alternative to the train and ship service available via Dover. The **Woodcock** had been available to reopen the weekly passenger service to Leith and that passenger service also seemed assured. The Mediterranean routes could carry on much as before, dependent for their income on cargo with up to twelve passenger berths available in some of the ships. In 1920 a new agency was opened far from the sea in Basle to facilitate through loads via Boulogne, and later to handle insulated containers of perishable goods.

Bordeaux was the problem, as the company found they had no suitable tonnage with which to maintain the passenger and cargo service offered prior to and throughout much of the war. Of necessity the service was downgraded to cargo with some passengers, and although it was still possible to sail to Bordeaux, the departures were no longer on a regular schedule, and the departure times were fixed to suit cargo needs not the needs of the passenger. In due course, the regular twelve day return schedule was resumed with a Saturday departure from both London and Bordeaux, but passenger accommodation was limited to twelve.

GSN, unlike many shipping companies at that time, did have some money in the bank, partly through the excellent housekeeping of Chairman Richard White. Those companies that survived the war with assets and goodwill, but no money, were destined to fall in the hard years ahead. Recompense for war losses was mean, companies being offered the pre-war market price of the vessel, barely enough to buy the steel after the war, let alone the services of the shipbuilder. The last newbuild, the **Philomel**, had left the Ailsa yard at Troon to be sunk within her first year, just seven weeks before the German capitulation and the signing of the Armistice. Nevertheless, GSN had gained financially from favourable Government charter fees and high freight rates throughout the war which had put money into the bank. Armed with the cash, GSN set about rebuilding its fleet, spurred by a post-war boom in trade, which none realised would have turned to depression by 1921. In the meantime, during 1919, GSN bought Leech & Company and its London to Ghent service and the goodwill of Messrs. G R Haller of London and its cargo service between London and the Humber.

Orders for six new ships were placed with the Ailsa Shipbuilding Company, now the preferred company shipbuilder, and four more were ordered from Bow, McLachlan & Company at Paisley. Five of the ships were to be of the conventional engines and accommodation amidships design, with limited but comfortable passenger accommodation. These were the attractive looking near sisters **Heron**, **Starling**, **Halcyon**, **Philomel** and **Drake**, which were delivered between 1920 and 1922, and intended for the Bordeaux, Lisbon and Mediterranean services.

**The Heron (1920)
was built for the Mediterranean trade.**

**The Halcyon (1921)
shared the roll of flagship of the fleet with
sister Philomel with comfortable
accommodation for 12 passengers.**

**The Drake (1922)
was the last of the five traditional steamers
built in the early 1920s.**

The other five were of the new engines-aft design, with the navigation bridge placed between holds one and two, and a design speed of 12 knots. These were the *Lapwing*, *Petrel*, *Auk*, *Teal* and *Gannet*, which were designed for the Antwerp and Hamburg routes but with the Havre service also in mind (now centred on the nearby port of Fécamp). These vessels came into service throughout 1920 and 1921 and cost up to £140,000 each reflecting a dramatic post-war hike in prices. In addition, the small engines-aft steamers *Blackcock* and *Oriole* were delivered in 1921, the former built at Southampton, the latter at Aberdeen.

The *Lapwing* (1920) was one of a quintet of engines-aft steamers built for the near Continental trade.

The sisters *Petrel* (1920) with *Teal* (1921) beyond, anchored in mid-Thames.

[Picture by A Duncan]

The *Teal* (1921) seen in dock was another member of the quintet.

The *Gannet* (1921) worked on the London to Hamburg service for much of her early career.

The *Blackcock* (1921) was one of a group of small engines-aft steamers either built for GSN or bought second-hand - she is seen here as the *Rora Head* after sale to Comben Longstaff in 1937 and resale to the North of Scotland Orkney and Shetland Steam Navigation Company in 1939.

The **Halcyon** and **Philomel** were destined for the Southampton to Bordeaux route and represented the flagships of the fleet. A W Younghusband talks fondly about them in an article which first appeared in Sᴇᴀ Bʀᴇᴇᴢᴇs in July 1954:

*"My first passage to Bordeaux was in February 1926, and at that period there were two sister ships in the trade, the **Halcyon** and the **Philomel**. Built in 1921 to replace two ships lost in the First World War, with straight stems, counter sterns and graceful lines, more like two large yachts than cargo carriers, they were 270 feet long oil-burning steamships of 929 net and 1,566 tons gross, with a service speed of 12½ knots. They carried twelve passengers who were accommodated with the officers amidships. There was a spacious saloon in the forward part of the flat, and although the accommodation was not modern by today's standards of convenience and comfort, the ships themselves radiated a sense of seaworthiness and strength, and engendered a feeling of security and wellbeing."*

The rebuilding programme became an immense burden on the finances of the company, inflated though they were by the profits of war. Richard White committed his company to borrow heavily on the strength of its assets and the positive vibrations, misguided as it turns out, of the early post-war commercial boom. However, ever since the 1880s the British India Steam Navigation Company, and more recently P&O as well, had informally and later formally adopted GSN as the preferred feeder company for Continental and east coast UK transhipments. By 1920 P&O had developed a vested commercial interest in the GSN cargo network and needed it to survive. Conscious that Ellerman Lines were making overtures to GSN, the Royal Mail Steam Packet made an offer, which was countered by Lord Inchcape, the Chairman of P&O and former Chairman of GSN, through his company Gray Dawes. The Inchcape offer was accepted, conditional on GSN retaining its independent management and its identity. When Lord Inchcape sold the shares at cost to P&O later in 1920, GSN Limited was placed firmly on its feet. Outwardly, nothing changed and GSN was once again the brand leader in the Home Trade. Lord Inchcape describes the deal in a memo to the P&O Board (Owen Phillips being, of course, Lord Kylsant of the Royal Mail Group):

"I had the opportunity a few days ago of buying the share of the GSN at £5-10-0 per £1 share. I looked into their position and found their cash assets and their freehold property at £5-10-0 per share would give me their fleet of 27 steamers and the goodwill of their business.... Sir Owen Phillips had got the offer of the shares at £6 open for a fortnight but he made a counter offer of £5-5-0 for the whole or £6 for 51%. This was refused and the Directors offered me the whole at £5-10-0. I accepted and I have got 93.78% up to now and the deal has gone through... The amount involved is about £1,959,375 but the cash and realisable assets are equal to this."

P&O acquired over 95% of the GSN ordinary shares[1] and this may have been the salvation of the company, for in 1921 depression set in. Besides, GSN could have gone down with Lord Kylsant had the Royal Mail Group managed to buy it. In May 1922, Lord Inchcape wrote to the GSN Board requesting that GSN ships try to reduce their running costs by £10 per day. But all was not doom and gloom, as Cope Cornford relates:

"In 1923, GSN together with T Small & Company (Great Yarmouth), formed a new company – the Great Yarmouth Shipping Company – to operate the Hull and Yarmouth steamship services and the services between Great Yarmouth, Lowestoft, Norwich and London, as well as the operation of some tugs, lighters and wherries on the rivers of east Norfolk and north-east Suffolk together with wharves and warehouses at Great Yarmouth, Lowestoft and Norwich."

The new company was incorporated on 15 June 1923 and chartered the two small twenty year old sisters **Goldfinch** and **Bullfinch**, which forsook their black funnels for yellow with a black top. On 28 June GSN invested £4,000 in the Great Yarmouth Shipping Company and by the end of the month GSN had acquired 47.5% of the company. On 31 December 1931 GSN transferred the interests of Jas. Harborough & Son to the Great Yarmouth Shipping Company so giving it a controlling interest of 71.7%. Jas. Harborough was acquired in 1929 and operated on the inland waterways of Norfolk and along the East Coast.

The London & Dunkirk Shipping Company, in which GSN owned a 35% interest, was incorporated through GSN on 8 May 1922. Its steamer the **Egham** (**Conifer** from 1932 when ownership was transferred to GSN) was managed by GSN.

The first victim of the downturn in trade was the passenger service to Ostend and the 'gentille' **Alouette** was sold for demolition at Rainham in 1924. However, on the positive side, the GSN Board were keen to benefit from very low prices on the second hand market which had over 2 million tons of British shipping laid up and 30,000 seamen out of work.

---

[1] The P&O shareholding was reduced to 75% by 1927, but was slowly increased to 85% after World War Two.

The *Adjutant* (1922) was one of a number of second-hand purchases made in the early 1920s.

A succession of purchases was made to bolster the fleet in anticipation of better trading conditions (Table 3). Ten of these were small vessels destined for the UK and near Continental routes, whilst the *Adjutant* and *Guillemot* were larger steamers for the Mediterranean and Bordeaux trades. The *Adjutant* had been built at Grangemouth in 1921 for J & J Denholm of Glasgow as the *Myrtlepark* and her yet-to-be-named sister was subsequently bought on the stocks and launched as the *Albatross* in 1924.

Another was the *Arbonne*, which became the *Peregrine*. She had been built in 1921 for Thomas C Steven and Company of Edinburgh for their wine trade between Edinburgh and Nantes/Bordeaux in competition with GSN. The export market was available from Scotland with washed coal 'nuts and pearls' in the lower hold at Leith, and linoleum and paper loaded at Kirkcaldy above the coal, whereas GSN's London based boats were fully loaded inbound but sailed generally only to half capacity with British exports. Thomas C Steven decided to call it a day in 1924, and sold off its entire fleet, the one vessel coming to GSN, the trading conditions being too difficult for them to continue.

The various purchases of the early 1920s were made at about half the book cost of the ships, so desperate were conditions becoming. GSN bought them using the compensation, received in 1924 at a rate of 15 shillings in the pound, against the three vessels improperly seized by the German Government just before war was declared. The remaining 5 shillings in the pound was received a year later. In addition the company was able to write off the value of its fleet a sum of money described as 'more than adequate'.

The company's Centenary was marked by a Celebration Dinner held on 24 June 1924 at Claridges Hotel. The guest list read like a who's who of shipping, with names such as R N Cayzer, J R Westcott and many others. For the staff and their families, free trips aboard the *Golden Eagle* could be enjoyed throughout July, and the company had also made the gift to staff the previous year of a sports and social club situated at New Beckenham.

In 1925 the fleet stood at 45 vessels representing a total gross tonnage of 47,000. The average age of the vessels was just under 17 years.

Remarkably, while other companies were struggling or giving up altogether, GSN was able to embark on a second massive rebuilding programme. This programme was to continue at a steady pace right through the depressed years of the second half of the 1920s, and the whole of the 1930s. It ensured that GSN was always able to offer a modern and fit-for-purpose fleet that was able to operate more efficiently and to smaller economic margins than virtually any other operator in the Home Trades.

Sadly, the man responsible for restoring the fortunes of the company from its poor prospects at the beginning of the century to its present role as market leader died in May 1926. Richard White as Chairman and Managing Director of GSN had been greatly assisted by his deputy Captain H Hooper, but he too had died in service some three years previously. Happily, W J McAlister had been understudy to the pair for a good many years, and McAlister, who had been a Director since June 1914, was unanimously elected to the role of Chairman in May 1926. It must have been a forbidding prospect to be given the wheel when all around was economic gloom, inflation and ever increasing industrial unrest. McAlister rose to the challenge and, as will be seen, brought his company through the depression not only in one piece, but with considerably enhanced assets and a variety of owned and managed subsidiary companies.

A number of innovative features now characterised GSN ships. Whereas the steam deck crane had been a hallmark at the turn of the century, the electric crane had taken its place. In addition, the company had been quick to realise the benefits of oil-fired boilers, and a number of ships were built with the capability to carry and burn either solid or liquid bunkers in the form of coal or oil. This enabled the company to buy whatever fuel was available at cheapest prices, to give it flexibility at times of fuel shortages.

The first products from the ongoing new building programme were two steamers for the Dutch routes, the *Roek* and *Merel* and for the Belgian and northern France services the attractive looking steamers *Fauvette* and *Hirondelle*.

**The *Roek* (1925)
was specifically designed
for the near Continent cargo services
usually operating to Antwerp.**

[Picture by A Duncan]

**The *Fauvette* (1925),
an intermediate sized steamer,
built by J Samuel White & Company
at Southampton.**

[Picture by A Duncan]

**The *Hirondelle* (1925)
looking every part a mini-cargo liner,
was normally rostered on northern France -
Belgium routes. She had a service speed
of only 11 knots.**

**The *Hirondelle* (1925)
alongside at Antwerp - she is best remembered
for her extensive association with the
London to Antwerp route. Her four deck cranes
and three derricks were continuously
in use at both terminals.**

The age-old problem of overcrowding on the Thames excursion steamers reared its head once again in 1924. The ticket collector aboard the ***Eagle*** was reprimanded and the Master given a ticking off when the ship was found to be overloaded. It appears that a simple issue like counting heads walking up a gangway was yet to be solved.

In 1925, J Samuel White at Southampton, delivered the first oil-fired excursion paddle steamer to the Thames, the magnificent and fondly remembered ***Crested Eagle***. She was ordered by GSN to counter the threat from the ever expanding services of the New Medway Steam Packet Company. The ***Crested Eagle*** quickly earned the name 'Greyhound of the River' with her service speed of 19 knots on the Fresh Wharf to Ramsgate service, with running-mates, ***Eagle*** and ***Golden Eagle***, still based at Greenwich. The new ***Crested Eagle***, which twice daily passed under London Bridge, had a three barrel concertina funnel as built, though this was modified to only two parts in her second year. The top part of the funnel was rarely fully extended, and the ship had a characteristic stumpy funnel throughout her career.

Like the ***Golden Eagle*** before her, the Promenade Deck ran almost the full length of the ship, and most public rooms occupied her full width. An innovative and popular feature was placing the first class dining saloon one deck higher than normal on the Main Deck. Situated forward, passengers were able to dine and enjoy the passing scenery, whereas on earlier ships they might see foaming green water and occasional glimpses of sky through the infrequently distributed portholes dotted along the water line. The ***Crested Eagle*** was licensed to carry 1,650 passengers, while her tonnage was 1,100 gross. A key safety feature was ten watertight compartments with nine bulkheads built up to Main Deck level.

The year 1926 was a particularly hard year for everybody. This was the year of the General Strike when the working forces demonstrated that ever diminishing disposable incomes could not continue. Although the strike was over quickly, the miners opted to stay out, and the so-called Coal Strike caused havoc to industry and the transport industry in particular, as it was still so dependent on coal. Oil burners like the **Crested Eagle** were unaffected by the shortage of coal as were the many modern steamers in the GSN fleet, equipped for either coal or oil burning. The remaining coal burners were of necessity either laid up or their owners had to seek inferior coal on the Continent at inflated prices. Nevertheless, the depression did not stop GSN taking delivery of one more new steamer, the **Grebe**, built by the favoured Ailsa Shipbuilding Company at Troon.

A variety of the older vessels less suited to the post-war trading conditions were disposed of. Although the ships that were sold were of no further use to GSN, they had been well maintained and others obviously thought well of some of them, as John Spilman reported in an article on Palgrave Murphy of Dublin which first appeared in SEA BREEZES in December 1962:

*"In 1926, despite the gloomy outlook, a steamer, the **Mallard**, was acquired from the General Steam Navigation Company and renamed **City of Dublin**, and continued to serve the company [Palgrave Murphy] over 22 years. At the ripe old age of 60, in 1942, the **City of Dublin** was despatched to Sao Thome Island on the Equator to load West African produce for Dublin. Notwithstanding the considerable difficulties occasioned by wartime conditions, the voyage was successfully concluded."*

The *Cormorant* (1927)
looking attractive in the colours adopted after World War Two when brown superstructure finally went and the company flag was adorned on the funnel.

The **City of Dublin** eventually succumbed to the shipbreaker's torches in Dublin in 1948. Of the same vintage as the **Mallard/City of Dublin** was the slightly smaller **Cormorant**, which was sold directly to the breakers in 1926. The **Albatross** dating from 1884 went to the breakers in 1924 after a brief spell under the Italian flag and the slightly younger **Grebe** also went to Italian owners, later to become a war casualty in 1941.

The company had already been able to rebuild its fleet with purpose-built and second hand additions, so that it was completely back to strength. Having completed the renewal of its assets, GSN found that it was trading in depressed conditions for low rates against ever increasing operating costs, notably port and dock handling charges. As time went on, the cost of second hand shipping plummeted even further, but there were few buyers, and most shipowners now found themselves with surplus tonnage on their books.

Convinced that a fleet of modern and efficient ships was the only way to survive, the new-building programme continued. The **Woodcock** was delivered for the Leith service in 1927, still offering good quality passenger accommodation but only for twelve passengers. A nice touch was to register the Scottish boat at Leith rather than London as was customary, both in respect for her builder at Grangemouth and as a counter to Scottish pride which would naturally prefer to use the rival Scottish boats rather than the interloper 'up from London'. The next vessel to enter the fleet was designed for the steel trade from Belgium and transit on the Ghent Canal. This was the engines-aft **Falcon**, another product of the Ailsa shipyard, but distinctive in that the bridge was set further forward than normal to create space for an enlarged hatchway to No. 2 hold to facilitate the carriage of long steel bars. By all accounts this arrangement made for lively handling when the wind was on her bow. A twin-berth cabin, the owner's cabin with priority for company staff, was always maintained and she offered a popular means of travelling, for those in the know, who had time available to wait on the unpredictability of cargo handling.

**The *Woodcock* (1927)
was built for the London to Edinburgh express
cargo service - note the port of registry,
Leith rather than London.**

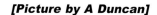

[Picture by A Duncan]

**The *Falcon* (1927)
was designed for the Belgian steel trade
and had the bridge set forward to create
a long hatchway to No 2 hold for loading
steel bars.**

Continuing the policy of amalgamation or co-operation with rivals, GSN was able to buy the Ellerman's Wilson Line service between London and Bremen in 1927 for £7,500, including their steamers, *Hero* and *Nero*. The Ellerman's Wilson Line had been particularly hard hit by the recession and a number of its ships were subject to a rolling programme of lay-up at Hull, and a contraction in routes clearly suited them. The purchase was also important to GSN, as it represented the only real enlargement in its trading operations since before the Great War. The *Nero* was originally F H Powell & Company's *Sussex Coast*, completed in 1907. After a variety of owners and names she was purchased by Ellerman's Wilson Line in 1924 for £5,250 and given the name *Nero*. In October 1927 her value had risen to £5,625, the price paid for her by GSN to help run the Bremen service, but, as she was found unsuited to the work, she was sold back to Ellerman's eight months later for just £4,150. She subsequently had a nomadic life based in the Mediterranean until an explosion amongst a cargo of drummed petrol destroyed her in 1936.

The *Hero* fared a little better with GSN. She was an attractive little steamer with a single hold forward with two hatches and a single hold aft. She had worked on a variety of services within the Ellerman group since her delivery from Earles shipyard at Hull in 1895. In fact, GSN actually bought her from the Westcott & Lawrence Line who were managing her on behalf of Ellerman Lines. She survived on the London to Bremen route until 1933, when she too was disposed of, this time to a scrapyard, as more modern purpose-built tonnage became available to GSN.

In 1929 GSN acquired an 80% interest in the London & Cologne Steamship Company, later also known as the Rhine-London Line. Control of the company passed to GSN in 1931 which allowed them to raise mortgages against the two ship fleet comprising the *Borussia* and *Badenia*. The mortgage was released in 1939 when GSN sold the company to A Kirsten, whilst the ships eventually became GSN owned in 1947 (Chapter 10).

Despite the difficult trading conditions, GSN had been able to rebuild its fleet and maintain its traditional role as brand leader in the Home Trade. It had almost completely given up its foreign going passenger carrying business, which was such a feature of the company before the Great War. None of the passenger packet services had resumed after the war as all the main passenger-cargo ships had been lost during the hostilities. GSN still maintained a weekly service for a small number of passengers to Edinburgh. However, this was small beer compared to the twice weekly and prestigious passenger service operated by the London and Edinburgh Shipping Company's *Royal Scot* and their new *Royal Fusilier*, the latter vessel offering 160 first class berths and 13 second class. The GSN Bordeaux service was also operated by twelve passenger berth steamers whilst the Lisbon and Mediterranean services could offer anything from just two to twelve berths.

The Coal Strike of 1926 had depressed freight rates even further on the east coast UK services as the railways had intensified competition during the time when ships had been unable to acquire bunkers. But on the Continental services it had actually had a beneficial effect for GSN whilst a number of rival companies were forced to withdraw from their long established trades against mounting losses, so leaving an increased share of the market for GSN. As the recession gathered pace, it appeared that GSN was set to ride out the storm and emerge as a buoyant and vibrant company, but the recession still had a long way to go.

TABLE 3 Second-Hand Purchases Between 1921 and 1924

Vessel	Year built	Original owners	Gross tons	GSN name	GSN service
Kinnaird Head	1921	Henry & Macgregor, Leith	445	Iris	1921 - 1927
Independance	1919	Ex-Neptunus Soc.d'Armement, Antwerp, ex-Controller of Shipping	500	Mavis	1921 - 1929
Glanton Firth	1920	G T Gillie & Blair, Newcastle	499	Ptarmigan	1921 - 1938
Chao Chow Fu, ex-Rajaburi	1900	South Asian owners	1,909	Guillemot	1922 - 1929
Glanmor	1920	Glanmor Shipping Company	462	Sheldrake	1922 - 1937
Beauly Firth	1920	G T Gillie & Blair, Newcastle	489	Ortolan	1923 - 1950
Peronne	1917	R & J Park, London	207	Peronne	1923 - 1946*
Picardy	1920	R & J Park, London	320	Picardy	1923 - 1953*
Arbonne	1921	Built for Thomas C Steven & Co, of Edinburgh; sold 1924 to J P Hutchison, Glasgow, no change of name.	933	Peregrine	1924 - 1938
Myrtlepark	1922	J & J Denholm, Glasgow	1,942	Adjutant	1924 - 1950
Pentland Firth	1920	G T Gillie & Blair, Newcastle	638	Alouette	1924 - 1936
Honfleur	1874	Built for London & South Western Railway, sold 1911 to Greek owners; sold 1916 to French Government.	429	Fauvette	1924 - 1925
Not named	1924	J & J Denholm, Glasgow	1,942	Albatross	1924 - 1939

* Transferred to Great Yarmouth Shipping Company 1931.

CHAPTER 7

RATIONALISE, ECONOMISE AND EXPAND

"Arrangements were made from time to time with other lines in various trades with a view to eliminating undue duplication of services and sailings. This rationalisation of sailings was not only in the interests of the shipping lines concerned but also the shippers and receivers inasmuch as they received benefit of an improved service provided jointly by all the lines operating in the trade. In other cases competing lines were taken over and amalgamated with existing General Steam services."

Hancock (1949)

The depressed years of the 1920s ground on towards the Wall Street Crash of August 1931. The pound fell overnight from $5 to $3-50 and within months over a third of British shipping was laid up in idle docks and in deep water estuaries and Scottish lochs. Seamen filed off to join the ranks of the unemployed. But the depth of this global depression made the depressed years of the 1880s and early 1890s look like a picnic. The lightermen's strike in 1932 did little to help the situation.

Despite the adverse trading conditions, GSN continued its ongoing fleet replacement programme with a handsome quartet of vessels coming from the Ailsa Shipbuilding Company between 1928 and 1930. Of these the **Groningen** and the **Leeuwarden** were placed on the joint services operated to Amsterdam and Rotterdam with William Muller's Batavia Line, their former namesakes having been lost in the Great War. The **Woodlark** was built for the Edinburgh service, and like the **Woodcock** before her, was registered at Leith. The **Starling** was destined principally for the Mediterranean services; she displaced her namesake which was sold in April 1930 to Andrew Weir's United Baltic Corporation for £17,000 and she went on to serve on their Estonian route under the name **Baltallin**.

The United Baltic Corporation was obviously pleased with their purchase as they also bought her sister ship, the **Heron**, when she was put on the sale list in February 1935, renaming her **Balteako**. Prior to this the **Heron** had carried out a charter to Strand Exploration in 1934 for a three month voyage to the South Atlantic on 'scientific research work'.

A number of smaller vessels were either built or purchased second hand for services to northern France and the Low Countries. One of these was the small steamer **Silverthorn**, dating from 1908 and transferred in 1928 to GSN from the Bennett Steamship Company of Goole as part of a shared agreement over the ownership and operation of the London and Dunkirk Shipping Company and the Rhine-London Line. Bennett, it will be recalled, was responsible for ousting GSN from the London to Calais service in 1899. But in the depressed years of the early 1930s John Bennett was forced to give up his share in the Rhine-London Line which GSN took over in 1931, having held a share in it since 1929, along with the small steamer **Volga**. Bennett also relinquished the London and Dunkirk Shipping Company and its small steamer, the **Conifer** in December 1932. GSN later renamed the company General Steam North France Lines. As a consequence, GSN was once again operating a cargo service from London to Calais and Boulogne, albeit still in competition with the Bennett Steamship Company.

**The *Swift* (1930)
seen in the Thames**

[Nautical Photo Agency]

John Bennett had been very satisfied with his former business relationship with the mighty GSN. As a small family owned business, the Bennett Steamship Company and its part-owned subsidiaries were particularly vulnerable to predators during the depression and John Bennett became wary of his larger partner. During 1931 the company had been ordered to modify its flag and funnel colours which were a red cross on a white ground, as these had been determined by the War Office to be in contravention of the Geneva Convention of 1911. That Bennett's father had adopted the red cross as the logo for his company back in 1873 cut little ice with the War Office. John Bennett (the son) wrote to his agents in London and Boulogne in 1931, with a warning about the likely change in livery: 'I expect if and when we have to make the change when it is first seen on the Thames there will be rumours amongst the water side interests that the GSN has acquired us'.

The Bennett Steamship Company did survive a little longer. However, its remaining steamers, the **Corea** and **Sparta**, were both lost in the Second World War, and company assets on shore at Boulogne and at Hull were also destroyed. John Bennett died in 1946, and the business and goodwill of what was left of his company was sold by the family to GSN.

On another front, rationalisation of the separate GSN services with those of the Great Yarmouth Shipping Company, the latter formed in 1923 by GSN and T Small & Company (Great Yarmouth), was long overdue. Hancock reports: *"In 1931 the Great Yarmouth Shipping Company, in which the General Steam had a controlling interest, absorbed the steamship services, wharves and river services operated by General Steam at Great Yarmouth, Norwich and Lowestoft, and the steamship services, shipbroking business carried on by T Small & Company (Great Yarmouth), at Great Yarmouth."*

On 31 December 1931 the little steamer **Picardy**, dating from 1920, was transferred into the Great Yarmouth Shipping Company, along with near sister, the **Peronne**, the **Yellowhammer** (built as the **Robin** in 1928 but immediately renamed) and the **Goldfinch**, bought by GSN as a two year old ship on the second hand market in 1929. T Small's ships on the service were also transferred along with the two-thirds interest in barge owners Jas Harborough and Sons, acquired in 1929. In all GSN transferred a total of 40 vessels to the Great Yarmouth company[1].

GSN was also looking to upgrade its share of the Thames excursion business, seasonal demand for which had remained buoyant despite a great reduction in family disposable incomes. In 1932 GSN took delivery of its only vessel built by Cammell Laird at Birkenhead, and the very last paddle steamer to be built for the company, the **Royal Eagle**. Eric Thornton in his book THAMES COAST PLEASURE STEAMERS excitedly reports:

"1932 was a year of great developments. First and foremost was the placing in service by GSN of the large paddle steamer Royal Eagle… equipped with triple expansion three crank engines and two oil fired Scotch boilers working on the forced draft closed stokehold principal. Whereas the earlier steamers had been rather stark in appearance, with long open decks, Royal Eagle was built up on the Promenade Deck with observation lounges and a Sun Deck on top. She was luxuriously fitted out…. Opinions will always differ in what constitutes beauty in a vessel, but in the writer's opinion her appearance was marred by the bridge being aft of the single funnel, which itself was rather too short. The effect was to give her a very heavy appearance amidships, but these were details which did not detract from her popularity on the Tower Pier, Southend, Margate and Ramsgate route on which she always operated. With her advent, Crested Eagle was placed on a new service between Tower Pier, Southend, Clacton and Felixstowe in opposition to Laguna Belle."

The Crested Eagle (1925) leaving the Pool of London with the Royal Eagle (1932) at the buoys.

[DP World P&O Heritage Collection]

[1] On 31 December 1931 GSN transferred to the Great Yarmouth Shipping Company:
       4 steamers: the **Picardy**, **Peronne**, **Yellowhammer** and **Goldfinch**
       4 steam tugs: the **Gensteam**, **Jeanie Hope**, **Jenny Wren** and **Royal Sovereign**
       2 steam wherries: the **Opal** and **Topaz**
       5 sailing wherries: the **Elder**, **Fir**, **Malve**, **Marble** and **Plane**
       3 sailing 'keels' (may not have been used commercially): the **Bloodstone**, **Moonstone** and **Sunstone**
       22 barge and lighters, of which 12 were 'dumb' and ten were 'towing'

THE
ROYAL THAMES

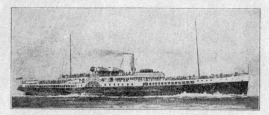

The "ROYAL EAGLE"

ONE-DAY LUXURY CRUISES
FROM THE HEART OF LONDON
(Weather and other circumstances permitting)
*Daily (except Fridays) from

TOWER OF LONDON PIER	9.0 a.m.
GREENWICH PIER	9.30 "
NORTH WOOLWICH PIER	10.0 "

TO	FARES. SINGLE.	DAY RETURN. Mon., Tues., Wed., Thurs.	PERIOD RETURN or DAY RETURN. Sats. and Suns. and Bank Holidays.
SOUTHEND	3/-	4/-	5/-
MARGATE	6/-	8/-	10/-
RAMSGATE	6/6	9/-	11/-

All Bank Holiday Day-Return Fares at Saturday Day-Return Fares.

CHILDREN UNDER 14 HALF-PRICE.

A supplementary charge of 1/- per single journey (1/6 return) for use of the Sun Deck, payable on board, including use of deck chairs available.
Passengers are carried only on the terms and conditions printed on the Company's Tickets.

Excellent Breakfasts, Luncheons and Teas. **Fully Licensed.**

The General Steam Navigation Co., Ltd., 15, Trinity Square, London, E.C.3.
Telephone : Royal 3200. Ext. 8.

Book to MARK LANE for Tower Pier

Do You Know?

THAT London is the greatest port in the world —that you can sail through it and see the shipping of the world on the most luxurious short cruise passenger steamer afloat.

THAT it is impossible to recount a fraction of the wonders and sights of the lower reaches of the Thames—that no river embraces more vivid history or gigantic industries.

THAT on this one-day cruise you experience the exhilaration of sea air and sunshine on the smooth waters of the Thames Estuary along the green Kentish coast.

THAT you can spend about 2 hours at Margate or remain on board all day and sail round the North Foreland to Ramsgate and back.

THAT excellent meals are served in spacious, well ventilated Dining Saloons at moderate cost.

THAT there are comfortable chairs in the glass enclosed deck lounge and on the exclusive sun deck.

THAT the Tower of London Pier is two minutes walk from Mark Lane Underground Station, and thus within easy reach of all parts of London.

THAT Tickets can be obtained from all the usual agencies or—

THE GENERAL STEAM NAVIGATION Co., Ltd.,
15, TRINITY SQUARE, LONDON, E.C.3.

Telephone: Royal 3200.

C.7.   Bradley & Son, Ltd., 115 Fleet Street, London, E.C.4 ; and Reading.

THE
ROYAL THAMES

"CRESTED EAGLE"

ONE-DAY LUXURY CRUISES
FROM THE HEART OF LONDON
*Daily (except Fridays), leaving

TOWER OF LONDON PIER	9.20 a.m.
GREENWICH PIER	9.50 "
NORTH WOOLWICH PIER	10.15 "

(Weather and other circumstances permitting)

SOUTHEND and CLACTON

FARES	SINGLE.	DAY RETURN. Mon., Tues., Wed., Thurs.	Sats.	DAY RETURN. Sundays.	PERIOD RETURN
SOUTHEND	3/-	4/-	5/-	5/-	5/-
CLACTON	5/6	6/-	6/-	8/-	9/-

CHILDREN UNDER 14 HALF-PRICE.

All Bank Holiday Day-Return Fares at Saturday Day-Return Fares.

Passengers are carried only on the terms and conditions printed on the Company's Tickets.

The General Steam Navigation Co., Ltd., 15, Trinity Square, London, E.O.3.
Telephone : Royal 3200. Ext. 8.

Book to MARK LANE for Tower Pier

The Catering Service.

The Catering on the Eagle Steamers is one of the corner stones upon which the popularity of the services has been built up.

There are no better breakfasts than those served immediately after leaving Tower Pier in the morning, and first-class lunches and teas later in the day. Grills, some hot dishes and cold buffet always available. The Steamers are fully licensed.

PART OF A MAIN DINING SALOON.

The Main Dining Saloon has large plate-glass windows, enabling passengers to watch the scenery and passing pageantry of Thames life.

A new feature is the Special Grill Room.

No luggage allowed to day-trip passengers. Personal luggage up to 100 lbs. accompanied by passenger carried free, at passenger's own risk, to holders of single or period return tickets.

C.6.   Bradley & Son, Ltd., 116 Fleet Street, London, E.C.4 ; and Reading.

Placed under the command of Captain W G Braithwaite (who was master of the *Peregrine* when she was lost in the Great War), the *Crested Eagle* carried 3 million passengers by the close of the 1938 season. The cost-cutting fare structure offered by the rival *Laguna Belle* was eventually seen as an opportunity rather than as threat and this one ship company was bought out by GSN in 1935.

The problems of navigation in busy shipping lanes and confined fairways in these days prior to the invention of radar were highlighted by four collisions. The *Raven* sank following a collision in May 1930, the *Tern* in the Humber in March 1931, and the smaller *Kingfisher* was lost in October 1931 under similar conditions. The latter was towed into port where she was declared a constructive total loss and sold for demolition. Then in October 1934 the modern twin screw steamer *Fauvette* sank in the North Sea after colliding with the steamship *Penelope* whilst on a voyage from Antwerp to London. Lessons on the importance of watch-keeping were never more necessary.

GSN had long been conscious of the arrival of the diesel engine in the short sea and coasting trades, but had so far resisted any temptation to experiment with the new propulsion system. Although proven to offer a greater deadweight because the engines were lighter and the bunker spaces smaller, a key drawback to the increased adoption of the diesel was a shortage of trained and certificated diesel engineers. This had been a serious problem for Paton & Hendry, the pioneer operator of diesel coasters in the UK, who introduced the motor coaster to the British register just before the Great War. But as time went on, Paton & Hendry's fleet (all of which had names with the prefix *Innis-*) thrived as the efficiency of the motor ship increased. By 1930 the average motor coaster was using less than one third the equivalent fuel of a steamer.

As it happened, in 1932, the yard of J Koster at Groningen was building a small motor coaster of just 213 tons gross to an accepted engines-aft design. Nearing completion, it became apparent that the intended owners of the vessel would not be able to take delivery due to the recession. The ship was offered to a variety of companies including GSN, and the company directors decided that this was the appropriate opportunity to test the new machinery. Launched as the *Tern*, the vessel had the distinction of being the first motor ship in the fleet and the first GSN vessel to be built at a foreign yard. She had a 4-cylinder Deutz engine with clutch reversing, and separate cylinders bolted to the crank case. The engine controls were in the wheelhouse allowing the engine room to be unattended for lengthy periods, save for checks on pressures, temperatures and the contents of the fuel oil gravity tank. Serving on the near continental routes, her success can be judged by the order of a larger vessel of 614 tons gross, the *Fauvette*, which on delivery was placed on the London to Antwerp service in 1934. In 1936 the smaller *Bullfinch* and *Goldfinch* were delivered to GSN and they took up duties on the northern France runs.

The *Fauvette* (1935) was the first motor ship to be built specifically for GSN.

The *Goldfinch* (1936) on the Ghent - Terneuzen Canal at Zelzate.

[A postcard issued by Huis Blondine, Zelzate]

The timing of the entry of the diesel ships compares favourably with other similar companies. The Coast Lines group of companies had the pioneer fast overnight diesel passenger ferries of the **Ulster Monarch** class in operation between Belfast and Liverpool from 1929 onwards, but their first motor coasters were the **British Coast** and **Atlantic Coast** which were delivered in 1933. The railway fleets stayed doggedly with steam until after the Second World War, having ready access to abundant bulk-purchased supplies of cheap coal, received in return for favourable transport costs for the collieries.

The fleet replacement programme allowed a number of vessels to be disposed of, the more modern ones at the most favourable rates. The **Drake** of 1922, which had spent 12 years going to and fro between northern France and London, was sold in 1934 to the Government of Zanzibar as an upgrade in their fleet of steamers serving the island. Renamed **Al Said**, she gave sterling service to Zanzibar until she was sold to breakers at Hong Kong in June 1956.

Other ships were disposed of because they were no longer economical to maintain in the depressed economy of the early 1930s. Such was the case when the magnificent sisters, **Philomel** and **Halcyon**, were withdrawn from the Southampton to Bordeaux service and replaced by the **Falcon** which had been built for the Belgian steel trade, and the ancient 1909-built engines-aft **Laverock**. As a consequence, the weekly Saturday departures from both Bordeaux and Southampton for twelve passengers was downgraded to an erratic service from London, with accommodation for just two passengers. The **Philomel** and **Halcyon** were sold to the Khedivial Mail Line of Alexandria, which P&O had acquired in 1919 and resold in 1924, and given the names **Zaafaran** and **Zamalek** respectively. As such, they sailed the eastern Mediterranean offering a regular feeder service to the longer Khedivial Mail Line services and to other main line ships connecting at Alexandria. The circuit offered by the twins was from Alexandria to Port Said, Jaffa, Haifa, Beirut, Tripoli, Lattakia, Mersin and Alexandretta, returning via the same ports. The Egyptian fleet was popular with Scottish officers, and without exception all the passenger units of the Khedivial Mail Line had Scottish masters during the 1930s.

In 1932 the government had charged P&O to undertake a thorough audit to ensure that capital assets were appropriately valued and that subsidiary companies were not double accounting. This was a precautionary measure that served to check that P&O was not on the same slippery slope that the Royal Mail Group had descended. The audit report to the Directors of GSN was prepared by Deloite, Plender, Griffith & Company and contains an inventory of the freehold properties[2] and the ships owned by the company as at 1932. The report writes the value of the fleet down to £1,306,947, approximately £125,000 less than its book value ten years previously. But it is the list of subsidiary majority-owned companies that is impressive, a list which illustrates the complex network of companies then held by both P&O and Royal Mail, and which highlights how difficult it was to account for overall group activities. The list of GSN shareholdings in addition to the London & Dunkirk Shipping Company, Great Yarmouth Shipping Company and the Belgian London Midland Line, was:

80% London & Cologne Steamship Company (acquired 1929)
66% Jas. Harborough & Son (acquired in 1929) - Norfolk inland waterways and east coast services
52% North Sea Steamship Company (acquired in 1929) - cargo services from Kings Lynn to the Continent
92% Thomas Trapp & Son - forwarding agents in London
99% Navigation Properties Company - owners of London properties
95% Irongate Lighterage Company - Thames lighterage services
75% Oceanic Stevedoring Company Société Anonyme, Antwerp
100% General Steam Shipping Agency, (Basle) - company agents
100% Agenza Marittima General Steam Societa Anonima, (Genoa) - company agents
86% La Société de Consignation Maritime Franco-Britannique, (Bordeaux, Havre, Dunkirk, Paris) - company agents
80% General Steam Société Anonyme Belge de Transport (Antwerp, Ghent, Terneuzen) - company agents
58% General Steam Transport Company (Rotterdam, Amsterdam, Harlingen) - company agents
85% General Steam Navigation Company, Hamburger-Agentur GmbH (Hamburg, Bremen) - company agents

Two separate but significant incidents took place in 1933. One was the opening of a new agency at Smyrna in Turkey. The other was the introduction of a life assurance and pension scheme for staff, officers and Directors. Previously, pensions had been 'a gift from the Board at their pleasure with no legal mandate'.

---

[2] Freehold properties: Irongate and St Katherine's Wharf, London; Brewers Quay, London; Deptford, London; ABC Wharf, Yarmouth; Crisp's Wharf, Lowestoft; Baltic Wharf, Norwich; North Albert Wharf, Leith.

As the global economy began to recover throughout 1934, trading conditions slowly regained the vigour that was last enjoyed back in the early 1920s. But GSN was in expansive mood, with interest earned on its shareholdings in other companies and from its investment in gilt edged stocks - it was almost as though the money it held was burning a hole in the company's pockets. Sale of the stocks yielded a profit on the investment in excess of £400,000 and this was available for reinvestment, ideally in an established shipping line whose business complemented that of GSN. As it happened, the clean up following the collapse of Lord Kylsant's Royal Mail Group had prompted the amalgamation of the Moss and Hutchison parts of that group ready for sale. The eternal desire of GSN Directors to trade from Liverpool, coupled with a business that connected both the Mediterranean and the near-Continental ports with Liverpool and Glasgow, clearly put the newly-formed Moss Hutchison Line in the frame for GSN (see Chapter 8).

Hancock, apparently oblivious to the background to the purchase, explains:

"The Moss Hutchison Line is a combination of two very old established companies, the Moss trade being then principally between Liverpool, Glasgow and Bordeaux and the Eastern Mediterranean and Black Sea, and Hutchison's between the west coast UK and Hamburg, Bremen, Rouen and French 'Bay' ports, Portugal and Spain. The fleet then consisted of sixteen modern steamers totalling over 52,000 tons, and the average age of the ships was about ten years. In addition to strengthening the General Steam's long-established trade between this country and the Mediterranean it was possible, of course, to effect a certain amount of rationalisation and interchange of tonnage according to requirements. This acquisition brought the total of subsidiary companies either owned entirely or controlled by GSN up to 31. Although the Moss Hutchison Line is now part and parcel of the General Steam, the former retains its own offices and management in co-operation with the GSN's services."

In truth the purchase of the Moss Hutchison Line by GSN was a shrewd move by John Morison of Thomas McLintock & Company, who had been appointed by the Bank of England to disentangle Kylsant's 'web of deceit' (Chapter 8) and raise cash for the surviving parts of the Royal Mail Group. The sale was approved by P&O and the Bank of England despite the fearsome competition that existed on the Moss Hutchison routes from fascist regimes of Germany in the north and of Italy in the Mediterranean.

But it was a marriage from heaven, and GSN had paid £388,859 for Moss Hutchison and still had change from their £400,000. It also provided GSN with some impetus to upgrade its own services from London to Bordeaux and the Mediterranean ports. The venerable **Laverock** and the equally unsuitable **Falcon** were in charge of Bordeaux, aided as required by the **Drake**, one of the conventional engines-amidships vessels built in the early 1920s. The **Drake** also supported the Mediterranean sailings along with the **Adjutant** and **Albatross**, also built in the early 1920s, and the **Stork** which had been built in 1904.

The upgrade comprised four new ships. These were the motor-driven twins **Crane** and **Stork**, with comfortable and modern accommodation for twelve passengers, and the big steamer **Philomel** and her near sister, the motor ship **Heron**, both of which were specifically designed for Mediterranean routes. A W Younghusband described the **Crane** and **Stork** in an article which first appeared in SEA BREEZES in July 1954:

*"They were smaller than their predecessors, being 214 feet in length and of about 785 gross tons. The **Crane** had a service speed of 10.5 knots, while her sister was faster and capable of 11.5. They were built to take six passengers only, in three very comfortable, well appointed cabins, all the accommodation being the then latest thing in modern luxury and veneer. From the moment of their 'coming out' the sisters were much sought after and were the toast of the town, but while the youngsters extolled their beauty there would always be some old grey head to lament: 'Ah, but if you had known the **Halcyon** and **Philomel**. When shall we see their like again?"*

The new Mediterranean ships **Philomel** and **Heron** were both built by the Caledon Shipbuilding & Engineering Company at Dundee for the Mediterranean routes. The reason why an order for one steamer and one motor ship should be given for a pair that were intended to work together is not apparent. It may be that GSN was still a little nervous about diesel propulsion for their larger units and wanted to compare the performance of the two vessels, like by like, or there may have been an influence from P&O for wider group experience. Whatever the reason, the **Philomel** was the last steamship ever to be built for GSN. She was in any case a much better proportioned vessel than her sister. Both ships carried twelve passengers in considerable splendour, compared with travel by the previous incumbents on the Mediterranean routes.

So that the GSN vessels would not be confused with those of the Moss Hutchison fleet, the company devised a new colour scheme for its new Mediterranean passenger and cargo ships. Whereas the Moss Hutchison funnel colours were black with a white band, GSN still wore all black (apart from the Thames excursion fleet which was buff with a thin black top). In order to identify properly the new **Philomel** and **Heron** as the London boats, each was given discreet sized plaques of the company houseflag which were affixed to their funnels – red globe, the letters GSN in each corner and the date 1824 on a white ground. In addition, the traditional brown superstructure, which by now was a little outdated, was replaced by modern white upperworks which with the white band on the ship's black hulls set them off a treat. So pleased were the Directors with their artwork that the new Bordeaux vessels were similarly adorned, and as time went on, some of the smaller, but newer vessels in the fleet also received the new scheme. And in order to make some of the old paddle steamers on the Thames look more like modern motorships, there were experiments in 1935 with corn coloured hulls, but black was soon reinstated to cover the rust streaks.

Then the Director's went overboard with their paintbrush, and the **Philomel** emerged from winter refit with an all-white hull. Whilst the effect was very attractive, the poor quality of the paints that were available in the 1930s meant that every time the ship was in port, any available men were sent over the side with paint and rollers. The rust streaks from just one winter of travelling across the Bay of Biscay were enough for the Directors to revert to the conventional hull colouring.

The steamer _Philomel_ (1936) was designed for the Mediterranean service and for a while she was painted all white as seen in this picture.

[R Ellis of Malta]

The _Mallard_ (1936) was one of a pair of small motor ships delivered by the Caledon Shipbuilding & Engineering Company, Dundee.

In August 1936, a GSN ship proudly flew the Royal Mail pennant once again – the first time for several decades. This was the **Auk** which made a special trip from Oporto to London with 60 mail-bags that could not go by their normal route overland because of the ongoing Spanish Civil War.

GSN then pooled its resources on the London to Hamburg route with the German Argo Line and with A Kirsten to allow a daily departure from both Hamburg and London.

In December 1936, GSN bought out the entire share capital of the New Medway Steam Packet Company, a feat it accomplished in just 24 hours. This was its second major acquisition in as many years, and this one placed its own Eagle Steamers line of Thames excursion steamers in collaboration with its arch rivals who traded as the Queen Line from Rochester. The Medway Steam Packet Company had long been family run and a minor player on the Thames, maintaining services on the Medway and across to Southend. The old company did not survive the Great War but was reconstituted as the New Medway Steam Packet Company after the war by a young and dynamic master mariner, Captain Sydney Shippick. The take-over deal included the associate Acorn Barge Building Company of Rochester as well as a number of tugs and three small passenger launches.

The subsequent ascendancy of 'Shippick's Navy' is well known (e.g. Burtt, 1949; Thornton, 1972). Needless to say, at the time of the GSN take-over in 1936, Shippick had commissioned a large day excursion motor ship for his continental routes, the **Queen of the Channel**, and had another larger motor ship on the stocks, the **Continental Queen**. Both ships were designed and built by William Denny & Brothers at Dumbarton, famous for fast coastal passenger ship design.

The innovative motor excursion ship
Queen of the Channel (1935)
seen at speed in this picture.

[Nautical Photo Agency]

Captain Shippick had been very careful to watch the pennies in developing his fleet and he had bought a number of vessels from other operators as opportunity arose (Table 4). These included three vessels from the former Belle Steamers fleet. He also bought two First World War paddle minesweepers which were otherwise destined for the scrapyard, and which were converted at his own yard at Rochester to become the popular steamers, **Queen of Thanet** and **Queen of Kent**. However, the favourite of all time was the paddle steamer **Medway Queen**, built for the company in 1924 to plough between Rochester and Southend, thence to Herne Bay and return.

The **Queen of Kent** (1916),
seen at Calais awaiting the return of her
passengers, was built as the World War I
paddle minesweeper HMS **Atherstone**
and joined the New Medway Steam
Packet Company after conversion to a
day excursion boat in 1927.

The New Medway Steam Packet
Company's **Essex Queen** (1897),
before enlargement of the
forward lounge in 1931.

The new motor ship known as the **Continental Queen** was considerably modified on GSN instructions, and went into the water in time for the 1937 season as the GSN crack motor ship **Royal Sovereign**, something of a coup for GSN. The modifications included flaring out the hull above the water line to provide enlarged deck areas and to provide enhanced stability in a beam sea. GSN now had a total monopoly on Thames excursions, although the separate trading names of Queen Line of Steamers and Eagle Steamers were retained and the vessels marketed under their separate banners (see Table 4).

The **Royal Sovereign** (1937)
showing off her flared out Main Deck arrangement.

In 1937 the first P&O placement was voted on to the GSN Board, Mr Donald Black, who was also Secretary of the P&O Steam Navigation Company[3]. This was felt expedient by P&O, as GSN had expanded its activities considerably since its original purchase in 1920. Not only had GSN expanded its various brands, its fleets and its holdings in wharves, warehouses and freight-handling agencies, but it had also expanded its continental agency business. These agencies now included nearly thirty different businesses via the various shore offices in all the major Continental and Mediterranean ports, representing virtually all the major UK liner companies and several foreign shipping companies as well. This was obviously also good for trade as these connections developed new contacts for freight-forwarding on a feeder basis to a range of different P&O group liner companies. In February 1937 the small steamer **Sheldrake**, dating from 1922, foundered on passage from London to Bridgwater in the Bristol Channel. She was carrying a cargo of cement, and sank rapidly once her watertight integrity was breached.

In 1937 William McAllister stepped down as Chairman and Managing Director, although he retained a place on the Board. His place was taken by Robert Kelso as Chairman who also assumed Chairmanship of Moss Hutchison. Kelso had first been elected to the GSN Board in 1924. Under Kelso's influence, the direction of the company was little changed and he carried on the vigorous fleet rebuilding programme and expansion by merger, take-over or collaboration wherever it was in the common interest of GSN and others.

The **Crane** (1937)
was a neat vessel with two holds.
She is seen loading at Tonnay Charente.

[DP World P&O Heritage Collection]

The motor ship **Heron** (1937)
was a quasi-sister of the **Philomel**
for service on the Mediterranean routes.

[Picture by A Duncan]

[3] Donald Black was appointed a Director of GSN in March 1937, and resigned as P&O Company Secretary in September when he was appointed an Assistant Manager. He remained on the GSN Board until he resigned from P&O in January 1943. He was succeeded as P&O's nominee by Mr Archibold O Lang, P&O's Deputy Chairman and a Managing Director. P&O was later represented at GSN by Sir Andrew Crichton. Conversely from 1955 onwards the GSN Chairman (first Mr I M Hooper, then Mr R G Grant then, after a short gap, Mr D L J Mortelman) was a member of the P&O Board.

By 1939 another six motor cargo vessels had been commissioned for the near Continental, Leith and longer distance routes of the GSN network. Three of these ships were built for the company by J Koster's 'De Gideon' shipyard at Groningen in the typical Dutch style of the day, with engines and accommodation amidships. These were the sisters **Kingfisher** and **Alouette** and the larger **Drake**, which were all commissioned specifically for the Rhine ports, Brussels and Bruges services and to work from some of the smaller Dutch ports.

The distinctive design of the *Alouette* (1938) belies her Dutch origin in this picture by *A Duncan*.

The *Drake* (1938) was a larger version of the *Alouette* and her sister *Kingfisher*.

The *Oriole* (1939) was a useful addition for the near-Continental trades.

The fine two funnelled motor excursion ship **Royal Daffodil** was completed by Denny in 1939, but spent only one season on the Thames before being requisitioned for official duties. Although the order had been placed for the new ship by the New Medway Steam Packet Company, the registered owner of the **Royal Daffodil** was GSN. Resplendent with two funnels, her dining saloons could accommodate 286 passengers out of a total passenger complement of 2,060. Unlike the two earlier motor driven excursion ships which had direct-drive engines, the **Royal Daffodil** had geared diesels that allowed the ship to go astern without having to stop and restart the engines in reverse. And unlike the two earlier motor excursion ships which were both lost in the Second World War, the new **Royal Daffodil** was to survive and later to please holidaymakers on the Thames until the mid-1960s.

The *Royal Daffodil* (1939)
at Southend in August 1962.

[Nick Robins]

A handbill from summer 1937
advertising sailings by the
first *Royal Daffodil*.

The new motor driven cargo vessels in the fleet in turn displaced several of the older steamers, which were disposed of. A number of the larger and potentially more useful units were transferred to Moss Hutchison. The elderly steamer **Corncrake**, the Edinburgh stalwart **Woodcock** and the smaller steamer **Grebe** were transferred to bolster the Moss Hutchison Line at little cost to GSN. The other associate company, the Great Yarmouth Shipping Company had taken delivery of two engines-aft diesel vessels in the mid-1930s which had been given the familiar East Anglian 'Trader' names that were to become associated with the company. These were the **Lowestoft Trader** and **Boston Trader**. In addition, two steamers were also purchased by the company in 1934 to support the upturn in trade towards the end of the depression.

One of the last business acquisitions made by GSN before the outbreak of war was the purchase of a majority interest in Turner Edwards & Company and their agency Edwards Bristol Channel Lines in March 1939. Turner Edwards connected Bristol Channel ports with the Continent via a variety of routes on a regular basis, and was particularly strong in the wine trade. The wine trade between Bristol and Bayonne stemmed from the twelfth century, with vessels carrying cloth outwards and wine back. Turner Edwards sustained imports of wine, sherry and port destined for Averys of Bristol and John Harvey & Sons. They had also acted as local agents for J & P Hutchison and later the Moss Hutchison Line (Chapter 8). It was an obvious company to complement the London based parent activities, and GSN acquired the balance of the shares in December 1947.

The *Starling* (1930)
in a late 1950s view showing her wearing the Turner
Edwards funnel colours.

GSN also controlled the lorry company, Blackmore's Motor Transport Company, and the freight-forwarding agency, Thos. Trapp & Sons. The latter dealt with the UK distribution of wine and brandy. GSN was a power to be reckoned with, and one that P&O was well pleased with.

As the shadow of war loomed once again, the **Philomel** was abruptly taken off the Mediterranean service as early as January 1939 for official duties. The **Heron** followed in July. Although war was only threatening at that stage, the business of the company was already being modified. The pleasure steamers enjoyed their last season on the Thames until September, when Neville Chamberlain's 'policy of appeasement' towards the dictators, Mussolini and Hitler, finally failed and war was declared.

MASTERS OF THE *HALCYON* (1920) AND *PHILOMEL* (1921) ON THE BORDEAUX ROUTE

To 'TO FRANCE IN GSN SHIPS', from an article by A W Younghusband, which first appeared in SEA BREEZES, July 1954:

"With a beam wind blowing from across the miles of Atlantic Ocean, the **Philomel***, light-loaded on her outward voyage commenced to roll 'rather more than somewhat' and the captain ordered a very small triangular sail to be set on the main mast. When in my very youthful ignorance, I asked if this sail really helped at all, he replied: 'Young man, that sail serves two very useful purposes, firstly, rigging it keeps the crew occupied and out of mischief, and secondly it keeps me amused'. The captain was one of that fine old school that is fast becoming only a memory, who served their time in sail. A kindly, erudite man with an extra master's certificate and a keen, if slightly disconcerting, sense of humour, he would tell inquiring passengers the most extravagant tales with such a dignified manner that disbelief was almost impossible. However, he, like his ship, will always be recalled with affection by his many friends.*

The master of our sister ship [**Halcyon** *] was another original character. Commodore of his company's fleet, he had served long in the Bordeaux trade, and knew more about the sands of the Gironde than many of the local pilots. During the war he had seen service in the RNR where he had acquired some quaint ideas of naval discipline and etiquette that would have left the Royal Navy speechless and marvelling. He was a relic of that time when shipmasters engaged in trade on their own account, and had a thriving trade in empty wine casks. In this matter of trade, it has been reported that a master mariner died recently leaving £50,000. This was entirely due to his hard work, steadfast honesty, and strict attention to his owner's interests, and to the fact he won £49,999 in a lottery.*

Later, another master of the old breed joined the trade. Also an extra-master with a square-rig certificate, he seemed to collect pilotage licences as a hobby. He was inordinately fond of dogs, and his knowledge of their ailments and the cures would have been the envy of many a veterinary surgeon. Hounds sent out to join the Duke of Westminster's pack outside Bordeaux were always his particular and personal care, and to see him in the hold surrounded by dogs used to bring to mind Saint Francis of Assisi."

The article was followed in press by a rather sheepish letter to the Editor of SEA BREEZES, February 1955, written by Captain Charles Birch, retired, of Seaford:

"...I was for 32 years master in the GSN's ships and in the summer of 1926 was master of the **Philomel** *and from February 1929 to December 1931, was master of the* **Halcyon** *between Bordeaux and Southampton. These ships were like large yachts, but the passenger accommodation was separate from the crew's.*

I do not think I could have been the master of either ship at the time of which the author writes, although I have an extra master's certificate, 'square-rigged' dated 1896, and seven pilotage certificates, among them one for Southampton, 1903. I am not fond of dogs, and have no veterinary knowledge. In both ships I used sail – a 'bounderous' jib and a very extensive spencer on the main."

Case proven – who knows? But it would appear that there were many colourful characters within the company who had spent the greater part of their careers with GSN, albeit still hankering for their youthful days under sail. The reference to a 'bounderous' jib apparently derives from the Victorian sea shanty 'Paul Jones': And 'neath the weight of a bounderous jib Her boom bent like a hoop."

TABLE 4   The Combined Thames Excursion Fleets of the New Medway Steam Packet Company's Queen Line of Steamers and GSN's Eagle Steamers in December 1936

Name	Built	Tons gross	Length (feet)	Speed (knots)	Comments
New Medway Steam Packet Company:					
Queen of Southend	1898	522	240	16*	Ex-*Yarmouth Belle*, bought from the East Anglia Steamship Company in 1928.
Essex Queen	1897	465	230	16*	Ex-*Walton Belle*, bought from the East Anglia Steamship Company in December 1925.
City of Rochester	1904	235	160	15	Built at J Scott & Company at Kinghorn Fife.
Royal Daffodil	1905	465	152	15	Ex-*Daffodil*, 1919, bought from Borough of Wallasey in 1934.
Queen of Kent	1916	798	235	16	Ex-HMS *Atherstone*, bought from Admiralty in 1927 and refitted at Rochester.
Queen of Thanet	1916	792	235	16	Ex-HMS *Melton*, bought from ship breakers in 1928 and refitted at Rochester.
Medway Queen	1924	318	180	15	Built at Ailsa Shipbuilding Company, Troon.
Queen of the Channel	1935	1,030	255	19	Built at Dumbarton by Wm Denny Brothers.
GSN:					
Laguna Belle	1896	570	249	18	Ex-*Southend Belle* 1929, bought from East Anglian Hotels in1935.
Golden Eagle	1909	790	275	18	Built at Clydebank by John Brown & Company.
Crested Eagle	1925	1,110	299	18	Built at Southampton by J Samuel White.
Royal Eagle	1932	1,538	290	18	Built at Birkenhead by Cammell Laird & Company.

* Formerly capable of 17 knots when built.
<u>Note:</u> The elderly **Isle of Arran** built in 1892 and acquired by GSN in 1933 from Williamson Buchanan Steamers on the Clyde had been sold at the end of the 1936 season.

CHAPTER 8

MOSS AND HUTCHISON

"...the Hutchison house flag is still flown while vessels of the Moss Hutchison Line are in French ports. Apparently the two brothers John and Peter Hutchison were great lovers of France and during the Franco-Prussian War medical stores for the French Army were carried freight free. In recognition of this service the French Government authorised the Hutchison ships to fly the French Tricolour, with the Scottish thistle superimposed, as a house flag – a privilege which has been valued ever since."

From an article by James Pearce,
which first appeared in SEA BREEZES, April 1949.

The Moss Hutchison Line was first registered on 6 April 1934. This was the outcome of the amalgamation of James Moss & Company (Moss Line) and Messrs J & P Hutchison, in the wake of the collapse of the Royal Mail Group, the UK's (and probably the world's) largest shipping concern. The association of the two companies was cemented in 1919 when Moss bought itself into the position of total shareholder of J & P Hutchison.

The origins of the Moss part of the union dated from a meeting in 1815 when Liverpool ship chandler, James Moss, invited friends to share with him in the charter fees and potential profits for a sailing vessel to voyage to the Mediterranean. None took up his invitation, so he alone undertook the charter and after a few voyages he was able to buy the vessel outright. One of his friends did join him in 1823, and the company traded as Moss & Hampson until 1833, when Thomas Hampson pulled out. He was replaced by James' nephew, William Miles Moss, and Richard Spencer, and trade resumed under the banner James Moss & Company.

The new company's first advertisement in July 1833 read as follows:

*"For Palermo and Messina, the well known fast sailing brig **Trinacria**, Antonio Lagana, Master. A1 at Lloyds, coppered, and 232 tons per register: has three fourths of her cargo now ready to be put on board, on owners account, and will be dispatched immediately.*

*For Constantinople, Smyrna and Salonika, the fine fast sailing brig **Comet**, E C King, Master. A1 at Lloyds, coppered, 120 tons per register, and an excellent conveyance for dry goods.*

*For Alexandria, with leave to call at Malta if required, the fine brig **William**, A Orfeur, Master. A1 at Lloyds, coppered, 130 tons per register."*

The management of the business passed to William Miles Moss following the death of James Moss in 1849. The first steamships for the company were the **Nile** of 340 tons and the **Orontes** of 530 tons, both delivered by Messrs Denny at Dumbarton. The steamers having proven their worth, orders were placed with a Bristol company in 1854 for three larger and more powerful ships: the **Meander** and **Scamander** of 780 tons and the **Araxes** of 1156 tons. A huge boost to the company was the rapidly growing cotton trade from Egypt, which required even bigger and faster vessels, built variously on the Clyde, the Lagan and the Mersey. The American Civil War had closed many of the cotton export routes from the Southern States by 1868, and growers in India had stepped in to satisfy the burgeoning demand. The Bombay and Bengal Steamship Company was created by the Indian merchants to ship cotton to Suez, then overland to Alexandria, where the Moss Line took over, and brought it to Liverpool. Two ships were specially built for this work, the **Magdala** and **Necra**, but they were sold once the Suez Canal opened and the need for transhipment ended.

In 1873 the company started to run a direct service to Bordeaux with the **Olinda**, a vessel bought second hand from Thos. & Jno. Brocklebank. The similarities in trading with that of GSN from London are indeed striking. When William Miles Moss died, later in the same year, the company took advantage of the new Companies Limited Liability Act to be reconstituted as the Moss Steamship Company Limited, with Messrs James Moss & Company as managers. There was even the same yen for distant waters that was displayed at this time by the likes of GSN, the Wilson Line and David MacBrayne, as there was a Moss service to north-east Canada for a while. The **Patroclus** of 1854 was lost off the Canadian coast soon after the transatlantic venture began, and when the brand new **Mareotis** was lost in 1900, the company saw sense, and soon withdrew from the trade.

On the eve of the Great War, the Moss Steamship Company possessed twelve steamers with an aggregate gross tonnage of 2,722 and an average age of just eight years. In 1916 the company was taken over by the Royal Mail Group. In 1918 the Moss Steamship Company emerged from the terrors of the Great War with just two ships. A majority share was purchased in J & P Hutchison in 1919 so also bringing that company into the Royal Mail Group.

Moss bought the wartime standard ship *War Leven*, which had been built at the Caledon shipyard in Dundee, and gave it the name *Limoges*. In 1922 the company did a deal with Coast Lines, also a part of the Royal Mail Group, whereby the *Lomoges* became the *Western Coast* and their similar wartime standard ships, another *Western Coast* and the *British Coast* (laid down as the *War Shannon*), which had been built by Swan Hunter, became the Moss Steamship Company's *Esneh* and *Etrib* respectively. Coast Lines preferred the Caledon-built wartime standard ships having already bought the *War Garry* and *War Spey*. They were all flush-decked vessels, with a squat deckhouse amidships topped by an open bridge.

The Moss Steamship Company weathered the onset of the depression, but could not survive the failure of the Royal Mail Group and its leader Lord Kylsant, and it was rebranded in the early 1930s under the title James Moss & Company (Moss Line) of Liverpool. The fleet had been largely upgraded as part of Lord Kylsant's over-building programme to keep his shipyards in business. Moss also had two pioneer motor ships, the *Kheti* and *Kufra*. These vessels were built by Harland & Wolff at Govan, which was also a part of Lord Kylsant's empire, with Burmeister & Wain engines, built locally under licence. The early move towards diesel propulsion reflects the close liaison within the Royal Mail Group particularly with the Lamport & Holt Line which then operated a fleet of largely diesel ships to South American destinations. The Moss Line provided an important feeder service for Lamport & Holt as well as for a number of other Liverpool-based liner companies.

The company went into the merger with the Hutchison Line with twelve ships:

Amarna (1919)	4,195 tons gross	*Lormont* (1920)	1,276
Assiout (1918)	4,215	*Kana* (1929)	2,743
Esneh (1919)	1,931	*Kantara* (1925)	3,237
Etrib (1919)	1,943	*Kavak* (1929)	2,743
Hatasu (1921)	3,198	*Kheti* (1927)	2,650
Landes (1920)	1,276	*Kufra* (1929)	2,608

**The *Kufra* (1929)
was the second of a pair of motorships to be
built for the Moss Steamship Company.**

**The *Assiout* (1918)
was part of the original merged fleet
and had been built for the
Moss Steamship company.**

**The *Amarna* (1919)
was the sister to the *Assiout*.**

The Hutchison family of Glasgow first became interested in shipping in the mid-nineteenth century when Hutchison & Brown started trading between Scotland, Ireland and France. In 1869 Brown withdrew from the partnership, and the company was rebranded J & P Hutchison, with the brothers John and Peter Hutchison in control. James Pearce (SEA BREEZES, April 1949) reported the development as follows:

"By the 1870s Messrs J & P Hutchison were well established in France, having a branch office in Havre. Later the office was transferred to Bordeaux, and other branch offices were also opened in Rouen and Nantes. The firm prospered, and by the early 1890s owned a fairly large fleet of small steamers engaged in trading along the west coasts of Britain and France, the range of ports covered including Glasgow, Garston, Bristol Channel ports, Dublin, Belfast, Rouen and south to Bayonne."

At the turn of the century the company built a series of engines-aft steamers of about 500 gross tons, but of only about 80 net tons. These included the **Hector**, **Paris**, **Achilles**, **Atlanta**, **Argo** and **Mercury**, and by all accounts they created great concern to any harbour authority which based its charges on net tonnage alone! Before the Great War, Hutchison purchased the Portugal and Spain services of the Dublin-based company Palgrave Murphy, and thereafter Hutchison acted as agent for Palgrave Murphy in Glasgow, whilst Palgrave Murphy acted as Hutchison's agent in Dublin. Immediately after the war, Palgrave Murphy's service via the Bristol Channel to Plymouth, Hamburg and Bremen was also taken over. By the time of the amalgamation with Moss in 1934 there was a fleet of ten ships:

Ardenza (1920)	933 tons gross	**Memphis** (1917)	1,033
Busiris (1929)	943	**Philotis** (1918)	1,037
Chloris (1921)	1,197	**Procris** (1924)	1,320
Endymion (1909)	887	**Sardis** (1928)	970
Fendris (1925)	1,309	**Smerdis** (1920)	815

J & P Hutchinson's *Procris* (1924) served the merged fleet of the Moss Hutchison Line until she was sold for scrap in September 1950.

The reason for the merger lay firmly at Kylsant's door. The prospectus for the building of two large diesel passengers liners, **Asturias** and **Alcantara**, at Harland & Wolff for the Royal Mail Steam Packet Company during the 1920s had alerted the Bank of England to financial malpractice within the Royal Mail Group. New ships for group members were ordered from the company owned shipyards but there was little money available to pay the bills. When Kylsant undertook to buy the White Star Line back from the American owned International Mercantile Marine, both he and 'his wonderful web of deceit' were at last exposed.

A leading firm of accountants, Thomson McLintock & Company of Glasgow, was appointed by the Bank of England to unravel the web and put the Royal Mail interests back on the rails. Government could not afford to see the shipping empire collapse nor could it allow the Harland & Wolff shipyard to go under in a newly partitioned and still very sensitive Ireland. A key to the reorganisation of the group was the settlement of claims in American courts over the loss of the Lamport & Holt liner **Vestris** just outside New York harbour in November 1928 with the loss of 112 lives. This work was finalised in 1933 by John Morison from Thomson McLintock & Company. The Moss and Hutchison interests were then finally available for sale to raise some desperately needed cash to support the core parts of the surviving Royal Mail Group, and both GSN and Andrew Weir's United Baltic Corporation had already shown an interest in both the Moss and the Hutchison interests. John Morison realised that a greater sum might be raised by selling the two companies as a single going concern and duly amalgamated Moss and Hutchison, which had previously been jointly owned but separately managed, to form the Moss Hutchison Line.

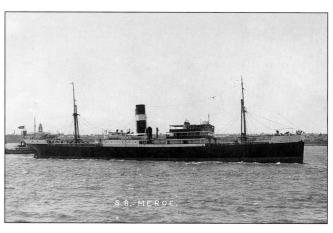

Hutchinson's *Fendris* (1925) seen in the Mersey.

[Picture by B & A Feilden]

The *Meroe* (1928) also seen in the Mersey.

[Picture by B & A Feilden]

The combined businesses of the newly formed Moss Hutchison Line shed a number of its older and less economical ships during the reorganisation. In truth it contained a number of vessels that normal business practice would never have ordered, had the Royal Mail Group not corporate shipyards to support. Two large former Moss vessels, ***Amarna*** and ***Assiout***, were disposed of, along with the two smallest units, the ***Landes*** and ***Lormont***. Three of the former Hutchison fleet also went, the elderly ***Endymion***, and the medium-sized engines-aft steamers ***Chloris*** and ***Philotis***. The ***Philotis*** actually went to rivals, the British and Continental Steamship Company, and served as their ***Nyroca*** on the Southampton and near-continental routes until 1950. She then passed into the Greek registry and was withdrawn and scrapped only in 1974 at the venerable age of 56. Two relatively modern steamers were brought into the fleet to bring it back to strength. These were the United Africa Company's ***Nigerian*** and ***Lafian***, which were given the traditional Moss Line names, ***Kyrenia*** and ***Meroe***, respectively.

The United Africa Company had been formed by soap manufacturer, William Lever, in 1929 by amalgamating the Niger Company and the African & Eastern Trade Corporation, for whom both the ***Lafian*** and ***Nigerian*** had been built. In 1949 the United Africa Company adopted the more familiar name of the Palm Line, whose ships are remembered discharging palm oil at Bromborough destined for Lever Brothers' Port Sunlight works (remember Sunlight Soap?).

Despite the sale of the newly combined Moss and Hutchison companies clearly being a sale of fire, GSN, in a shrewd move devised by John Morison and approved by both Montague Norman of the Bank of England and by P&O, completed the purchase. The political aim was to secure the future of the remains of the Royal Mail Group, which after all represented a sizeable chunk of the British Merchant Marine and a significant stake in British shipbuilding. The United Baltic Corporation never really got a look in. The Moss Hutchison Line had actually been one of the few profitable parts of the ailing Royal Mail Group, and it remained profitable until its disappearance within the P&O empire in the 1970s. Kylsant, whose imaginative accounting and deceit had led to the Royal Mail Group debacle in the first place, was jailed for twelve months prior to retiring from business altogether.

And so, on 17 October 1935, GSN became the owners of the entire share issue of the newly created Moss Hutchison Line and the long standing GSN vision to operate from the UK west coast ports was finally fulfilled. More importantly came the opportunity to streamline services from north and south Britain to continental and Mediterranean ports. This was the perfect example of the GSN policy of combination with other companies, provided it would promote economies and efficiencies in both businesses. For the next few years GSN stood back from its new acquisition, and did not directly interfere with its day to day management other than to act as co-ordinator of pooled services such as shore agents and freight-forwarding companies. To this end Moss Hutchison acted on behalf of GSN and vice versa, and wherever offices of both companies existed in one port, they would combine their resources and act as one agent.

Business was good from then on, as the years of the depression were over, and competition from Italy and Germany lessened whilst these states concentrated on their political agendas. Trade with the Mediterranean was buoyant. During 1937, two GSN steamships, the ***Corncrake***, then a 27 year old veteran, and the much younger ***Grebe*** were transferred to Moss Hutchison, and respectively renamed ***Chloris*** and ***Philotis***. The former London to Leith steamer ***Woodcock*** was transferred two years later, adopting the name ***Lormont***. Outwardly the appearance of the former GSN steamers was greatly improved when the GSN brown superstructure was painted in Moss Hutchison white, the funnels, of course, remaining black but for the addition of a broad white band. As the clouds of war blew across the sky, the Moss Hutchison fleet stood at seventeen ships with an average age of 15 years and an aggregate 33,665 tons gross.

Eight of the fleet were lost in the Second World War, along with the company offices at Liverpool and the dedicated company berth at No. 2 Branch Huskisson Dock, both of which were victims of the blitz. Three of the ships were lost in collisions during 1940, the motor ship **Kufra** and the steamship **Philotis**, during black-out night time convoy manoeuvres, and the **Lormont**, the former **Woodcock**, which sank on collision whilst on guardship duties off the Humber. The **Kavak** was lost to a submarine with the loss of 25 men in December 1940 in the Atlantic, just five days before the **Lormont** was sunk.

The **Kantara** was one of five allied ships to be destroyed by the German battle cruisers **Scharnhorst** and **Gneisenau**, on 22 February 1941 in heavy seas in the Western Atlantic. The raiders opened fire from a distance of eight miles, and closed on the **Kantara** at high speed. All the merchantman could do was to fire her one and only gun in rage. Radio calls for help were blocked by the Germans whilst the crew were taken on board the **Gneisenau** and later transferred to the prison ship **Ermland**.

Tales of bravery and hardship are summed up in another incident in an account by ship's carpenter Walter Manning, one of only six survivors from the torpedoed **Hatasu**. The vessel had lost contact with her convoy during a night of very heavy weather, and went down some 600 miles east of Cape Race (taken from a crew member's report to the Marine Superintendent):

The **Kantara** (1925)
was a handsome Moss Line steamer that was lost in
World War II to the German raider **Gneisenau**.

[Picture by John Clarkson]

"It was hell for 15 days after we got away from the ship. We put up a canvas sheet for shelter, but the boat was always streaming with water. Four days out frostbite got me in both feet. I kept down the water supplies for each man to one small 'dipper' morning and night. It just lasted, but we suffered raging thirst all the time. On the seventh day a Scottish fireman died. On the fifteenth day the gale was unabated. We crept under the canvas for shelter. Then, when I chanced to come out of the shelter and found we were in the trough of a mountainous wave I heard a ship's siren. An American vessel had spotted us. We could not get alongside because of the heaving seas, but as each wave threw us up to the level of the ship's deck sailors snatched a man out of the boat until we were all off."

In June 1942, whilst in a homebound convoy from Gibraltar, the steamer **Etrib** was torpedoed and sank. Whilst all but two of the crew were saved, one man, Liverpudlian William Swinchin, survived after being adrift on his own for 75 days, fortunate in that the raft he had managed to climb on to was provisioned for 25 men. Although his food ran out after about 50 days, he did have water. He was rescued by a German submarine and taken prisoner.

In May 1941, a skeleton crew aboard the **Busiris**, which had a partially dismantled engine and was under repair at Liverpool, found themselves adjacent to the bombed and burning munitions carrier **Malakand** of the Brocklebank Line. The Second Officer resolved to warp his ship as far from the stricken vessel as possible, and aided by the Bo's'un, two able seamen, the second engineer and two firemen plus six co-opted soldiers, managed to save the ship. As the **Malakand** finally blew up at 7.30 the next morning, the **Busiris** was secure even though pieces of heavy debris were strewn across her decks. Acres of dockland were flattened in the incident.

The **Meroe** never came home during the war. She was requisitioned as a supply ship, and spent five and a half years in the Mediterranean, Red Sea and in East African waters before returning to Liverpool in November 1945. Amongst other military duties, the **Kheti** served in the Pacific for part of the war as a munitions ship. The company also managed the **Empire Antelope** during the war, built for the Americans in 1919 as the **Orphis**, and which was torpedoed in November 1942. The Liberty ship **Samouri**, never actually reached Britain after being built in the United States in 1943, and was torpedoed in ballast on a voyage from Bombay to New York in January 1944 also with a Moss Hutchison crew aboard. Other actions included the **Procris** under Captain Wigg, which took part in the landings in southern France in 1944.

Reconstruction of the post-war fleet was assisted with the transfer of the **Hirondelle** and **Swift** from GSN to Moss Hutchison in 1948. These old stalwarts were given the names **Landes** and **Lormont** respectively, and put in charge of the Liverpool and Glasgow to Bordeaux service.

Three new motor ships were ordered for the Mediterranean routes and these were delivered by Harland & Wolff at Belfast and William Pickersgill & Sons at Sunderland during 1947 and 1948. The sisters **Kantara** and **Karnak** came from the Lagan and the near sister **Memphis** from the Wear. Another pair of similar ships, the **Amarna** and **Assiout** came from Harland & Wolff, one from Govan and one from Belfast, each with two holds forward and two aft of the machinery space. Pickersgill delivered the **Kypros** in 1949 whilst the **Tabor** belatedly emerged in 1952 from the Caledon Shipyard at Dundee some three years after she was ordered, a reflection of the materials shortages still being experienced in the post-war years. Both ships had Doxford oil engines, and a distinguishing feature was that all the crew was accommodated amidships. As each was delivered, so the older pre-war vessels were systematically disposed of, the last being the **Sardis** which was sold in 1954. The former **Hirondelle** and **Swift** were disposed of in 1953.

The *Memphis* (1947) seen in the Mersey.

[Picture by John Clarkson]

The *Kantara* (1947) in a fine study.

[Picture by A Duncan]

By way of example, the **Assiout** was described by James Pearce in SEA BREEZES January 1950:

*"In addition to being equipped for the carriage of general cargo, the **Assiout**'s holds can be arranged for carrying grain, while four cargo spaces in the shelter 'tween deck amidships are insulated for refrigerated cargo. She has two cargo holds forward and two abaft the machinery space, served by large cargo hatches, while the cargo handling equipment consists of 11 tubular steel derricks, all operated by electric winches, of which there are two at each hatch. The holds are arranged for the carriage of grain by a combination of steel centreline bulkheads, wood shifting boards, and wood grain feeders. Accommodation of a high standard is provided in deckhouses amidships for the master [Captain John Slade] and officers, and includes a spacious dining room and smoke room. Accommodation for the crew is provided in a deckhouse on the Shelter Deck amidships, with a recreation room aft."*

The *Amarna* (1949) seen in the Liverpool dock system.

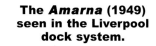

The *Assiout* (1949) in the docks on the Mersey.

In 1956 the former GSN Mediterranean motor ship *Heron*, one time partner to the steamer *Philomel*, transferred into the Moss Hutchison fleet as the *Kufra*. By 1959 the *Kufra* had been sold for further trading and the fleet stood at seven modern ships. As time went on and as trade demanded, a number of GSN fleet members took up the Moss Hutchison colours for a variety of periods although they retained their bird names and GSN registry. These included the *Adjutant*, *Auk*, *Laverock*, *Seamew*, *Ringdove* and *Corncrake*, all of which had been built since the war, the *Crane*, which had been built in 1937, and the *Woodlark* of 1928 vintage.

The *Woodlark* (1928) was built for the GSN London to Leith service and was registered at Leith. She is seen here in July 1950 in the Queen's Dock at Glasgow on Moss Hutchison business.

[Picture by Dan McDonald of Glasgow]

In 1961 the company took delivery of its largest ship. This was the 24,000 ton tanker *Busiris*, placed under Moss Hutchison Line ownership by parent P&O and managed by the British India company, while P&O attempted to gain a share of the blossoming tanker market, in this case on a lucrative long-term bare boat charter to Shell. In December 1962 all the different P&O tanker companies were gathered under the banner of Trident Tankers, and this new company then became responsible for the management of the *Busiris*. During 1967 and part of 1968, the *Amarna* was chartered to the Cunard Line as the *Assyria*, and the *Kypros* made two voyages to the Great Lakes in the last half of 1967 with the Cunard name *Aurania*.

In 1971 and 1972 the three oldest ships, *Memphis*, *Kantara* and *Karnak* were replaced by two new ships, the *Melita* and *Makaria*, supported by modern chartered tonnage as required. However, on 1 October 1971 the management of the Moss Hutchison fleet, together with other cargo liner companies in the P&O group, was transferred to the newly formed P&O General Cargo Division[1]. The Moss Hutchison vessels, including the two new sisters, were allowed to retain their black and white funnels to the end. The *Melita* and *Makaria* offered sufficient capacity for the *Assiout* to be sold in 1973, and shortly afterwards the two new ships were registered under the ownership of the P&O Steam Navigation Company. The *Amarna* and *Tabor*, spared the indignity of wearing the new corporate colours of blue funnel on to which the logo P&O was outlined in white, were sold shortly afterwards. The *Kypros* finally closed the Moss Hutchison books in April 1976, when her ownership was also transferred to P&O, although she was sold just four months later. The *Melita* and *Makaria* were left to supervise the final demise of the Mediterranean traders, after which, in 1978, they were laid up side by side at Liverpool. Fifteen months later they were both sold to Panamanian owners, as the *Siboney* and the *Los Teques* respectively. Together they went to a breaker's yard in Mexico in 1987, and with them went the last vestige of the Moss Hutchison Line.

GSN's *Auk* (1949) in Moss Hutchison colours.

[Picture by Michael D J Lennon]

The GSN vessel *Adjutant* (1954) in Moss Hutchison colours.

[Picture by Michael D J Lennon]

[1] These were: Avenue Shipping Company; British India Steam Navigation Company; Federal Steam Navigation Company; Hain-Nourse; Moss Hutchison Line; New Zealand Shipping Company and P&O Steam Navigation Company. Strick Line followed when P&O bought out the minority shareholders in 1972.

The P&O General Cargo Division sported two former Moss Hutchison names in 1979, the **Vendee** and **Vosges**, which were 'pallet-reefers' built originally for the British India company as the **Zaida** and **Zira** respectively. For a while the Moss Hutchison interest in the Mediterranean service was maintained by the chartered German motor ship **Widukind**, which carried the Moss Hutchison colours, but ran in partnership with Ellerman City Liners and Zim Lines of Israel on a direct service to Haifa.

The demise of the Moss Hutchison Line, like so many companies at this time, was simply due to its dogged retention of break-bulk cargo systems. This reflected the earlier fleet rebuilding programme that had taken place in the immediate post-war years. All seven of this generation of break-bulk ships, modern and efficient though they once were, were all due for replacement at about the same time, a time when neither the money was available to undertake a fleet rebuilding programme nor the will to redirect the business strategy. Besides, foreign shipping companies registered in countries which offered favourable tax concessions, and with crews who were satisfied with only modest wages, were fast taking over the trade of the seas. It was time too for P&O to consider withdrawal from many of its traditional services.

Although the **Melita** and **Makaria** did provide limited container capacity, it was too little too late. The once-proud subsidiary of the GSN and its distinctive pedigree passed into history in 1979, as it happened in the very same year as the last vessel to work under the GSN banner was also sold, and GSN too became nothing but a legend. However, there remains much to tell of GSN's history as it prepares for the Second World War.

The *Tabor* (1952)
seen on trials resplendent in white hull with blue line and
green boot topping. She reverted to the more manageable black hull
and red boot topping in the late 1950s although fleet mates
***Assiout* and *Kypros* remained white.**

THE *MELITA* AND *MAKARIA*

A short article by John Young which first appeared in SEA BREEZES, February 1972, described the arrival into service of the **Melita**, one of the last ships to be ordered by the Moss Hutchison Line:

*"Latest vessel to join the fleet of the Moss Hutchison Line, of Liverpool, is the motor ship **Melita**, 3,850 tons deadweight, the first of two ships ordered by the company from Hall, Russell & Company, Aberdeen. ...the **Melita** and her sister **Makaria**, which will enter service shortly, have been designed for service between Liverpool and East Mediterranean ports. On her maiden voyage the **Melita** called at Malta, Cyprus and Israel. The new ship has a length of 345 feet and a beam of 53 feet. Propulsion is by a Crossley-Pielstick oil engine developing 5,670 bhp, driving a controllable pitch propeller to give a speed of 15 knots.*

*In common with many modern ships the engines can be controlled from the bridge. The **Melita** is equipped with an extensive system of cargo handling facilities, including deck cranes, heavy lift derricks, press-button operated hatch covers and hydraulically operated side-loading doors. The ship has been built with flush 'tween decks throughout to enable fork-lift trucks to be used. Variable general and perishable cargoes can be carried in break-bulk or unitised form."*

CHAPTER 9

SUCH BRAVE LITTLE SHIPS

"When in August 1939 it was seen that war was inevitable, Mr Kelso, Chairman of the company, who had had the misfortune to be held as a prisoner of war in 1914-18, was determined that none of the General Steam staff afloat or ashore should be caught in a similar position, and he gave Captain Hutton, the Marine Superintendent, strict instructions that none of the company's ships should be in any danger of being seized should war break out."

Hancock, SEMPER FIDELIS, 1949[1]

David and Stephen Howarth in their book on the history of P&O (see reference section) highlight the impending hazards of the Second World War:

"In the twenty years since the Treaty of Versailles, merchant ships had grown larger and swifter, more capable of doing their job well. But they were not really any more capable of doing a war job, with complete efficiency, and weapons were more deadly than ever. Submarines and their torpedoes could travel farther and faster. Though it was not yet known elsewhere, Germany had developed a magnetic mine, far superior to the contact mines of World War I. Under the terms of the Versailles Treaty, the German Navy had devised its infamous pocket battleships, vessels with the tonnage of a cruiser and the fighting power of a battleship – ideal weapons for commerce raiding. Aircraft had been transformed: no longer the ponderous Zeppelins or fragile biplanes of the Great War, they were now huge long range bombers and speedy, well-armed fighters."

The first job for GSN was to help evacuate women and children from the capital in the wise belief that air raids would shortly be taking place. Eight of the company's excursion ships were responsible for taking nearly 20,000 children from Gravesend and Tilbury to Felixstowe, Lowestoft and Great Yarmouth between Friday 1 and Sunday 3 September, the day on which war was declared. For this duty, the bridge of each ship was protected by wooden padding and each master was issued with a firearm.

For the second time in the twentieth century, the British Mercantile Marine was chartered to the Nation on firm contract rates. Captain S W Roskill in his book A MERCHANT FLEET IN WAR described the rising situation:

"On 26 August 1939 there was issued in Whitehall an order which established the pattern under which the whole of the British Merchant Navy was to work for the next six years. It stated that the Cabinet Committee responsible for 'Defence Preparedness' had, in consultation with the Foreign Office and the Board of Trade, authorised the Admiralty 'to adopt compulsory control of movements of merchant shipping which... should extend to the Baltic, Dutch Danish or Mediterranean ports, and should include the routing of ships in the Atlantic. Parallel with this assumption of operational control by the Admiralty, other Government directives transferred the responsibility for the loading and unloading of all merchant ships from their owners to the Ministry of Shipping."

During August the Germans had dispatched the pocket battleships, **Admiral Graf Spee** and **Deutschland**, along with their supply ships, to the Atlantic. By the start of September, 39 of the 57 strong fleet of U Boats were already in position around Britain. Just four hours after war was declared, **U30** sank the Donaldson Line's **Athenia**, but fortunately 1300 survivors were picked up, although over 100 souls were lost that day. The incident convinced the Admiralty that the Germans would not abide by the rules they had been made to sign up to, although Germany later claimed that the sinking was an accident.

Immediate provision for convoys was put in place. GSN was affected by coastal convoys between Southend and Methil on the Forth (designated FN and FS as in Forth North and Forth South), through the English Channel (OA) and at first homeward Gibraltar convoys only (HG). In the early days the Atlantic convoys could be escorted only up to 200 miles west of Londonderry but vessels were alone and vulnerable beyond longitude 12.5º W. The convoys were organised in columns and each ship had a convoy number, for example, 47 would be stationed seventh in line in the fourth column. The columns were spaced 1,000 yards apart and each ship kept station 400 yards behind the vessel in front. The speed of the convoy was set at the speed of the slowest ship. Imagine the chaos when a large Channel convoy approached the Thames, and reformed in line ahead during a dark night in the blackout. It is not surprising that Moss Hutchison lost both the **Kufra** and **Philotis** during convoy manoeuvres.

---

[1] The greater part of Hancock's text covering the 25 year period of GSN's history up to 1948 is devoted to the years of World War Two, as it was fresh in his mind at the time he was writing. Reference to his work should be made for the detail of selected incidents suffered by GSN during the war.

The submarines did not have it all their own way, as 18 U Boats were destroyed during the first five months of hostilities. But this was little compensation for the merchantmen Britain had lost, including GSN's **Merel** off Ramsgate to a mine in December 1939 with considerable loss of life.

On 9 February 1940, the Great Yarmouth Shipping Company's **Boston Trader** was attacked by enemy aircraft and holed, even though there had been no direct hit. The master was able to beach the ship at Blakeney and later with the help of the Sheringham lifeboat, the master and the Great Yarmouth Shipping Company's Superintendent were able to salve the vessel and tow her to safety.

On the 12 May the **Roek** was sunk by a mine, this time off Vlaardingen, having left Rotterdam on passage to London. She had been at Rotterdam during the German parachute invasion, and Captain Parkinson, with a party of refugees on board, was ordered to leave port when the **Roek** hit a mine in the harbour. As the **Roek** began to sink she was tied to a tree to prevent her from sliding back into the fairway. The crew was repatriated aboard HMS **Mohawk**.

The evacuation at Dunkirk took place at the end of May 1940 as the Allied troops were forced back to the sea by the German advance. The week before, while Dunkirk and later Calais were being bombarded, the **Mavis** was bombed off Calais, severely damaging her engine and boiler compartments. Although the crew were picked up by a French fishing boat and taken to Calais, an attempt by Captain Watson to tow his crippled ship to port the next morning was abandoned when his rescue tug was mined off the harbour entrance. Two sinkings in twenty four hours earned him the MBE. While all this was going on, the **Stork** was attacked off Boulogne. She fared better and managed to destroy a German plane with the ship's gun.

The Thames excursion ships of both the GSN and New Medway Steam Packet Company performed wonderfully at Dunkirk. They included the paddle steamers **Royal Eagle**, **Crested Eagle**, **Golden Eagle**, **Queen of Thanet** and **Medway Queen**, and the motor ships, **Queen of the Channel** and **Royal Sovereign**.

The *Royal Sovereign* (1937)
discharging troops at Cherbourg on 16 September 1939.

[Imperial War Museum]

The ack-ack ship *Royal Eagle* (1932).
Note the protective cladding to the
very exposed bridge wings.

In addition, the small diesel vessel **Bullfinch** had been ordered to attend at La Panne beaches just west of Dunkirk. The pioneer motor ship **Queen of the Channel** and the **Crested Eagle** were both lost during the evacuation and very nearly also the brand new **Royal Daffodil**. The **Queen of the Channel** was bombed and sunk, although all on board were taken off, but the bombing of the **Crested Eagle** set her fuel oil alight, causing heavy loss of life and only 150 men were able to clear the vessel, many with serious burns. The **Royal Daffodil** survived a bomb alongside her port engine room. Taking on a serious list, she was able to limp home where temporary repairs were effected, repairs that in the event carried her through the war. She made seven return trips accounting for 9,000 men. The New Medway company's smaller **Medway Queen** also made seven trips and retrieved 3,000 troops whilst the **Royal Eagle** was able to make three trips with 1,000 aboard on each return journey.

Of the exploits of the little **Bullfinch**, Hancock tells us in SEMPER FIDELIS:

The little *Bullfinch* (1936)
took 1,500 troops off the beaches
at La Panne near Dunkirk whilst waiting
for the tide to float her off.

"Whilst at anchor in Small Downs the **Bullfinch** received orders at 10.20 am on 28 May 1940 to sail at once for La Panne beaches. The ship arrived off the beaches at about 4.50 am on 29 May. The beach was crowded with troops, but there were only a few boats bringing off small numbers. The master received orders to beach the ship, and accordingly he let go the kedge anchor and headed slowly for the beach. The vessel grounded about 5.45 am, but owing to the kedge anchor not holding, her stern swung round to the eastward and the ship was aground fore and aft with the beach. After the first boatload came aboard one of the troops swam ashore with a line. Two five inch ropes were run ashore and hauled boats off and back to the beach. When the tide receded the troops waded off and embarked up the ship's ladders. Embarkation proceeded until the ship had about 1,500 on board, during which time the ballast tanks were pumped out. The ladders were then pulled up as the ship could take no more."

Once afloat again the ship headed for home, by all accounts protected from accurate aerial attack by two Bren guns that the troops had brought aboard and mounted on the Boat Deck. One of the gunners, Sergeant Head, downed two dive-bombers in quick succession, and, arriving in port calmly walked down the quayside as if this sort of thing happened every day.

The evacuation soon progressed to western France. The little motor ship **Goldfinch** took 500 men off the beach at St Valery, using her own boats, and transferred them to the troopship **Princess Maud**, a ship better known in peacetime as the Stranraer to Larne ferry. As the evacuation continued down as far as Bordeaux, the GSN fleet continued to play their part, with the motor vessels **Bullfinch**, **Drake**, **Crane** and **Stork** as well as the steamers **Groningen**, **Falcon**, **Cormorant** and **Woodlark** all actively involved. This was indeed Britain's 'darkest hour'.

Amongst the French ships to escape to Britain on the fall of France was the **Penestin**. She was none other than the former Hamburg steamer **Teal** which GSN had sold in 1939 to Cie. Navitaise of Nantes for £12,000. The **Penestin** was placed under the management of GSN for the duration of the war and later returned to her French owners after the cessation of hostilities. In July 1940 the Dutch motor coaster **Caribe II**, which had been delivered from the yard of Van Diepen Brothers at Waterhuizen only in March that year, was bombed and damaged 13 miles south-south-west of Portsmouth. She was towed into port, repaired and put under the British flag, and with the name *Empire Daffodil* was placed under the management of the Great Yarmouth Shipping Company.

On 15 May 1940 the Ministry of Shipping bought the *Abukir* which was then placed under GSN management. She had been built in 1920 as the *Island Queen* for service between London and the Channel Islands. She was sold initially to Monroe Brothers as the *Kyle Queen*, before she passed to the Khedivial Mail Line of Egypt, who gave her the name *Abukir*. Her next two owners were also Mediterranean based, before she again returned to the British registry to receive a GSN crew. Within two weeks, on the 28 May 1940, the *Abukir* was on passage from Ostend to The Downs with military equipment and vehicles and their associated personnel when she got caught up in the Dunkirk operation and was spotted by an E Boat which sank her with a torpedo. The *Abukir* had tried to ram the E Boat during the encounter, and once the passengers and crew were away in the ship's boats the E Boat returned to strafe them with machine gun fire.

During June and July 1940 two further ships were lost, the *Kingfisher*, returning from Nantes, and the *Mallard*, returning to London from Newlyn with a cargo of stone. The *Kingfisher* was torpedoed and one man was killed instantly. As the crew took to the boats, it was realised that a second man was absent, probably trapped in his cabin. The man was rescued from his bunk in an unconscious state by the Second Engineer, and all the survivors were later safely picked up. The *Mallard* was sunk by an E-boat. The *Mallard* sank in under two minutes taking with her a fully loaded lifeboat that was still attached to the falls as she rolled over.

Sadly the veteran of Dunkirk, the *Royal Sovereign*, pride of the GSN fleet, was mined in December 1940. Her war had been brief but intense. Acting first as a troopship on cross-Channel duties, she then excelled at Dunkirk, before assuming the title HMS *Royal Scot*, though retaining her crew and her master Captain Tommy Aldis. She had been up to the Gareloch, and was returning to the Thames when she struck a mine in the Bristol Channel and sank. Her smaller consorts then acted in a variety of capacities. The First World War minesweepers, *Queen of Thanet* and *Queen of Kent*, took up their old duties at Dover and later on the Forth, the *Royal Eagle* and the *Thames Queen* became anti-aircraft guardships, the *Essex Queen* became an emergency hospital ship, still under Captain W G Braithwaite, and the *Laguna Belle* an ambulance ship. The *Royal Eagle* was commissioned for a total of 730 days, of which only 101 nights were spent in port - she engaged enemy aircraft 52 times.

The motor ship *Royal Daffodil* helped to maintain the military ferry service between Stranraer and Larne until 1945, when she transferred to cross-Channel duties. A plaque was presented to the *Royal Daffodil* in January 1945 by the London, Midland & Scottish Railway in recognition of the vessel's services to the Stranraer to Larne mail service - she had also carried 2 million service personnel between the two ports whilst on service to the Ministry of War Transport. Duties were not all routine, and on 26 February 1941 she put out from Stranraer in the teeth of a gale to recover the crew of a sinking flying boat.

The heavy losses to submarines incurred during 1940, despite the convoy system, led to the introduction of convoy rescue ships in January 1941. The role of these little ships was twofold: firstly, they, rather than the escorts, were responsible for effecting rescue work from casualties, and, secondly they were there to boost the morale of the merchant seamen, now conscious of the devastating losses their profession was suffering. A total of 27 vessels were converted for the work, all characteristically low freeboard vessels normally of the coastal liner type. Six of the newly converted convoy rescue ships were put under the management of GSN. These were:

Zamalek	Captain O C Morris
Zaafaran	Captain C K McGowan
Tjalder	Captain R Campbell Watson
St Sunniva	Captain C K McGowan
St Clair	Captain R M Wolfenden
Pinto	Captain L S Bloggs

Not all of them were fully crewed by GSN. The *Pinto*, formerly of the MacAndrews & Company fleet, was crewed by MacAndrews apart from the Second Mate who was a GSN staff member. The *St Sunniva* was crewed by her peacetime owners, the North of Scotland Orkney and Shetland Shipping Company, save for the First and Second Officers and the Chief Steward. The ship went missing on her first mission, presumed capsized due to severe icing two days out of Halifax, Nova Scotia. The *Tjalder* had been captured earlier in the Faroes, but was found to be unsuitable in the role of convoy rescue ship, and was discharged after only two months. The *St Clair*, also of the 'North Company', arrived on the scene too late to act as a convoy rescue ship, and adopted the role of 'medical aid and advice' following her commissioning in July 1944.

The old friends *Zamalek* and *Zaafaran* , formerly GSN's *Halcyon* and *Philomel*, had been bought from the Khedivial Mail Line by the Ministry of War Transport and registered in London. The pair had an extra 150 ton oil tank fitted to allow them to cross the Atlantic but on 27 June 1942 they set out from Reykjavik together in convoy PQ17, along with a third rescue ship, the Clyde Shipping Company's **Rathlin**. On 4 July the convoy was instructed to scatter and the following day the **Zaafaran** found herself alone and under air attack. One man was killed by falling debris, and as the ship sank the remainder of the crew took to the boats to be picked up later by the **Zamalek**. The **Zaafaran** had rescued about 220 men during seven separate incidents as a rescue boat, whilst the **Zamalek** took part in a total of 19 rescues involving 617 men. At the end of it all, in June 1945, the **Zamalek** was offered back to her former owners.

GSN survived the first half of 1941 relatively unscathed, although Brewers Quay was totally destroyed during the London Blitz. But on 14 August the **Stork**, **Lapwing**, **Starling** and **Petrel** set sail in an outbound Gibraltar convoy of 22 ships. The **Stork** was torpedoed on the eighth day, bursting immediately into flames, so that there were only three survivors. On the return trip, both the **Petrel** and **Lapwing** were torpedoed. One survivor from the **Stork**, the ship's carpenter, went down with the **Petrel**, was rescued by the **Lapwing** and finally lost his life when she too was sunk. Sadly, the **Lapwing** was hit whilst hove to, rescuing men from the water from both the **Petrel** and MacAndrews' **Cortes**, which had also been torpedoed. Only 22 men ended up in the surviving lifeboat, which fourteen days later put 19 survivors ashore in Ireland.

**The Belgian Government's fast motor ferry *Prince Baudouin* (1934)
was managed by GSN for nearly a year on behalf of the Ministry of War.**

Between September 1941 and November 1942 GSN managed the Belgian Government's fast passenger motor ferry **Prince Baudouin** on behalf of the Ministry of War Transport. For the duration she was engaged on trooping duties, but was later converted, as HMS **Prince Baudouin**, to a Landing Ship Infantry Small. The **Empire Creek** was also under GSN management in 1941 when she was attacked by enemy aircraft. With her engines damaged, Captain K R Nicholls was able to summon a tow, and later reached Aberdeen safely.

In January 1942 the Great Yarmouth Shipping Company's **Norwich Trader** was mined and sunk in the Thames approaches, with the loss of all hands including her master Captain Conolly. The intensity of the war at sea slowly declined after that winter and through much of 1943. Although there were casualties and GSN had its scrapes, fortunately no further ships were lost that year. The **Crane** was part of the invasion force on the Azores, whilst the **Woodlark** had accompanied the Fourth Cruiser Squadron on the bombardment and landings on the Italian coast, and was later involved with the landings in southern France. At the end of the year, the **Swift** was converted for use as a Port Repair Ship leaving Liverpool in May 1944, ready to take up duties in Cherbourg following the D Day Normandy Landings.

Meanwhile in 1943, the **West Coaster** was bought from British Isles Coasters to help make up numbers, but could not be given a corporate name until well after the war, when she became the **Mallard**. The previous **Mallard**, delivered to GSN in 1944, had been transferred to the Great Yarmouth Shipping Company in 1948 to become the **Norwich Trader** so freeing up the name.

GSN was heavily involved in the Normandy Landings in June 1944. Hancock reports:

*"Among the ships of the General Steam which assisted in the success of the D-Day landings and the subsequent build-up were the **Drake** (Captain Pirch), **Oriole** (Captain Wighting) and **Ortolan** (Captain Davis) which were taken over by the Sea Transport Division of the Ministry of War Transport in the early months of 1944 and fitted as case petrol carriers. The **Oriole** left the Solent for the beaches on D+2, the **Drake** on D+3, and the **Ortolan** on D+4, all three thereafter making numerous subsequent voyages between the beaches (and later the smaller French ports) and Southampton, Poole and Plymouth. The **Goldfinch** (Captain Lowe) was taken up a little later, also as a petrol carrier, leaving Milford Haven for the beaches for the first time on 8 June 1944."*

Shortly afterwards the **Auk** struck a mine while carrying petrol in the Adriatic, with devastating consequences. She was the last war loss to the company.

A number of Ministry of War Transport ships were placed under GSN control including the Liberty ship **Sammex**, which later adopted the name **Franz Boas**. The **Sammex** was built in 1943 at the emergency Bethlehem Fairfield Shipyard at Baltimore, and came to Britain under the lease-lend terms as one of the 'Sam' ships. She was a standard wartime Liberty ship, with a gross tonnage of 7,200, a triple expansion engine and a speed of 11 Knots. The **Sammex** travelled widely during the war years, and the GSN house flag was flown, albeit only briefly, in many harbours and in many countries that the company had never previously visited. Four F-class standard coasters, the **Empire Fable**, **Empire Fang**, **Empire Facility** and **Empire Farringay**, were also put under GSN management when they were delivered during 1944. The company was also successful in obtaining licences to order a number of new ships: the small motor ships, **Mallard**, **Lapwing** and **Kingfisher**, were delivered in 1944 and the **Stork** and **Petrel** in 1945.

The *Lapwing* (1944) was a valuable addition to the war-ravaged fleet.

The *Petrel* (1945) was a near sister to the *Lapwing*, both ships coming from the Goole Shipbuilding & Engineering Company.

Shippers on the east coast cargo route had now gained sufficient confidence in the future to restart talks within the London-Edinburgh Conference regarding a merged service. This proposition had been discussed in 1939, but that discussion had been shelved of necessity. The loss of both passenger and freight business to the railways meant that none of the four stakeholders in the trade had worked profitably for some years. Harvey and Telford described the events in their book THE CLYDE SHIPPING COMPANY, GLASGOW, 1815-2000:

"With victory in sight the London-Scotland Conference was resuming some primitive form of what could be called normality and had reopened discussions on the situation they had planned to address at the outbreak of hostilities. On 1 December 1944 they acted and incorporated a private joint stock company 'To own and operate the interests which they severally conduct in the trade between Glasgow, Grangemouth, Leith and London areas'. The new venture was designated the London, Scottish Lines Limited, with capital subscribed by the four owning firms, in proportion to their pre-war carrying in the trade:

London and Edinburgh Shipping Company	*36%*
General Steam Navigation Company	*26%*
Clyde Shipping Company	*20%*
Carron Company	*18%"*

The inaugural sailing of the new company eventually took place in October 1946.

In March 1945 the **Woodlark** loaded munitions in Morocco and sailed for the Far East as munitions supply ship to the French battleship **Richelieu**. This was a voyage of some 2,000 miles calling only at Suez and Aden for bunkers and stores. At the end of the war the Port Repair Ship **Swift** was the first Allied merchant ship to enter Ghent, where she was welcomed by GSN's pre-war shore staff. She was also the first to enter Antwerp. After a short refit she was dispatched to the Far East arena, not returning to her owners for commercial duties for some time.

The movements of the big Mediterranean trader **Heron** illustrate the diverse nature of many of the activities during the war. She was initially stationed in Scottish waters as a munitions store ship for the Home Fleet. During the Norwegian campaign in 1940 she was stationed off Narvik and was able to evacuate Fleet Air Arm personnel from Harstad during June. Refitted on the Clyde for tropical duties, she went next to Alexandria via the Cape and Suez. Several vessels were lost in her convoy and at one time an enemy submarine dived beneath the **Heron** badly scraping her bottom plates. The journey through Suez was also eventful as she was trapped for a while, when the Germans mined both ends of the canal. Still as a munitions store ship, she next saw duty on the east African coast and in the Red Sea, before going to Colombo and back to Aden, where she served for 14 months as a depot ship. It was in this capacity that she moved to Mombasa for much of 1944, then taking up station in early 1945 at Sydney with the armament supply section of the Pacific Fleet. She was eventually returned to her owners in 1946. Like the **Heron**, her smaller consort the **Starling** spent much of the war away from home, in this case, on bareboat charter to Elder Dempster Line on the West African coast.

Company records state that all staff members who were absent from company duties but serving with HM Forces for any part of the war would have their pension made up for the duration.

A rather nice postscript was reported by Hancock in SEMPER FIDELIS:

"After the [First World] war ended Mr Coats returned to Hamburg and reopened the Company's office there, a duty he was again to perform when the last war ended in 1945. There was amongst the staff serving with the Company's former agents at Hamburg when the General Steam opened its own office there, a man who has now [1948] just celebrated his seventy first birthday. Mr Coats got him back in 1918, and when the last war ended, this man was there to receive him when the office was again reopened in 1945. The office was still there, the Company's nameplate was affixed to the door, and the pictures of the Company's ships and portraits of the Directors were hanging on the walls in preparation for a resumption of business. During the course of conversation, Mr Coats asked him if he had ever thought Hitler was going to win. The answer was 'No, I was always an optimist'."

**The _Kingfisher_ (1944)
was another useful replacement for war losses.**

**The _Stork_ (1946)
was an identical sister to the _Kingfisher_,
both products of Henry Robb's yard at Leith,
and ordered during the war but not delivered
until 1946.**

[Picture by John Clarkson]

**The _Empire Daffodil_ (1940),
managed by the Great Yarmouth Shipping
Company, became GSN's _Greenfinch_ in 1946.**

[World Ship Society Photo Library]

THE *PRINCE BAUDOUIN* AND HER FLEET MATES

The Belgian Marine Department, the 'Zeewezen', decided in May 1940 to protect their ferry fleet, which had been inactive at Ostend, and make the ships available to the war effort. The fleet was normally engaged on Ostend to Dover and Folkestone duties. On the morning of 16 May the *Prince Philippe*, *Prince Leopold* and *Prinses Josephine Charlotte* left for Folkestone. On board were Belgian civilians, part of the British expatriate community and valuable archives. On 17 May the *Prinses Astrid*, *Princesse Marie-José* and the *London-Istanbul* left for Folkestone, and on 18 May the *Prince Baudouin* followed, along with the French *Côte d'Azur* and *Côte d'Argent* formerly employed on the Dover-Calais service but temporarily also laid up at Ostend. When commissioned in 1934, the *Prince Baudouin* was the fastest motor ship in the world - 25.25 knots on trials - and the first motor ferry to serve on the Channel crossings.

In December 1940 the Admiralty decided to have the vessels converted to Landing Ships Infantry Small. In the meantime several of them saw service as transports and were involved in the evacuations at Dunkirk and Cherbourg. The *Prince Charles* and *Prince Leopold* were then brought to the Silley Cox yard in Falmouth for conversion, the *Prince Albert*, affectionately known as 'Lucky Albert', and *Prince Philippe* were converted at Penarth, and the *Prince Baudouin* was converted into a military unit in October 1943 at Tilbury. Subsequently the *Prince Philippe* was lost in a collision in the Irish Sea and the *Prince Leopold* was hit by a torpedo in June 1944 at Normandy.

Before her conversion to a military role, the *Prince Baudouin* was temporarily placed under the management of GSN and flying the Red Ensign on behalf of the Ministry of War Transport. GSN, of course, was one of the few British companies then with any experience of operating fast motor ships. The *Prince Baudouin* was given a part GSN crew under Captain W Hatcher in September 1941. Conditions aboard were anything but pleasant with seamen and stewards accommodated either side of the propeller shafts below the tourist class galley.

After running sea trials on 23 September the *Prince Baudouin* took up duty as a troop transport to North Africa via the Cape. Two days out of Greenock heavy weather put 5 feet of water in the fore-peak store and 18 inches on the forward troop deck. Bunkering firstly in the Azores and then at St Helena, an oil slick revealed where the bunkering tanker had been earlier when she was torpedoed with the loss of 40 lives. With the hostile submarine believed still to be in the vicinity, oil in drums was loaded from the shore to provide an estimated 12 knots for about 24 hours; the *Prince Baudouin* set off to rendezvous with a stores ship. At dawn, a flash of an Aldis lamp was followed by 'Heave to or I will open fire' as the armed merchant cruiser *Derbyshire* of Bibby's fleet slowly became recognisable as she came nearer. Bunkering alongside the bigger ship immediately damaged the bridge wing of the *Prince Baudouin* in the heavy swell, although she was soon thankfully on her way.

Approaching Durban during darkness the funnel exhausts caught fire, with flames and sparks advertising the target to all and sundry. On arrival at Durban 50 troops were take on board for Mombasa. After traversing the Suez Canal 1000 troops embarked at Alexandria and were shipped to Tobruk. This became a regular run with an occasional Cyprus to Haifa trip with refugees. Returning to Port Said for engine repairs the *Prince Baudouin* was straddled by bombs which damaged the propeller shaft. Whilst the Africa Corps threatened Egypt and the vital port of Alexandria, the immobilised troopship could only watch the withdrawal of her fleet-mates back through the canal. Several weeks later, and much to the relief of her crew, the *Prince Baudouin* was also able to retreat through the Canal to Aden and onwards via the Cape eventually to return her consignment of troops to Londonderry.

GSN management ended with a final voyage from Londonderry to London arriving on 27 November 1942, after a 48 hour passage that was undertaken at an average speed of 19 knots. Later prepared as a Landing Ship Infantry (Small), HMS *Prince Baudouin*, as she became, was then involved in the Normandy Landings and the invasion of Sicily. She was returned to the Belgian Government at Ostend in October 1945.

ENGINEER'S LOG.   No. 1

The General Steam Navigation Company Limited

Motor Vessel *Prince Baudouin* 1941

Departure from *Greenock* | Arrival at *On trials*

Hour	Day	Month	Hour	Day	Month
7·15 A.M.	23rd	September	2-30 P.M.	23 rd	September

On Passage .... Hours .... Minutes.

Opening page of the Engineer's Log,
Prince Baudouin

The year 1947 also saw the purchase of a former military landing craft which was rebuilt as the small excursion vessel **Rochester Queen**, and designated for the Sheerness and Herne Bay service which she commenced in the 1948 season. Her Davey Paxman engines gave her a useful speed of 12 knots. She could accommodate 425 passengers and offered a Fore Deck and after Main Deck, and Promenade Deck. There was a cosy dining saloon, lounge and refreshment bar. Other ships were inspected and decisions made on whether necessary upgrades were justified or whether the vessel should be disposed of. Of these, the elderly excursion steamers, **Laguna Belle** and **Queen of Southend**, were sold for scrap, whilst the **Essex Queen** was sold for further service on the South Coast.

The Great Yarmouth Shipping Company's **Peronne** was also disposed of, being considered by 1946 to have become too small for the trade on offer and deemed to be inefficient on the continental runs. She was sold to the Tay Sand Company, who used her profitably as a sand dredger for a further 14 years. Similarly the steamer **Yarmouth Trader** was sold as no longer being suited to the traffic on offer.

The large Mediterranean traders **Philomel** and **Heron** were released and available for civilian duties only in 1946. Both had travelled widely during the war years under a variety of different roles, and they finally met up at Christmas 1945 in Singapore. Their return to civilian duties required extensive refurbishment and the opportunity was taken to upgrade facilities aboard both vessels, which were given accommodation for just four passengers each.

Once the **Starling** returned from her wartime charter on the West African coast, she was put on the service of associate Turner Edwards & Company of Bristol for use on the Continental trades from Bristol Channel ports. For the remainder of her career she was the Bristol boat, and from 1956 was time chartered to Turner Edwards and carried Edwards' red house flag and staff with the letter 'E' in black in a white five pointed star on her funnel rather than the GSN house flag. Regular imports were port from Oporto and sherry from Cadiz, both destined for Harveys of Bristol. The **Starling** was always a popular ship with the dockers, perhaps reflecting their habit of springing the casks to 'test' the contents – such happy days! GSN gained the controlling interest in Turner Edwards in 1947, following the death of company Director Phillip Fowler, and bought the remaining shares in 1950.

The troopship *Empire Parkeston* (1930) was managed by GSN. She is seen here in the original black livery adopted in 1947.

In 1947 GSN was given yet another Ministry of War Transport vessel to manage. This was the 23 knot turbine steamer **Empire Parkeston**, one-time Canadian National Steamships' luxury coastal liner **Prince Henry**. The **Prince Henry** and two almost identical sisters ran between Vancouver, Seattle and Victoria in the early 1930s, interspersed with Alaskan summer cruises. The three Princes were found to be a bit too large to manoeuvre comfortably in the confines of Victoria Harbour. They ran in direct competition with the Canadian Pacific Princesses – and failed, being transferred to Atlantic cruises in 1932, whilst sister ship **Prince Robert** was laid up. In 1937 the **Prince Henry** was at first chartered for St Lawrence cruises, and then sold outright to the Clarke Steamship Company of Quebec, who gave her the name **North Star**.

She was requisitioned by the Royal Canadian Navy in 1940, and renamed HMCS **Prince Henry** after conversion at Canadian Vickers in Montreal. Apparently whilst stationed at San Juan in Puerto Rico her crew created so much mayhem ashore that the ship was sent away to nearby St Thomas where there was far less temptation. Converted for the invasion of Europe during 1943, the **Prince Henry** finally earned her keep when her landing craft were instrumental in establishing the bridgehead at Juno Beach, where she was designated HQ ship. She was also involved in Operation Dragon, the invasion of southern France, and later the liberation of Greece. At the end of the War in Europe the **HMCS Prince Henry** was paid off and loaned to the Royal Navy for use in the Pacific. However, she never sailed under Naval commission and was bought outright by the Ministry of War Transport in 1946, and given the innocuous name **Empire Parkeston**. Her two sisters, the **Prince David** and **Prince Robert** were sold to the Charlton Steam Shipping Company of London in 1948, to become the emigrant ships **Charlton Monarch** and **Charlton Sovereign** respectively. They were resold in 1951, the former for scrap, the latter eventually becoming the Italian cruise ship **Lucania**, until she too was scrapped in 1962.

The **Empire Parkeston** had ended the war as an accommodation ship at Wilhelmshaven and after a short spell laid up in the Fal was taken in hand for conversion to a cross-Channel troop transport. John Isherwood describes her entry into trooping in SEA BREEZES, September 1982:

"Renamed **Empire Parkeston** *she was converted in Southampton into a cross-Channel ship, guns and LCAs [Landing Craft Assault] removed, given a large bridge and wheelhouse and a new range of lifeboats under gravity davits, and put on the trooping service between Harwich and the Hook of Holland carrying men on leave and replacements between Britain and the British Army of Occupation.*

She started her service in early 1947, at first with a black hull and black funnels. But this was later altered to a sort of troopship uniform, light grey hull with a broad blue band and light grey funnels, relieving her former rather oppressive appearance. Later she was given the trooper's yellow funnels, though retaining the light grey hull, and at the same time her funnels were highlighted and fitted with Thornycroft tops. She ran the service with two others, the **Vienna** *of 1929, an ex-LNER ship and the* **Empire Wansbeck**, *ex-**Linz**, a former German."*

Whilst on the service she used only four of her six boilers as an economy measure. This gave her an adequate speed of between 16 and 17 knots. She was not a particularly popular ship with GSN officers although most did serve aboard her at some time or another. This dislike reflected the monotony of the run and the fact that she operated only at night. She carried a large complement of staff: master, three mates, two radio officers, 20 seamen, plumber, 18 engine room hands, purser, two ship's policemen, and 27 catering staff under a chief steward. In addition there were resident army staff as well as a Dutch pilot in residence for the passage up to Hook of Holland every second morning.

There was also huge rivalry with the smaller motor troopship **Empire Wansbeck** which was managed by the rival Ellerman's Wilson Line. Apparently inter-vessel football matches were feverish battles on which many a week's wage was lost and won.

In those first eighteen months after the Armistice, GSN had managed to re-equip its fleet and claw back much of its pre-war trade. Commercial trade to the Continent was slow to pick up, but it was satisfactorily topped up by the need to supply the British forces then stationed in Germany. By December 1947 the new and prestigious motor excursion ship **Royal Sovereign** was nearing completion at the yard of Denny's at Dumbarton, while the plans for a slightly smaller consort were well advanced in the design loft. Of equal importance were orders for a further four major cargo units that had been placed with Henry Robb at Leith, S P Austin at Sunderland and the Grangemouth Dockyard.

Two further post-war vessels.

The *Woodcock* (1948), was a product of the Grangemouth Dockyard along with sister *Ptarmigan*.

The *Ptarmigan*(1948) heads down the Thames with a full load.

The **Empire Celtic** (1945)
on passage from Tilbury to Hamburg,
was one of the many Landing Ships Tank
adapted by Frank Bustard to pioneer
roll-on roll-off freight services after
World War Two. Note the military
vehicles as deck cargo.

While GSN, and others like it such as Coast Lines and its various associate companies, felt secure in their post-war expansive mood, a man called Frank Bustard was setting about their ultimate destruction. Bustard founded the Atlantic Steam Navigation Company which was successful in chartering three LSTs (Landing Ship Tanks) from the Ministry of War Transport at peppercorn rates. Given the names **Empire Baltic**, **Empire Cedric** and **Empire Celtic**, the ships initiated a roll-on roll-off freight vehicle service between Tilbury and Hamburg in the autumn of 1946 as part of the supply chain to the British Army. By 1948 there was a regular service between Preston and Larne, the fleet was expanded to four with the addition of the **Empire Doric**, and the freight ferry was born and expansion of the fleet continued. Once restrictions for UK commercial vehicles travelling on the continent were lifted, the cross-Channel services would flourish. But of this prospect the Directors of GSN, and for that matter of Coast Lines as well, were oblivious. Yet within less than twenty years the inevitable development of the vehicle ferry would be the downfall of both companies.

In other fields, GSN was ahead of its time. It had fitted various new and innovative aids to its vessels and by the end of 1947 all ships had Decca Navigator positioning equipment and Marconi TV5 wireless sets, the latter not only enabling radio conversations, but also providing access to weather reports. Even echo depth sounding equipment and direction-finding gear had been installed in all the foreign going vessels. One ship, the **Crane**, had so far received a radar set, and this was explained by the company as a need to gain experience with the equipment before the Board of Trade made its installation compulsory. Apparently the Directors were duly impressed when the **Crane** left Bordeaux two days after a rival vessel had left Santander, yet the **Crane** was able to negotiate the murky depths of the Channel safely and arrive at London before the other ship!

Late in 1947 a Government propaganda film was released to cinemas around the country featuring the **Corncrake**. Under the title 'Passage to Bordeaux' the objective of the film was to highlight the important role of the mercantile marine in peace time, much as it is recognised to be in war time. That GSN proffered a brand new ship as the star of the film, rather than one of its more traditional steamers, reflected its pride in its post-war lead in the innovative development of the short sea trader. The company probably thought too that a crew living under relatively modern and civilised conditions aboard the **Corncrake** might make a better impression on the unenlightened cinema-goer than the hard-working crew aboard one of the company's elderly steamships, fraught with leaking steam valves and failing machinery!

The **Empire Parkeston** (1930)
later adopted yellow funnels with
Thornycroft type funnel vents and a
grey hull with a blue line.

THE *EMPIRE PARKESTON*
AND THE HARWICH-HOOK TROOPING RUN

The following is taken from an article by G L Harvey which first appeared in Sᴇᴀ Bʀᴇᴇᴢᴇꜱ, December 1982:

*"We used to sail from Parkeston Quay, Harwich, shortly before midnight and arrived at the Hook of Holland at about 7 am. Our sailing time from the Hook was 10 pm to arrive back at Harwich at around 6 am... Our course crossed some busy traffic routes and there was usually plenty of fishing craft around. This kept the officer of the watch on his toes most nights and avoiding action involving changes of course was frequent. On the homeward trip there was the added complication that we had to give precedence to the railway packet **Amsterdam** to ensure that we did not delay her arrival alongside Parkeston Quay to connect with the waiting boat train.*

*The **Amsterdam** left the Hook nearly an hour after us and was supposed to overtake us before we got to the Sunk. Very often she failed to do so and we had to keep a sharp lookout for her lights astern of us. For some reason to do with our boiler pressures the engineers preferred us not to reduce speed too much, except in emergency, so instead of slowing down by a few knots, it was quite frequent a practice to steer the ship round in a circle, if circumstances permitted, to enable the **Amsterdam** to catch us up and pass us...*

After a while the service became intensely tedious. The Hook of Holland was a bleak spot indeed and Parkeston Quay was not much better except for the presence there of the Eastern Hotel, where the bars were staffed by a bevy of most attractive young ladies; it is difficult to imagine that they are all probably grandmothers now.

After 50 round trips on the Hook and back, totalling 11,600 miles over this dreary stretch of water, I was glad to see the last of the Beach End Buoy at the entrance to Harwich Harbour when the ship eventually left to undergo her annual survey in London. Within a fortnight I was off to the more congenial waters of the Mediterranean in another of the company's ships."

**The *Laguna Belle* (1896),
formerly the *Southend Belle* of Belle Steamers, was sold at the end of her useful life in 1947.**

THE *GREBE* (1948)

This vessel came from the Henry Robb shipyard in Leith and her design was a variation on the **Woodcock**. The series of photographs of life on the ship was taken by a Mr Topham and all have come from the D P World P&O Heritage collection.

A fine view of the *Grebe*, taken by J K Byass.

The engine room and telegraph.

In the wheelhouse, with the Master and, presumably, a pilot keeping a careful look out on a dark night.

Peeling potatoes - an important but mind-numbing task.

.... and so to the galley

A well-equipped cabin, complete with splendid GSN bed cover.

.... from the galley to the officer's messroom.

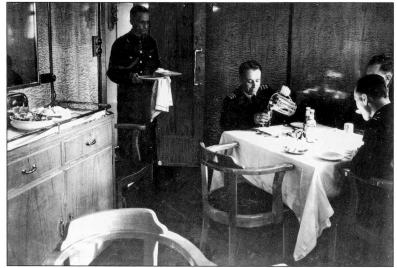

At leisure ....

in the crew's mess room.

..... checking details.

..... and so to bed.

CHAPTER 11

WHILST THE ECONOMY IS BOOMING

"...GSN owned about 40 cargo vessels, most of them smart little motor ships... The fleet was divided into two groups. Vessels of over 500 tons gross were classified as 'graded ships' and their officers and engineers were required to have the appropriate foreign-going certificates of competency. Ships of under 500 tons, known as the 'toshers', of which there were about ten, were officered by men with Home Trade only certificates."

From an article by G L Harvey which first appeared in SEA BREEZES, February 1986.

The years 1948 to 1950 were good years both for the nation as a whole, while the civilian economy recovered, and for GSN in particular. Despite materials shortages and labour problems in certain sectors opportunities for business development and growth were there for the taking. During these three years, GSN took delivery of four large engines-amidships vessels and two smaller engines-aft units.

In addition the two prestigious excursion ships **Royal Sovereign** and **Queen of the Channel** took up station on the Thames in 1948 and 1949 respectively, joining their pre-war counterpart the **Royal Daffodil**. GSN had even bought a small excursion vessel from the Forth which it commissioned under the famous name **Crested Eagle**. This vessel, which had originally been built in 1938 for Scarborough owners, was able to reopen the London Docks cruises for school children and morning cruises down to Gravesend and back for the general public. It also had a former landing craft converted into the small excursion ship **Rochester Queen**, and registered under the ownership of the New Medway Steam Packet Company (Chapter 10). Her main duties were excursions from and between Herne Bay and Sheerness.

The **Queen of the Channel** (1949)
was the last of the big excursion ships to be built for the Thames excursion services. In her early days, as shown here, she wore the colours of the New Medway Steam Packet Company rather than those of GSN.

All this new tonnage clearly displaced some older units in the fleet. Indeed the excursion fleet was now considerably overstocked and the elderly paddle steamers cum minesweepers, **Queen of Thanet** and **Queen of Kent**, were sold for further use at Southampton and Bournemouth. The **Golden Eagle** remained out of service in 1950 and her partner the **Royal Eagle** joined her in mothballs on the Medway during August before the season had ended. The **Golden Eagle** was sold for scrap the following year whilst the **Royal Eagle** was retained in lay-up in the vain hope somebody would buy her for further service. Alas, she too went under the breaker's torches late in 1953.

During 1948 the pension scheme was widened to include non-clerical staff. Senior staff members formed the General Steam '35' Club for those of suitable long service and each new member was gifted £35 by the company. A trust fund was added to supplement the provision of pensions following the dramatic inflation of the pound in the immediate post-war years.

The company's first motor ship, the **Tern**, was sold in 1949 as too small a unit for the post-war trade. Nevertheless size did have its advantages, and the **Tern** was the only vessel of the fleet that could get up the Thames as far as Kingston, a destination to which she occasionally took coal. Indeed, as the **Hindlea** she spent a lot of her later career under charter to Wm Muller on their joint service with the Compagnie de la Seine on the London-Paris Line route. The elderly **Ringdove**, onetime stalwart of the Rhine-London Line, was sold for scrap in 1950. Parts were stripped from the vessel's machinery and stored at Deptford in order to help her sister, the **Woodwren**, survive a few more years. In 1953 the **Woodwren** also succumbed, and was reduced to a coal hulk initially stationed at Gravesend and later at Ramsgate.

The big steamers **Hirondelle** and **Swift** were transferred into the Moss Hutchison fleet in 1948 in a move to concentrate the Mediterranean services under that brand. As the **Landes** and **Lormont**, they were soon overtaken by new builds for Moss Hutchison and both were sold out of the company in 1953. In a similar move the motorship **Mallard** went to the Great Yarmouth Shipping Company also in 1948 and adopted the name **Norwich Trader**. The need for more new tonnage was solved in 1950 when the four year old **Yarmouth Trader** joined the fleet on sale from Craggs & Jenkins' Hull Gates Shipping Company. Her arrival displaced the veteran **Lynn Trader**, one time GSN steamer **Yellowhammer**, which was sold for further service. Finally, the two year old **Somersetbrook** was purchased from Comben Longstaff & Company, and placed in the Grand Union (Shipping) Company fleet as the **Marsworth**.

The **Swift** (1950)
fitting out in September 1950 at Henry Robb's yard in Leith.
Note the low profile and hinged masts designed
for passage beneath the Rhine bridges.

[Photo by Mary Love]

The Great Yarmouth Shipping Company continued to operate its fleet of lighters and wherries, which were used largely for transhipment from Yarmouth to Norwich. Two small steam tugs, the sisters **Gensteam** and **Cypress**, each of just 32 tons gross, were the key to the lighter services. The operation was gradually run down under competition from road transport, and finally closed in the mid-1960s.

Robert Kelso stood down as Chairman of GSN in 1949 and the company was then voted under the leadership of J W Coats. Coats had been with GSN since 1907, when he joined the company as a freight clerk, later managing the Hamburg office with Kelso before the Great War, and serving at Hamburg for much of his career. Coats joined the Board in 1937, and was an obvious choice to take over the reins.

The long service of many individuals, and even whole families with GSN, reflected the care with which the company had always managed its personnel. And the stories of the wonderful food routinely supplied to the crews in the post-war years, whilst the rest of us were still on ration cards. It even introduced the GSN NEWS LETTER – clearly GSN was not the worst employer on the high seas.

For the most part, GSN and its associate companies were well placed to take on the boom years of the 1950s. Modern and efficient tonnage was rapidly displacing the less efficient steamers. Unit loads for onward transhipment were initiated on some Continental routes using sturdy wooden boxes or small wooden containers which were made at Deptford. The oldest member of the fleet was the **Gannet**, a relic from the post-World War I rebuilding programme, whilst the **Ortolan**, dating from 1920 and the **Adjutant** of 1922 were sold out of the fleet only in 1950. The big steamers from the late 1920s and early 1930s still had plenty to give, and the **Groningen**, **Woodlark**, **Falcon**, **Cormorant** and **Starling** were in many ways the backbone of the fleet.

In 1951 the company bought the **Helen Seabright**, which had been under GSN management in the war as the **Empire Seabright**, and gave her the name **Ortolan**. A new lighter tug, the **Gull**, was built for the company in 1952. She later adopted the quasi-GSN names **Teal** and later still **Thrush** after she was bought by a dredging company and ended her days as the **Niparound** with Westminster Dredging – having outlived many of her former Navvy colleagues on the Thames by many a year.

The refrigerated vessel **Tern** was commissioned in 1953. The **Tern** was a singleton built by Cook, Welton & Gemmell at Beverley in Yorkshire, and her engines were aft along with the accommodation. All her 45,000 cubic feet of cargo space was refrigerated and there was a large refrigeration plant prominent on the Main Deck between holds 2 and 3. The plant was not a success, as reported in the October 1954 company Minute Books:

*"Reported that the refrigeration installation of mv **Tern** continued to be unsatisfactory and that the builders had accepted responsibility to us for the failure of the vessel to attain her specifications. As a result of the faulty refrigeration the ship had been restricted in trading and had failed to earn a good reputation."*

**The *Tern* (1953)
was distinctive in being the only fully refrigerated ship in
the fleet and the only vessel with a grey hull.**

[Picture by John Clarkson]

She had been designed specifically for the chilled and frozen meat export trade to the British Army of the Rhine in West Germany. This trade peaked in the late 1950s and she then carried out some extensive charter work between ports in Central America. Before she was sold, she was hastily brought back into service for seven voyages between France and the Baltic carrying frozen beef to the Soviet Government. The beef was part of a fine paid by the Hungarian Government to Russia following the Hungarian Uprising, which had taken place in the autumn of 1956.

The **Tern** was a distinctive member of the fleet in that she wore a grey hull with a blue band, an attempt to reduce the black body radiation of her hull to assist in maintaining the desired temperatures in the holds. Towards the end of her career, she was honoured by being allowed to wear an excursion steamer yellow funnel, rather than cargo ship black, but still adorned with the company house flag. The 5-cylinder Polar diesel engine drove the **Tern** at a gentle 10 knots on her short Channel crossings.

GSN was represented amongst the great and the good at the Spithead Coronation Review on 15 June 1953, which was inspected by the newly crowned Queen Elizabeth and the Admiral of the Fleet, the Duke of Edinburgh. The **Whitewing**, fresh from the builder's yard, was the representative for GSN. Whilst the monarch took the salute aboard **HMS Surprise**, the Government guests were generously accommodated aboard the liners **Orcades**, **Strathnaver** and **Pretoria Castle**. The convoy was led by the Trinity House flagship **Patricia**, as it passed up and down the nine lines of shipping, each some seven miles long! Another Royal encounter took place on 15 May 1954, when the Queen returned from her tour of Australia and New Zealand directly to the Pool of London aboard the royal yacht **Britannia**. As the **Britannia** approached the Pool, the **Royal Sovereign**, moored at George's Stairs Pier just below Tower Bridge, sent the following message by signal lamp:

*"The General Steam Navigation Company with humble duty welcomes Your Majesty home. Last reigning Queen to arrive London by sea was Queen Victoria in our ship **Trident** 112 years ago."*

The brand new *Whitewing* (1953) represented GSN at the Spithead Coronation Review on 15 June 1953.

In November 1953 disaster befell the Grand Union (Shipping) Company's six year old *Bosworth*. Loaded at London with cement she was on her way up the east coast destined for Stornoway in the Outer Hebrides. Feeling her way gently in a dense fog bank off the East Anglian coast she collided with another vessel sustaining damage beneath the water line. Her dense cargo took her down like a stone giving the crew barely time to leave the stricken ship. She was replaced early the next year when the two year old single decker *Brier Rose* was bought from Hughes Holden Shipping and given the name *Marsworth*.

A new service from Southampton to Copenhagen and Gothenburg commenced in December 1954 with the *Adjutant*. This was founded on the P&O Group's New Zealand Line transferring its terminal to Southampton, but as it reverted to London only twelve months later the new service, with expensive port charges in Scandinavia, became redundant.

The Great Yarmouth Shipping Company also received new tonnage when the Empire F Class wartime standard ship *Helen Fairplay* was acquired and given the name *Lynn Trader*. Another secondhand ship, the *Norfolk Trader*, joined the fleet in 1956 bringing the complement up to a total of six ships.

The little *Lynn Trader* (1945) was built as the Empire F Class standard ship *Empire Fairplay* and joined the Great Yarmouth Shipping Company fleet in 1951.

The *Norfolk Trader* (1954) came into the Great Yarmouth Shipping Company fleet in 1956.

[Picture by John Clarkson]

The contrast between the newer ships in the GSN fleet and the elderly *Gannet* could not have been more extreme and it was no surprise in 1953 when she was sold for demolition. She had spent much of her post war days working on the former Edwards Bristol Channel Lines' routes. Her basic duties were Bristol Channel ports and Southampton, largely with military stores, to Antwerp, Rotterdam, Bremen and Hamburg with calls at London on inducement. G L Harvey reported in SEA BREEZES, February 1986:

*"The steamer **Gannet** was something of a museum piece when I joined her as first mate in June 1952. The last of a class of ship which her owners GSN had once owned a considerable number, she was surely of an obsolescent design even when she was launched at Paisley in 1921...*

Obviously the export trade from South Wales to the Continent was at a low ebb. There was only 40 tons for us to load at Barry, including NAAFI stores for the Army, some chests of tea and two tons of chemicals, all consigned to Hamburg. This was soon aboard and at 1 pm we shifted under the coal tips to fill up our bunkers...

Outside the Maas pierheads we encountered a moderate northerly gale and a heavy sea right on the beam. It was not long before we were getting the usual tale of woe from the engine room about seas driving up the ash chute and drenching the firemen and flooding the bilges by choking the pump suctions with ashes and small coal. I often wondered why, in thirty years, no one had ever got around to remedy this obvious design defect."

The other steamers in the fleet were slowly displaced between 1954 and 1961. The Mediterranean steamer **Philomel** was sold in 1957 whilst her Sulzer engined partner the **Heron** had been transferred in 1956 to the Moss Hutchison fleet, after a major refit at Liverpool, to become the **Kufra**. Their replacements were a succession of attractive looking, engines-amidships, cargo vessels. Variations on a theme, it is these ships that many of us remember with affection today as the GSN mini cargo liner. Each had a character and appearance dictated by the builder's design team. Ailsa built the sisters **Whitewing** and the **Ringdove**, S P Austin at Sunderland delivered the one off **Adjutant** complete with a Sulzer engine, whilst the identical sisters **Gannet**, **Woodlark** and **Heron** came from the Grangemouth Dockyard and Charles Hill at Bristol. The ultimate member of the class was the magnificent **Sandpiper**.

The **Gannet** *(1956)*
was one of three similar sisters - she is
seen here whilst on the South African
coastal service in Table Bay at Cape Town.

[World Ship Society Photo Library]

The **Woodlark** (1956)
was identical to the **Gannet** save for the after
cargo handling gear - both ships built by the
Grangemouth Dockyard.

[Picture by John Clarkson]

The mini cargo liners offered up to 70,000 cubic feet of general cargo capacity and some had up to 13,000 cubic feet of refrigerated space with a deadweight up to 950 tons. They suited the Bordeaux and Mediterranean trades as well as the Hamburg, Rotterdam and Antwerp services. They were joined in September 1956 by the Clyde Shipping Company's **Eddystone**, which adopted the name **Woodwren** on joining GSN. Just two years old, her sale to GSN reflected the downturn in the coastal trades, and only four years later the Clyde Shipping Company had to withdraw from its Glasgow to Waterford and Cork cargo service, severing a link between Scotland and Ireland that was well over 100 years old. But what was the Clyde company's loss was GSN's gain. The **Woodwren** had a large deadweight capacity of 1,180 tons, which made her a valuable unit for the carriage of bulk cargoes. She was also comparatively fast and her 8-cylinder British Polar engine could provide 13 knots at full revs.

The **Ringdove** (1954)
was one of a pair of ships
delivered by S P Austin at Sunderland.

The last in the amidships accommodation class
of ships was the **Sandpiper** (1957).
She came from Henry Robb's yard at Leith.

Employment for some of the larger cargo ships was found through investment in Canada in the subsidiary company St Paul Shipping Company, newly formed in 1955. GSN made a successful offer for the entire capital of Newfoundland Canada Steamships and its subsidiary Chebucto Steamships in August 1958. Their two small ships **Bedford II** and **Belle Isle II** traded principally between Halifax, St Johns and Montreal. During this period the **Woodcock** was deployed to Canada for a number of years, even finding her way up to Labrador at one stage, while other GSN vessels enjoyed shorter tours of duty across the Atlantic. The Canadian venture was never profitable and Newfoundland Canada Steamships was sold in 1963 to F K Warren of Halifax, Nova Scotia. Before that the St Pauls company had been closed and the Chebucto Steamships' shares transferred to GSN so that GSN could charter the one remaining vessel, the **Bedford II** to F K Warren. The **Belle Isle II** had earlier been lost. Chebucto was described as having been 'dormant for some considerable time' in the January 1968 company minutes.

The small excursion vessel **Rochester Queen** was sold before the start of the 1956 season, access to Sheerness having been prevented since 1954 by building work. She had operated for a time from Clacton, but had become barely profitable. 1956 was also the last year that the **Crested Eagle** ran on the Thames, her docks cruises having been taken over by Odell's motor launches in 1952. The **Crested Eagle** was then chartered to P & A Campbell for use on the South Coast in 1957 and sold thereafter.

In the mid-1950s GSN bought an interest in short haul aviation including part-ownership of Silver City Airways. This company ran an 'air ferry' service between Lydd in Kent and Le Touquet for passengers and their cars, freight and even cattle. It later became a separate entity within the P&O Group together with companion companies operating flying boats, air trooping contracts and regional airlines within the UK. By the early 1960s many of its services had closed and the rest were merged with other operators to form British United Airways.

In 1956 the Suez crisis provided an excellent business opportunity for the Mediterranean trade. The **Empire Parkeston** forsook her furrow between Harwich and the Hook of Holland to become a troop transport in the Mediterranean, based temporarily at Malta. Other ships in the GSN fleet were deployed on servicing the needs of the military, ensuring full employment for all the larger units of the fleet.

Smeeton and Morris (1982) report an incident that occurred in August 1956:

*"The **Gannet** under Captain A J Pirch, in heavy weather in the North Sea, effected a very gallant rescue of ten members of the crew of the **Traquair** before she foundered, and later the then Minister of Transport, Mr Harold Watkinson, acting on behalf of Her Majesty the Queen, presented Emblems of the Queen's commendation for Brave Conduct to the Chief Officer, Mr R Turnbull, the ship's carpenter and three able seamen for their part in the rescue."*

In February 1957 the **Adjutant** struck a floating World War II mine off the Dutch coast which disabled the ship. The **Gannet** was nearby and came to assist, towing the **Adjutant** to IJmuiden for repairs. This was an unfortunate incident, and an unhappy reminder of the early 1940s.

The Grand Union (Shipping) Company received one new purpose-built ship, the **Blisworth**, in 1957. She was built as a single decker but had 'tween decks added in 1959 to provide potential for interchange with the GSN fleet. The company then had four vessels in operation to maintain the London to Dutch and Belgian ports services under the trading name Regent's Line; the funnel colours being a black 'RL' on a yellow funnel with a black top.

The *Blisworth* (1957) was purpose built for the Grand Union (Shipping) Company.

[Picture by John Clarkson]

In 1958, unit load facilities were at last offered on the Felixstowe to Rotterdam route operated by the Great Yarmouth Shipping Company under the banner Hinterland Container Service. Whilst this was a major acknowledgement that trading patterns were on the move, it was a small step that was not transferred to other routes quickly enough for the group ever to hope it could maintain its market share. Bearing in mind that Frank Bustard's Atlantic Steam Navigation Company (Chapter 10) was now trading as the Continental Line using brand new roll-on roll-off freight and passenger ferries (the *Bardic Ferry* was running daily between Tilbury and Antwerp, and the *Ionic Ferry* between Preston and Larne), GSN really did have its head firmly stuck in the sand. Even the normally conservative railways had introduced two ships to the Heysham to Belfast service in 1958 which were able to carry up to 65 'B' Type large railway containers. The ships were the *Container Enterprise* and *Container Venturer* and they were the world's first purpose-built cellular container ships. But GSN was not alone in pursuing a traditionalist policy; so too did Coast Lines and virtually all their old rivals on the Continental services.

1958 was also the year during which William Muller withdrew its 37 year old steamer *Batavier V*. This delightful vessel offered 50 first class passenger berths, and her withdrawal finally closed the passenger connection between London and Rotterdam.

The massive stern doors and cargo handling crane of the *Ionic Ferry* (1958) reflect her status as the pioneer British roll-on roll-off freight vehicle ferry. She is seen on the Ribble on 4 September 1966.

[Nick Robins]

World's first cellular container ship *Container Venturer* (1958) approaching Heysham on 16 August 1970.

[Nick Robins]

The **Whitewing** and the **Gannet** were somewhat surprisingly deployed on a new African coastal service in 1957. They were later joined by the **Adjutant**. This new service clearly tried to emulate the successful coastal cargo liner service that Coast Lines had introduced around the coasts of Southern Africa in 1949. The new GSN route connected many of the smaller ports that were not served by the liner companies along the African coast from Lorenço Marques (now Maputo) on the east coast, via South Africa, and up the west coast as far as Takoradi on the Gold Coast. The service suffered almost a mortal blow in its second year when the West African states introduced an embargo with South Africa over its policy of apartheid. Cape Town was the main base and was the centre for transhipment to the big cargo liners. The **Adjutant** was the last GSN ship at Cape Town, and, having become too small for the trade on offer in 1962, was replaced by the Danish vessel **Lily Nielsen** in a collaborative service with two Danish companies. The service was later absorbed into the Union West Africa Line which survived until the mid-1960s.

In 1960 the Great Yarmouth Shipping Company was given the elderly **Plover**, having already disposed of the **Yarmouth Trader** and **Lynn Trader** in 1959 and 1960 respectively. Sadly the **Plover** was sunk after a collision in the New Waterway in November 1961, and when raised was deemed unworthy of repair. The wartime standard ship **Peregrine** was then chartered from GSN to fill the gap. The appearance of both ships had been improved when they adopted the buff funnel with a black top and the black hull topped by a thin white line that neatly picked out the bulwarks on the Great Yarmouth company's vessels. The advertised services were from Great Yarmouth, Boston and Kings Lynn to Antwerp; Great Yarmouth to Rotterdam; and Felixstowe to Amsterdam and Harlingen.

The year 1960 was also when GSN forsook its old offices at Trinity Square and moved to new and palatial accommodation at Three Quays on the old Brewers Quay site. This move prompted the minority (10%) shareholders to question the modest dividends they were receiving. P&O eventually bought them out at £9 per £1 share in 1971.

There was also the curious incident that occurred on 30 November 1960 as reported by Smeeton and Morris:

*"…at a time when the master was not on the bridge, the **Teal** collided with the South Goodwin Lightship, a vessel unable to take evasive action, which incident led to an official enquiry being held. Visibility was said to be clear for the time of year with good weather, and, of course, the **Teal** was held to blame. The Company's Minute Book succinctly records the outcome 'The report of the recent enquiry… had now been issued and was being studied by the Marine Superintendent; the action taken against the Junior Deck Officers was noted.' On the unofficial side on the morning following, one of the masters then fulfilling a shore appointment in the Marine Department imparted the news to a colleague in the terms 'Do you know the **Teal** hit a lightship last night', and it is said there was more envy in the voice than surprise or dismay."*

Two interesting second hand purchases were made in 1961 to sustain the strength of the GSN fleet as older members were withdrawn. These were the **Texelstroom** from the Hollandsche Stoomboot Maatschappij and the **Manchester Venture**, which came from Furness Withy's associate company Manchester Liners. The **Texelstroom** had started life in 1947 as the **Dorrit Clausen** for C Clausen of Copenhagen. Much of her early career was spent on time charter to the Yeoward Line of Liverpool on their Canary Island service. In 1949 she was bought by the Dutch and given the name **Texelstroom**, under which guise she had been the mainstay of their Manchester and Liverpool to Amsterdam route on which she carried up to six passengers. Taken over at Amsterdam in February 1961, and given the name **Swallow**, she was taken in hand ready to start work on the Bordeaux general cargo service, complete with her four passenger berths.

The **Swallow** (1947)
was built as the **Texelstroom** for the Hollandsche
Stoomboot Maatschappij and was bought by GSN in 1961.

Manchester Liners' *Manchester Venture* (1956) was built for the Welland Canal service and joined GSN as the *Philomel* in 1961.

Sister vessel *Manchester Vanguard* (1956) became *Sheldrake* in 1963 - she is seen at Southampton on 9 August 1964.

[Nick Robins]

The **Manchester Venture** was one of a pair of diesel ships to be built at Bremerhaven for Manchester Liners for their transatlantic services up the Welland Canal between Lake Ontario and Lake Erie. The pioneers of this route were the **Manchester Prospector**, and the sisters **Manchester Explorer** and **Manchester Pioneer**, their size and draught dictated by the canal. There are various stories of these little ships nosing up creeks to small wharves, and of apologies having to be made at one town where the vessel had been greeted by a large crowd including the mayor, for breaking the mayor's trees as the ship turned!

Winter ice meant the service had to be suspended seasonally and the sisters, **Manchester Venture** and **Manchester Vanguard**, were normally chartered to the Yeoward Line each winter - an unlikely link with the newly acquired **Swallow**, one time **Dorrit Clausen** chartered also to the Yeoward Line. Once the St Lawrence Seaway was opened there was no longer a need to use small shallow draught vessels on the Great Lakes service and they were sold. The **Manchester Venture** was acquired by GSN in 1961, and given the name **Philomel** and the **Manchester Vanguard** following her two years later when she became the **Sheldrake**. The attraction was the large hatches, some 20 feet by 42 feet, which were ideal for the Mediterranean trade.

The Rhine ports service from London, sometimes calling at Rochester, and from Felixstowe up the Rhine as far as Cologne, was pooled with the Hamburg company A Kirsten in 1961. The service had always been undertaken on the understanding that masters would hand the conning of the ship to the Rhine pilot above Dordrecht. From here to Cologne the currents and shifting sands could make navigation tricky and there were also numerous bridges that constricted the waterway.

The **Empire Parkeston** was finally paid off on 26 September 1961 having completed the last ever troop transport voyage from the Hook, and discharged from GSN management on 4 October.

The assets of the London Scottish Lines were distributed back to their owning consortium when the company ceased trading in 1962. The decision was taken not to reinvest in new tonnage and to withdraw entirely from the UK coastal cargo liner routes, the victim of fierce competition from rail and more recently from road transport. The elderly **London Merchant** and **Edinburgh Merchant** were both sold. The company was dissolved in 1965.

At the end of the 1963 summer excursion season on the Thames, the press followed the movements of the old Dunkirk veteran *Medway Queen* in true paparazzi style. Her normal routine was Strood, on the Medway, to Southend for Herne Bay, back to Southend for Herne Bay again and return to Strood via Southend. But with her five year survey due it was considered a good time to withdraw, and amid a great hue and cry the *Medway Queen* sailed up the Medway for the last time on 8 September 1963. Despite the furore that followed her withdrawal, she was sold to Forté & Company for use as a floating restaurant, and the New Medway Steam Packet Company ceased to be shipowners. As plans fell through, she was left to rot in a millpond on the Isle of Wight with only a few ducks for company, but she remains the one ship of the GSN family now left in Britain. Now returned to the Medway, National Lottery monies are at last helping to re-establish this fiesty little paddler.

The *Medway Queen* (1924)
in her last but one season seen leaving Southend Pier in August 1962.

[Nick Robins]

Despite the dock labour strikes of the early sixties which played havoc with schedules, and despite the move towards roll-on roll-off traffic, the first of a series of six new, but conventional builds joined the company in 1963. These were small ships with two holds and two hatches uncluttered by any cargo handling gear and engines and accommodation aft. They were designed to accommodate the contemporary ISO cargo containers although not in the cellular principle in use today. The first pair were identical sisters, the *Oriole* and *Ortolan* and they were delivered from the yard of J Lewis & Sons at Aberdeen in 1963 and 1964 respectively. Of just 430 gross tons, they were useful units for the carriage of both general and bulk cargo and found employment on a variety of the shorter routes to the Continent including the Cologne service for which they were equipped with hinged masts. The *Oriole* and *Ortolan* were considered to be the ultimate in modernity, with all the engine controls operated directly from the bridge, and much of the operation of the engine room protected by a sophisticated alarm system.

The *Ortolan* (1964)
was the second of two new ships to joing the fleet in 1963/64 and proved to be the last of the 'Navvies' when she was sold in 1979.

Their success was followed by repeat orders for a further pair from Aberdeen, the slightly larger **Albatross** and **Avocet** of 654 gross tons, and the **Petrel** and **Plover** which were built at Bolson's yard at Poole and were of 496 tons gross. These four ships were delivered in 1965, providing a sextet made up of three pairs of identical twins.

A number of pre-war and 1940s built vessels were displaced by the arrival of the new ships. However, the company was essentially still engaged on all its traditional routes, employing in 1965 a cargo fleet of 33 ships with an average age of 13 years and an aggregate 26,123 gross tons. The oldest members in the fleet were the **Drake** and **Alouette** dating from 1938, whilst the smallest were the new ships **Oriole** and **Ortolan**. The cargo services at that time (passenger berths having largely been discontinued in the mid-1950s) were broadly as follows:

From London to:
> French ports;
> Hamburg, Bremen and Rhine ports as far as Cologne;
> Antwerp, Ghent and occasionally Terneuzen;
> Amsterdam, Rotterdam and Harlingen;
> Oporto;
> Hull and Grimsby.

From London, Newcastle and Middlesbrough (also from Northern French ports) to:
> Mediterranean.

Bristol to:
> Tonnay-Charente.

Bristol Channel ports to:
> Hamburg and Bremen.

Southampton to:
> Hamburg, Bremen, Antwerp, Rotterdam, Le Havre, Danish ports and Gothenburg.

Shoreham to:
> Tonnay-Charente and Bordeaux

During 1964 Reginald Grout, who with Mr Hooper had become joint Chairmen after J W Coats, was succeeded as Chairman of the Board by the very last Chairman the company was to have. This was Douglas Mortelman, and it was he who commented, 'We have let 150 years of tradition get in the way of developing our future'. Things had to change and change they did.

THE *SANDPIPER* OF 1957

The **Sandpiper** was the last of the mini liners to be built with engines and accommodation amidships and was delivered from the yard of Henry Robb & Company at Leith in July 1957. She was designed for either the shorter sea routes to the Continent or the longer services to Oporto and Bordeaux. Given the rapidly changing nature of the trade in the 1960s, she was to enjoy only a short ten year career with GSN. She was sold in 1967 to Paturel Frères for just £135,000 to become supply ship to the St Pierre & Miquelon Islands off the Newfoundland coast. Strengthened for navigation in ice, she was ideally suited for this role. The following technical description of the ship is taken from an article by B M Leek which first appeared in SEA BREEZES, January 1996:

"The propelling machinery provided was a British Polar 8-cylinder diesel engine developing 1,280 bhp, constructed at Govan and installed by the shipbuilders. Two alarm systems were installed in the engine room to provide both visual and audible alarms covering both the propelling machinery and steering gear. The alarm system provided protection against any one of the following defective conditions:

- *A drop in the salt water circulating pressure for the freshwater coolers*
- *A rise in the cooling water temperature above a certain limit*
- *A circuit breakage in the supply of electricity to the steering motor*
- *A drop in the main engine lubricating oil pressure*
- *A drop in the generator oil pressure*
- *A drop in the double bottom fuel oil tanks below a predetermined level.*

The master was provided with a dayroom, bedroom and bathroom at the after end of the Navigating Bridge Deck, adjacent to the chart room and wireless room. The chief, second and third officers were accommodated on the Boat Deck, where there was also an officers recreation room. The chief, second and third engineers were berthed on the Shelter Deck and the remaining members of the crew were provided with single cabins on both the Shelter and Upper decks.

A spacious messroom for the officers was located across the forward end of the Shelter Deck and the crew was provided with a messroom on the after starboard side of the Shelter Deck. A focal point of interest in the officers saloon were two opaque glass panes set in the panel which separated the pantry from the dining area. One of these panels depicted the coat of arms of the port of Leith, where the ship was built, and the other featured the crest of GSN. Mechanical ventilation was provided throughout the accommodation areas through directional louvres. A mechanical exhaust system was installed in the galley and battery locker.

On the Shelter Deck Nos. 1, 2 and 4 hatches were fitted with MacGregor watertight steel hatch covers... No. 3 hatch cover, forward of the accommodation, was fitted with side-rolling, watertight, steel hatch covers. In the 'tween decks the hatchways were fitted with MacGregor flush type, watertight steel covers arranged to open and close by pivoted hinged sections at each end of the hatch. For serving the hatchways six 5 ton derricks and one 15 ton derrick were fitted. The derricks were powered by six Laurence-Scott Selector type electric winches."

CHAPTER 12

NAVVIES NO MORE

The realisation by the Chairman that GSN was letting its long standing tradition inhibit its future, heralded investment in consortia that were to revolutionise various short sea routes. North Sea Ferries and Normandy Ferries were the earliest examples of international co-operation in the development of short sea vehicle and related passenger routes, both consortia included GSN as a major driving force, and both were highly successful.

In August 1962 GSN led a meeting in Amsterdam with German, Dutch and other British operators to discuss the development of unit load services between the UK and the Continent. They considered routes between the Wash and Portsmouth in Britain and between Rotterdam and the France-Belgium border, and also considered whether to invite Belgian participation following that country's withdrawal from the Congo. There was some doubt on how to combine roll-on roll-off operations and the carriage of containers. Further talks, however, were suspended until the following year because of the imminent sale of the shipping interests of the British Transport Commission

During 1963 GSN's General Manager in Holland, Ian Churcher, convinced a variety of shipping companies to take up his vision of a revolutionary roll-on roll-off freight and passenger service to run overnight between Hull and Europort, Rotterdam, with departures six nights a week from each port. This would compete head to head with the conventional cargo and passenger ships operated by Associated Humber Lines, also offering an overnight service. By May 1964 a consortium of two German, two Dutch and two British companies - respectively the Argo Line and A Kirsten; Hollandsche Stoomboot Maatschappij and Phs. van Ommeren; and the General Steam Navigation Company and the Tyne-Tees Steam Shipping Company - was in place and by October it had reached agreement on operational details and the design of two vehicle and passenger ferries. The consortium was initially 40% British owned (GSN had 35%), 40% Dutch and 20% German.

These were the early days of the roll-on roll-off freight business that had been successfully pioneered by Frank Bustard since the war. Any shipping company willing to support the idea would have to be wholly convinced that the future of the short sea routes lay in the carriage of lorries and their drivers combined with passengers and their vehicles, be they cars or coaches. GSN was one such company, having already seen much of its business eroded by the arrival of other new services operating from Tilbury, Great Yarmouth and, of course, Dover, while the Tyne-Tees Steam Shipping Company was the representative of the Coast Lines Group, also suffering eroded business levels from roll-on roll-off carriers. GSN was supported by parent P&O who agreed that GSN should put up a proportion of the costs once the two Dutch and two German companies were on board.

**The *Norwave* (1965)
leaving Hull on 22 August 1967.**

[Nick Robins]

The new initiative, to be called North Sea Ferries, inaugurated its first service when the brand new British registered ferry ***Norwave*** sailed from the King George Dock in Hull on 17 December 1965. Nightly services began three months later when the Dutch-registered sister ***Norwind*** was delivered. In the first year they carried, on average, about 40 freight units each voyage and within five years were running to capacity. Within the first six years of service, the ***Norwave*** and ***Norwind*** had put the Associated Humber Line's nightly passenger service out of business, and its ships, the ***Melrose Abbey*** and ***Bolton Abbey***, were laid up almost in sight of the new North Sea Ferries terminal. The 54,000 passengers carried that first year was very satisfactory to the six investors in North Sea Ferries, and by 1973 the number had risen to 138,000. The success of the business was obvious.

Robins reported in FERRY POWERFUL:

"They [the **Norwave** and **Norwind**] had a service speed of 16 knots, and were susceptible to heavy weather, with little reserve of power; heading into Force 7 would delay the ships by anything up to 1.5 hours.

Although only of 4,038 tons gross, they had substantial accommodation for freight vehicles and cars (60 cars and 65 trailers or 200 cars), and a total passenger capacity of 235. There were berths for 187, mainly below the vehicle deck, and couchettes and reclining seats for the remainder. The fare included all meals whilst on board. The company also boasted fresh fruit in every cabin, a touch that set the service apart from others. The set breakfast had a rigid variety: bacon, sausage and egg fry into Rotterdam and bacon, tomato and egg fry into Hull!"

Encouraged by success on the North Sea, GSN decided to try to do the same thing on the English Channel. In collaboration with the French company SAGA (Société Anonyme de Gerance d'Armement), GSN agreed to target the Southampton to Le Havre route with a joint service under the name Normandy Ferries as outlined by a formal agreement dated June 1967. Business was developed preparatory to the new service by placing the little **Oriole** on a Southampton to Le Havre unit load route in May 1964. This coincided with the withdrawal of the railway operated passenger and cargo service when the turbine steamer **St Patrick** was transferred to the St Malo route until that too was withdrawn four months later. The new GSN cargo service was maintained until 1968, when the **Oriole** was displaced to the London to Cologne service via other Rhine ports in collaboration with A Kirsten. Business was so good once the roll-on roll-off ferries were established that the unit load service had to be reinstated – this time using the chartered German vessel **Falcon**. Robins again:

**The Dragon (1967)
as first commissioned, seen at Southampton.**

[Nick Robins]

"The GSN, conscious that its fleet of break bulk coasting vessels had little future, was also instrumental in setting up another new consortium. This was Normandy Ferries, who inaugurated a new service between Southampton and Le Havre in 1967. Two identical sisters were built at Dubigeon-Normandie in Nantes, the **Dragon**, registered at Southampton, and the **Leopard**, at Le Havre. The **Dragon** commenced service on 29 June 1967 in direct competition with Thoresen Ferries.

The **Dragon** was stern loading and could accommodate 276 cars or sixty 12-metre trailers. There was comfortable passenger accommodation for 846, with light and airy public rooms and a reputation for good quality catering. The ship was driven by twin 12 PC2V Pielstick engines, which provided 6,600 kW to maintain a service speed of 16 knots."

With the first arrival of the **Dragon** at Southampton, several open days were held. The passenger accommodation was certainly second to none; in addition to the day accommodation, there were 500 berths. She had an uncluttered vehicle deck, which to those of us who visited her during the open days, seemed as big as the inside of an aircraft hanger by comparison to anything seen before. There was also a small open freight deck aft, which was partly reclaimed by additional cabin accommodation during the 1968/69 refits.

Much of the Normandy Ferries initiative was driven by William Wilson who had been with GSN since 1930. However, he was greatly assisted by the removal of GSN's tourist travel department from London to Southampton following the final closure of the Thames excursion services at the end of the 1966 season. GSN had gained cross-Channel experience with the **Royal Daffodil**, which ran from the Thames to Calais with a connecting overland 'package' to Barcelona in 1965. Traditional 'no passport' day trips to Calais and Boulogne had been operated over a number of years by the **Royal Daffodil** and the smaller **Queen of the Channel**, and in 1966 also by the **Royal Sovereign** which ran cruises from Great Yarmouth to Calais. Expertise so gained was invaluable in the creation of the new company.

Commenting on the last Thames excursion season and its subsequent closure, GSN could make no mention of the creation of Normandy Ferries as this had not yet been announced. Neither was there any mention of the disastrous competition caused by Stena Line's introduction of 'The Londoner' service between Tilbury and Calais in 1965. This featured the brand new car and passenger ferry **Stena Naudica** which completely outshone the facilities offered by the **Royal Daffodil** and her two younger cohorts. A GSN spokesman said:

"...it had been 'grim'. The seamen's strike had affected party bookings and the weather was bad before the season closed in mid-September. The services were also in severe competition with car and coach traffic to the coast and via Dover and Folkestone to France as well."

So ended 142 years of excursion vessels on the Thames. The **Royal Daffodil** was quickly sold for scrap, the **Royal Sovereign** became the Dover based freight ferry **Autocarrier** in the Townsend Car Ferries fleet, and the **Queen of the Channel** became a Greek ferry. The **Autocarrier** retained a passenger certificate for use on excursions from Margate and Ramsgate. In the event truck business was so demanding on the Dover to Zeebrugge roll-on roll-off freight service that no excursion trips were ever rostered, and the plan to install portable seating on the freight deck was never put to the test.

But worse was to come. GSN knew well that in promoting the new roll-on roll-off technology in direct competition with its own conventional break-bulk and partly containerised services, something had to go. And go it did - ship after ship was sold out of the fleet until by 1967 there was just 18 left. These included the six newly built 'push button ships' of the **Oriole**-class, the two big former Manchester Liners **Philomel** and **Sheldrake** and a mishmash of post-war ships from the **Mavis** and the larger **Redstart**, both dating from 1946, to the **Heron** dating from 1957. The Grand Union (Shipping) Company's **Blisworth** and **Marsworth** had been transferred to GSN when the Regent's Line ceased trading in 1965, and they were also now part of the GSN fleet, although the **Blisworth** was on charter work in the Mediterranean for a long while running between Morocco and Greece. Their yellow and black funnels lost the RL logo at this stage and were painted all black. Overall, the average age of the 18 vessels was 10 years and the aggregate gross tonnage was down to 14,889 tons. The company had already sold one of the prides of the fleet, the **Sandpiper**, when the French Government had offered £135,000 for her the previous year.

The company's last casualties occurred in 1967 when the **Woodlark** went aground on rocks at Mort Point in North Devon. Towed to safety, she was unloaded at Swansea and then taken to Charles Hill's yard at Bristol for replacement of badly damaged bottom plates. The ship was out of service for several weeks. The **Lapwing** was in collision in the Thames and later condemned to the scrap yard, and the **Grebe** was withdrawn after major mechanical failure deemed her unworthy of repair.

The packaged timber carrier *Tanmerack* (1967) seen as S William Coe's *Quickthorn* at Birkenhead.

[Picture by A Duncan]

In addition, the 1,596 gross ton, engines aft, timber carrier **Tanmerack**, which was owned by P&O's Bermuda-based Charter Shipping Company, had been put under GSN management when she was delivered in 1967. She was employed on the timber import run to Liverpool for the Canadian Transport Company in association with Canadian Pacific Steamships. She was not a success. Designed specifically for the packaged timber trade, the size of the packages was changed prior to her delivery so that the consequent broken stowage led to lighter loads and lost revenue. She was an embarrassment both to her owners and the timber trade and soon resorted to the charter market. The **Tanmerack** was sold in January 1973 to S William Coe & Company of Liverpool and given the new name **Quickthorn**.

The Great Yarmouth Shipping Company struggled on, now with only one ship, the **Norfolk Trader**, their other vessel, the **Peregrine**, having been sold in 1965. The duties of the **Norfolk Trader** took her on a regular circuit between Great Yarmouth and King's Lynn, with Antwerp, Rotterdam and Amsterdam and occasional calls at

Felixstowe and Harlingen. Eventually overwhelmed by the container and roll-on roll-off vehicle revolutions, the company withdrew in 1970 and the ship was sold. However, during the 1960s the company acted as agents for the burgeoning offshore support industry for the North Sea gas and oil boom, a business that led to the formation of P&O Offshore Services which later became an international operation. The Great Yarmouth Shipping Company also bought a 50% interest in the stevedoring company W A Drake in 1970 and remained profitable during the sale of land assets including river frontage at Norwich.

The *Swift* (1950)
was designed with low air draught for
the Rhine ports service and was
finally retired out of the fleet in 1967.

In 1968 the Deptford yard was taken over by GSN's subsidiary Blackmore's Motor Transport Company for use as a heavy lorry depot. The site has subsequently been developed for housing. Companies such as the Irongate Lighterage Company and its fleet of barges had already been sold off. In addition the Belgian steel importing agency Wilkinson, Wall & Company, acquired in the 1930s, was renamed AUL Ascania Unit Loads to become a Tilbury-based freight forwarding company.

During 1967 and 1968, GSN set up a new company to operate thrice-weekly container services between Tilbury (No. 43 berth) and Dunkirk and Tilbury and Rotterdam under the banner European Unit Routes using chartered tonnage such as the *Impala* and *Eland*. The antelope nomenclature was chosen to reflect the speed of delivery! European Unit Routes was created simply by renaming the now dormant Grand Union (Shipping) Company. Routes were expanded in February 1969 to include a three-times-a-week service to Antwerp, but in November 1969 the Dunkirk service was suspended for nearly a year due to port labour problems. The company colours were dark blue funnel and black top with a matching blue hull with the EUR logo in white amidships. A part of its business was transhipment of containers from the liner services that terminated at Tilbury.

Typical of the tonnage then on charter to EUR were ships such as the *Sassaby*, built for the J Weigman Shipping Company of London for time charter to GSN, and a development of the earlier *Caribou* also designed for charter to EUR. The *Sassaby* served the Tilbury to Rotterdam route when delivered in 1971, and had a capacity of 106 standard 20 foot containers. This route was taken over by the *Fallow Deer* when the Sassaby transferred to the Antwerp route. The *Fallow Deer* was completed in 1972 for the London & Rochester Trading Company specifically for charter to GSN for the EUR service from Tilbury. The cellular container ship, *Roe Deer*, formerly North Sea Ferries *Norbrae*, was also used by EUR from 1973 onwards and ironically was registered under the ownership of Tyne-Tees Steam Shipping Company, which by then was just another branch of the P&O family (see below). The remainder of the vessels were chartered from foreign flag owners as required. In January 1974 the EUR service to Antwerp was taken over by the *Roe Deer*, and the *Sassaby* transferred to the Tilbury to Zeebrugge route to be operated in collaboration with British Rail as a through unit load service.

The *Roe Deer* (1962)
was owned by Tyne-Tees Steam Shipping
Company and used on the EUR services.
She had been built for Coast Lines' Link Lines
container routes on the Irish Sea as the *Buffalo*
but served North Sea Ferries from
1972 to 1973 as the *Norbrae*.

[John Clarkson]

The *Sassaby* (1971) was the mainstay of the European Unit Routes services from Tilbury to Rotterdam until transferred to a new route to Zeebrugge.

Other partnerships also displaced conventional GSN ships. For example, in December 1968 the Hamburg/Bremen/London conference comprising GSN, A Kirsten and the Argo Line announced that their conventional unit load liner services would be replaced early in 1969 by a dedicated container service running from Ipswich. The service started in the Spring using the *Antares*, which was owned by the Argo Line, and had been delayed from starting the Ipswich route by a collision whilst working the Hull to Bremen service for the Argo/Associated Humber Lines consortium. In the event, the Felixstowe and London based vessels were retained until the success of the new container service, marketed as the Hanseatic-Ipswich Line, had been proven.

The outcome of all this progress was a mass clearout of all the traditional liner vessels by 1969 apart from the six new *Oriole*-class vessels, leaving GSN with a small modern fleet of break-bulk carriers with an aggregate tonnage of just 3,083 tons gross. Nevertheless, the company was heavily committed to two thriving passenger and vehicle companies based at Hull and Southampton, and was involved in a variety of near-Continental container services and several old style general cargo routes, including the traditional service to Bordeaux.

With Britain on the verge of joining the European Community, the GSN Directors were mindful both of Coast Lines' share in North Sea Ferries and of its very large road haulage interests. The road haulage network was ideally poised to develop door to door transport options between Britain and the Continent. Following a meeting between Sir Donald Anderson, the Chairman of P&O, and John Turner of Coast Lines in August 1971, the Coast Lines Board agreed to a buy out of £5.6 million by P&O, ultimately bringing the residue of the once mighty Coast Lines Group and their senior managers alongside GSN. An early indication of the attrition of Coast Lines was the transfer of two of its vessels, the *Bison* and *Buffalo*, to the now 50% owned North Sea Ferries' service between Hull and Rotterdam in 1971 as *Norbank* and *Norbrae*, the latter later becoming the *Roe Deer*.

The so-called 1971 'October Revolution' at P&O, planned by management consultants McKinsey & Company and implemented under the chairmanship of Ford Geddes, changed the structure of P&O into Divisions. Instead of the hundred or so well known subsidiary companies, there were to be five operating divisions, each specialising in related trades or business sectors - GSN (and Coast Lines) fell neatly into the European and Air Transport Division. Although quite a few of the old companies remained shipowners, at least for a while, their former identities were soon to disappear. Also in October 1971 P&O made a successful offer to buy out the minority shareholders in GSN, a necessary preliminary to any merging of its operations with those of Coast Lines. GSN management, was used to near independence despite being owned by P&O for the previous 51 years, and was less happy at the prospect than the Coast Lines managers were. What neither management realised was that the end of both companies was now inevitable.

Coincident with this reorganisation, GSN pulled out of its agreement with A Kirsten to run the London to Cologne and other Rhine ports service. As a consequence the newest of the *Oriole*-sextet, the *Plover*, was sold. The remaining ships still maintained the Bordeaux service for which the UK terminal had been transferred to Shoreham, though much of the Mediterranean trade had long since been ceded to the Moss Hutchison Line. In December 1971 the Bennett Steamship Company, still a wholly owned GSN trading company, opened a new regular service between Goole and Antwerp with the *Petrel*. The service was partially successful but was soon overtaken by roll-on roll-off services on the shorter sea routes. Wine imports to Bristol ceased in 1971 and Turner Edwards & Company transferred to Shoreham with a road connection onwards to Bristol. The related Edwards Bristol Channel Lines had been put into liquidation back in 1961.

The basic Le Havre service of Normandy Ferries was supplemented by a summer only Le Havre to Rosslare service in 1971. Occasional off-season cruises were operated to Rouen in the early days of the company. In 1971 GSN took delivery of a third ship, the magnificent cruise ferry *Eagle*, for operation by its subsidiary company Southern Ferries. Another product of the Nantes yard, the *Eagle* carried her traditional GSN name with pride, having a gross tonnage of 11,609, and accommodation for 650 passengers. Built at a cost of 55.43 million French francs to a specification that satisfied the stringent United States regulations then in force there was a possibility of winter trading in the Caribbean, a prospect that was never taken up. The *Eagle* opened a new service to Lisbon on 18 May and to Tangier on 22 May. In October 1973 she was joined by the *SF Panther*, formerly the Travemünde-Trelleborg Lines *Peter Pan* and built in 1965. She made her first voyage on the Normandy Ferries service to Le Havre on 20 November 1973, before transferring to Southern Ferries ownership, and then opened a new route to San Sebastian in northern Spain on 22 December. The *Eagle*, however, was retained under GSN ownership.

The fortunes of Southern Ferries' long distance services fluctuated with the seasons and the two new ships struggled to break even. The *SF Panther* rolled badly in the Bay of Biscay, and was sent to have stabilisers fitted in 1975. At the same time the *Eagle* was temporarily laid up as political troubles in Portugal combined with a short recession at home rendered further operation uneconomic. A plan to extend her route to include the Canaries in

1976 was curtailed with her sudden withdrawal and sale to French owners, Croisières Paquet, Nouvelle Compagnie de Paquebots, Marseilles in December 1975. Although the winter 1975/1976 brochure read '1975 has been a marvellous year for the *Eagle*...', the head of P&O's European and Air Transport Division revealed that the *Eagle* had never made a profit since she had entered service in 1971, and that P&O had continually evaluated the problem until a favourable offer for the ship had been made by the French company. The *SF Panther* was also withdrawn late in 1975 when the Southampton to San Sebastian service was closed. After a period on charter in the Baltic, she then became, in March 1977, the first roll-on roll-off ferry on the former Coast Lines Seaway route between Aberdeen and Lerwick as the *St Clair*.

**The *St Clair* (1965)
formerly Normandy Ferries' *SF Panther*
seen leaving Lerwick on 23 July 1991.**

[Nick Robins]

The McKinsey reorganisation triggered many changes in the P&O Group. Behind the new divisional structure, many companies and interests formerly owned by the major operating subsidiaries such as GSN were transferred to be directly owned by P&O itself. A number of dormant companies were re-named for re-use, and dozens of ships changed owners and/or managers. Apart from a desire to simplify reporting relationships and introduce new trading identities, these changes are believed to have been primarily related to tax, but surviving documents do not make this clear.

GSN was affected as much as any of P&O's other major subsidiaries. In March 1972 management of *Dragon* and *Leopard* was transferred to Southern Ferries, now directly owned by P&O. Douglas Mortleman, never much in favour of the divisional reorganisation, resigned as Chairman of GSN and as a P&O director in July 1972. In October the GSN and Tyne-Tees interests in North Sea Ferries were taken over by P&O, and in December the remaining conventional GSN ships were re-registered under a new company entitled General Steam Navigation (Trading), actually the dormant former Coast Lines subsidiary J J Mack & Sons under a new name. This left the *Eagle* as the only ship actually owned by GSN. Without undue fuss, Thomas Brockelbank's 150-year-old vision of trading worldwide in competition with the mighty sailing ships of the East India Company, and the less exotic but nonetheless valiant pageant that had followed, was coming to an end. In 1975, the Normandy Ferries partnership was replaced by a limited company owned 50:50 by P&O and SAGA, and in March 1976 the General Steam Navigation Company was renamed P&O Ferries (General European). GSN had ceased to exist as such, but its story would not be complete without considering what happened to its services, its ships and its heritage.

While all this was happening within the P&O Group, a rash of new roll-on roll-off services were cashing in on the cross-channel commercial vehicle traffic boom. Few of these services were introduced by well-established firms, and most were under-capitalised using chartered ships flying flags of convenience. The more successful might attract the interest of an investor and eventually flourish, while others fell by the wayside. Between August and November 1973 alone, the Thanet Shipping Line started running between Ramsgate and Flushing, DD Ferries between Felixstowe and Dunkirk, and the Rotterdam/Ipswich Line started the roll-on roll-off vessel *Ipswich Pioneer II* on their new service. Ironically one of the failures at that time was the Norfolk Line route between Sheerness and Scheveningen, who retrenched to the Great Yarmouth to Scheveningen route under the ownership of the Unilever Group. With the mighty soap giant behind them, the Norfolk Line was one company that was able to develop ultimately to the major ferry operator we know today.

With this massive competition building against the traditional and unit load services it was inevitable that the former GSN services would contract. Others suffered as well, and the Hollandsche Stoomboot Maatschappij ceased trading to the UK early in 1974 with their Felixstowe and Hull services taken over by KNSM, the Royal Netherlands Steamship Company. The British and Continental Steamship Company managed to struggle on for a few more years, but using foreign chartered tonnage. Like the Dutch before them, however, they soon terminated their services from the Mersey to the continent. Even the Compagnie Maritime de la Seine had been forced to give up their cherished London-Paris Line in 1970 – the onward march of the roll-on roll-off ferry was unforgiving.

Within the P&O Short Sea Shipping sector (renamed P&O Ferries at the end of 1974, when Ian Churcher was appointed sector head) there was a growing flexibility in the employment of former GSN and Coast Lines vessels. In 1973 the *Dorset Coast*, built in 1959 for the Dagenham to Cork car export trade, introduced a new container service between Shoreham and Bordeaux, and was later transferred to GSN (Trading) ownership. During April that year the remaining ex-GSN services, to Portugal, Spain and the Western Mediterranean, were altered to terminate at Shoreham where faster turnarounds were possible than in London, and the GSN (Trading) vessels began to appear elsewhere. The *Ortolan*, for example, found herself running between Aberdeen, Orkney and Shetland alongside the ferry *St Clair* for part of the second half of 1974, having carried out an inaugural run in late June. During this period some of her trips terminated at the Flotta Oil Terminal in the Orkneys. In 1975, the *Ortolan*, *Oriole*, *Petrel* and *Dorset Coast* were deployed on the islands services from time to time. The *Petrel* and the *Dorset Coast* were in the north again for June 1977, and the *Dorset Coast* operated out of Aberdeen during the period July to September 1978. This increased Scottish activity reflected the rapid development of the North Sea oilfields in the mid-1970s. In September 1976, the *Ortolan* replaced the *Stormont* on the former Tyne-Tees Steam Shipping Company routes between Newcastle and Hamburg and Bremen, later being replaced by the slightly larger *Petrel*. The one time GSN fleet had become quite nomadic, although between them they still maintained the Shoreham-based service to Bordeaux.

In April 1976 the GSN (Trading) ships *Dorset Coast*, *Oriole*, *Ortolan* and *Petrel* were transferred to P&O Ferries (General European) together with the small container ships *Norbank* and *Roe Deer*. What had once been GSN, now owned ships once more, and *Avocet* and *Albatross* from GSN (Trading) as well as the ex-Coast Lines *Stormont* followed in June, but this was little more than a book-keeping exercise as a prelude to their disposal over the next few years.

One by one the remaining members of the *Oriole* class were disposed of as the traditional liner trades were withdrawn and charter work diminished. The larger pair, the *Albatross* and *Avocet*, found new owners in 1976, the *Oriole* herself followed in 1977, the *Petrel* in 1978 and lastly the *Ortolan* in 1979. Of the six *Oriole*-class ships, four were subsequently wrecked, the *Maral R*, formerly the *Ortolan*, following a serious engine room fire in the North Sea.

The *Maral R* (1964)
after drifting ashore at Seaton Sluice. The former *Ortolan* had been sold to
Boston Offshore Maintenance in 1979 and resold to Gearstyle, of Hull, when was
abandoned by her crew on 26 August 1987 off the Farne Islands after fire broke out in
the engine room during a voyage south from Berwick-upon-Tweed.

The last of the 'Navvies' were no more, but the story does not end there. North Sea Ferries was going from strength to strength. From 1970 it operated freight ferries in support of the Hull to Rotterdam service, and in November 1972 announced that the *Norwave* and *Norwind*, the two original ships, were to switch to a new service between Hull and Zeebrugge. The transfer was completed in 1974 following the arrival of the much larger sisters *Norland* and the *Norstar* which took over the Europoort service. North Sea Ferries had originally inaugurated the Hull to Zeebrugge link on 20 November 1972, using the chartered German stern-loading freighter *Norcape*.

The **Norwave** and **Norwind** had a gross tonnage of only 4,038, a length of 110 metres and a breadth of nearly 18 metres. They were drive-through ships, bow loading at Hull and stern-loading at Europoort and Zeebrugge. The public rooms were on B Deck; a large lounge and bar at the forward end, reception area amidships, and the cafeteria aft. By way of contrast, the new British-registered **Norland** and Dutch-registered **Norstar** were 153 metres long and had a breadth of 25 metres. They were designed with a passenger complement of 1,200, and vehicle accommodation for up to 135 twelve metre freight trailers or 252 cars.

North Sea Ferries added a new Ipswich/Rotterdam freight service in 1977 (it was closed in 1995) and became a 50:50 partnership between P&O and the Dutch company Royal Nedlloyd in 1979. In 1987 the 1,200 passenger, 183 trailer **Norsea** and **Norsun** joined the Hull/Rotterdam route with the 'second generation' **Norland** and **Norstar** moving to Hull/Zeebrugge and **Norwave** and **Norwind** being sold. Freight services out of Middlesborough were added, to Zeebrugge in 1988 and to Rotterdam in 1995, and in 1996 P&O acquired full control of North Sea Ferries and added 'P&O' to its name.

Meanwhile, Normandy Ferries, now managed by P&O Ferries, had inaugurated a new service between Dover and Boulogne in April 1976 using the **Lion**, formerly the Burns and Laird Lines (Coast Lines Group) vehicle and passenger ferry from the Ardrossan to Belfast route. Two former Danish ferries joined her on the route, the **nf Tiger** in June 1978, and the **nf Panther** in January 1980 by which time P&O had increased its share in the operation to 90% and rebranded it P&O Normandy Ferries.

Designed with shallow 'Baltic draught' of just 14.4 feet, the two Danish ships had stabilisers added before starting at Dover. Whilst naming the **nf Tiger** at Dover, the former Foreign Secretary Lord George Brown commented that 'an old colleague of mine also had close connections with a ship called **Tiger**...' - a reference to the meetings between former Prime Minister Harold Wilson and Prime Minister of Rhodesia, Ian Smith, aboard **HMS Tiger**.

The **Dragon** and **Leopard** persisted on the Le Havre service, and at the end of 1979 P&O increased its share in Normandy Ferries from 50% to 90%. The vessels at Southampton and Dover then adopted the corporate P&O livery. The UK terminal for the Le Havre service transferred to Portsmouth in December 1984. The following month, however, the company was sold to the European Ferries Group (Townsend Thoresen) for £12.5 million and the five ships (two at Portsmouth and three at Dover) were integrated into the Townsend Thoresen fleet. Normandy Ferries, with its annoying advertising gimmick 'Norman D Seagull' was no more.

A final irony in the Normandy Ferries story came in December 1986, with the announcement that the P&O Group was to buy European Ferries for £450 million. The deal completed in January 1987 saw the combination of P&O's remaining ferry operations with those of Townsend Thoresen to form P&O European Ferries. The **Dragon**, by now renamed **Ionic Ferry**, returned to the P&O fleet on the Irish Sea, as did **nf Panther** which became **St Sunniva** on the Aberdeen/Lerwick service. The **Ionic Ferry** was sold to Greek owners in 1992, as was the **St Sunniva** when the service to the Northern Isles was closed in 2002. By then the possibility of **Eagle** rejoining P&O had come and gone, with a failed takeover bid in the summer of 2000 for the French-owned Festival Cruises in whose fleet the former GSN-owned ferry now served as the cruise ship **The Azur**.

Following the takeover of European Ferries the freight services of North Sea Ferries from Felixstowe to Rotterdam and Zeebrugge were transferred to P&O North Sea Ferries. In 2001 two of the largest passenger ferries in the world, the Dutch-flag **Pride of Rotterdam** and the British **Pride of Hull**, entered service on the Hull/Rotterdam service, with the traditional 'Nor-' prefixes displaced by P&O's 'Pride of' style. P&O European Ferries' services out of Dover became the P&O Stena Line joint venture between 1998 and 2003, but when they returned to P&O the name P&O Ferries was adopted for all P&O ferry services, and the North Sea Ferries identity disappeared.

GSN (or at least company number 75764) still exists – just. On 24 March 1976 the General Steam Navigation Company had become P&O Ferries (General European) Limited. This in its turn on 21 February 1980 became Beaufort Insurance Company Limited, which used to operate as P&O's in-house insurance company for non-marine risk, but is now dormant. Beaufort Insurance no longer trades, and neither does P&O, absorbed by Dubai Ports World in 2006. But P&O Ferries still operates, and it is P&O Ferries, both at Dover and Hull, that retains the last vestiges of what was once General Steam and its wonderful century and a half of sea trading.

REFERENCES

Several journals including SEA BREEZES, THE ILLUSTRATED LONDON NEWS and GSN NEWS LETTER contain information about GSN. The main source of information is contained within the 'GSN' Archive at the National Maritime Museum at Greenwich and is accessible through the Caird Library. The Moss Hutchison archives are held at the Merseyside Maritime Museum at Liverpool.

Blake G 1956. BI CENTENARY 1856 :1956. Collins, London.

Burtt F 1949. STEAMERS OF THE THAMES AND MEDWAY. Richard Tilling, London.

Cable B 1938. LONDON'S OWN LINERS. HISTORY OF GSNC 1924 TO 1938. Unpublished manuscript,
    GSN Archives, National Maritime Museum.

Cope Cornford L 1924. A CENTURY OF SEA TRADING 1824-1924. A & C Black Ltd., London.

Duckworth C L D & Langmuir G E 1968. RAILWAY AND OTHER STEAMERS. Second edition.
    T Stephenson & Sons Ltd., Prescot.

Duckworth C L D & Langmuir G E 1977. CLYDE AND OTHER COASTAL STEAMERS. Second edition.
    T Stephenson & Sons Ltd., Prescot.

Duckworth C L D & Langmuir G E 1990. CLYDE RIVER AND OTHER STEAMERS. Fourth edition.
    Brown, Son & Ferguson, Glasgow.

Farr G 1967. WEST COUNTRY PASSENGERS STEAMERS. Second edition. T Stephenson & Sons Ltd., Prescot.

Forrester R E 2006. THE GENERAL STEAM NAVIGATION COMPANY C1850-1913: A BUSINESS HISTORY.
    Unpublished PhD thesis, University of Greenwich.

Green E & Moss M 1982. A BUSINESS OF NATIONAL IMPORTANCE. Methuen & Company, London.

Greenway A 1986. A CENTURY OF NORTH SEA PASSENGER STEAMERS. Ian Allan Ltd., London.

Gurnett P A T 2001. A BRIEF HISTORY OF THE GENERAL STEAM NAVIGATION COMPANY.
    An Historic Deptford Publication, Deptford.

Hancock H E 1949. SEMPER FIDELIS, THE SAGA OF THE 'NAVVIES' (1924 TO 1948).
    General Steam Navigation Company, London.

Harrower J 1998. WILSON LINE. World Ship Society, Gravesend.

Harvey W J & Telford P J 2002. THE CLYDE SHIPPING COMPANY, GLASGOW, 1815-2000. P J Telford, UK.

Howarth D & Howarth H 1986. THE STORY OF P&O, THE PENINSULAR AND ORIENTAL STEAM NAVIGATION
    COMPANY. Weidenfield and Nicolson, London.

Hubatsch von W, Bernartz H, Friedland K, Galporin P, Heinsious P & Kludas A 1981. DIE ERST DEUTSCHE FLOTTE
    1848-1853. E S Mittler & Sohn, Herford and Bonn.

Jordan S 1998. FERRY SERVICES OF THE LONDON, BRIGHTON & SOUTH COAST RAILWAY.
    The Oakwood Press, Usk.

McNeill D B 1969. IRISH PASSENGER STEAMSHIP SERVICES, PART 1 NORTH OF IRELAND.
    David & Charles, Newton Abbot.

Middlemiss N L 1999. 'THE NAVVIES', HISTORY OF THE GENERAL STEAM NAVIGATION COMPANY.
    Shield Publications Ltd., Newcastle.

Palmer S 1982. 'The most indefatigable activity' the General Steam Navigation Company, 1824-50. THE JOURNAL
    OF TRANSPORT HISTORY, Vol. 3, No.2, pages 1-21.

Parsons R M 1985. 150 YEARS OF HISTORY IN THE WINE TRADE. Turner Edwards & Co Ltd.
    (P&O Wine Services), Bristol.

Robins N S 1998. THE BRITISH EXCURSION SHIP. Brown, Son & Ferguson Ltd., Glasgow.

Robins N S 1999. TURBINE STEAMERS OF THE BRITISH ISLES. Colourpoint Books, Newtownards.

Robins, N S 2003. FERRY POWERFUL - A HISTORY OF THR MODERN BRITISH DIESEL FERRY.
    Bernard McCall, Portishead

Roskill S W 1962 A MERCHANT FLEET IN WAR, 1939 - 1945. Collins, London

Smeeton E & Morris G 1982. THE GENERAL STEAM NAVIGATION CO LTD. Unpublished manuscript lodged with
    P&O History and Archives, DP World, London.

Thornton E C B 1972. THAMES COAST PLEASURE STEAMERS. T Stephenson & Sons Ltd., Prescot.

A letter from former GSN master Captain Gordon Renshawe, FNI

This letter was written to the author by the late Captain Gordon Renshawe following publication of an article by the author in SEA BREEZES called "The Day of the Dragon", February 1988.

12²/88

GORDON RENSHAWE
ASHLEY ROAD
NEW MILTON

Dear Mr Robins,

Just to congratulate you on the excellant article "The Day of the Dragon".
I stood by her at Nantes, and was deputy Master until I went to North Sea Ferries
and then returned to bring out the "EAGLE" (for my sins). I did the first
trial run of Dragon to Lisbon, to keep her occupied during the French
strikes if 1968, I also did a spell on the "Leopard", in fact started
the run Rosslaire/Le Havre.   In 1973 I started the"Peter Pan" off
when she became the "Panther". We had on board a glass painting of the
1851 Panther leaving Ostende on a days outhing from Ramsgate, but it was
'borrowed' by someone in the Company while on the Swedish charter. After the
first six months I returned to the "Eagle" until she was sold. Thence the
"Dorset", Poole to Cherbourg for Truckline charter, thence "Lion" in Dover.
I also dropped back to Dragon now and then to relieve, and keep my Southampton
licence.   I am afraid though, the "Eagle" never made the Canaries run, before
being sold to Paquet Lines. I had good training for the ferries on the "
"Golden Eagle" and "Royal Sovereign", which were great fun even though hard
work.   Again many thanks for an enjoyable article.

Best wishes, Your's sincerely

Gordon Renshawe FNI

FLEET LISTS

Formal records of ship registration were only maintained from 1850 onwards. Prior to that it is not always apparent whether vessels mentioned in reports were owned or chartered by GSN. Cope Cornford's fleet list is not entirely accurate and modifications to that list have been made where evidence to the contrary is available. Disposal dates of the early wooden hulled ships are also vague as many were hulked and left to rot in some quiet corner rather than formally dismantled. The Return of Registered Steam Vessels for 1851 and 1860 provide some information on ships out of service as does the first archived timetable for 1876 (Forrester, 2006). When known, second hand ships show the company the ship was purchased from, which may not be the original owner, and ships sold for further service show the name of the purchaser.

The dedicated excursion ships, rather than early river steam packets, are listed separately, as are the fleets of Moss Hutchison Line, New Medway Steam Packet Company, Great Yarmouth Shipping Company and Grand Union (Shipping) Company.

General Steam Navigation Company (Also owned numerous smaller vessels, e.g. owned and co-owned forty tugs, lighters and wherries in 1930. GSNC was, from 1913 onwards, also the registered owner of the small former John Crisp & Son vessels: *Emerald* (1879), *Topaz* (1893), *Amethyst* (1895), *Opal* (1896), *Diamond* (1899) and *Crystal* (1903) of which only the *Topaz* and *Opal* survived long enough to transfer into the Great Yarmouth Shipping Company in December 1931.)

Name	Built	GSN Service	Gross Tons	Hull/Propulsion/Engine	Comments
Earl of Liverpool	1823	1824-?	262	Wood/paddle/steam	Ex-William Joliffe and Edward Banks; out of service by 1860
Lord Melville	1822	1824-?	116 net	Wood/paddle/steam	Ex-William Joliffe and Edward Banks
Royal Sovereign	1822	1824-?	220	Wood/paddle/steam	Ex-Thos. Brockelbank
City of London	1824	1824-?	213	Wood/paddle/steam	Ex-Thos. Brockelbank; out of service by 1860
Victory	1818	1824-?	160	Wood/paddle/steam	Possibly chartered and not owned
Superb	1824	1825-1834	125	Wood/paddle/steam	Wrecked on passage to Hamburg
Mountaineer	1821	1825-1837	200	Wood/paddle/steam	Wrecked off Shoreham
Brockelbank	1825	1825-?	125	Wood/paddle/steam	
Rapid	1820	1825-1841	85	Wood/paddle/steam	Chartered initially and purchased in 1825; scrapped
Eclipse	1821	1825-?	88	Wood/paddle/steam	
Waterloo	1819	1825-1847	133 net	Wood/paddle/steam	Sold
Talbot	1819	1825-1833	97	Wood/paddle/steam	Wrecked near Ostend
Belfast	1820	1825-?	204	Wood/paddle/steam	Ex-George Langtree, precursor to Belfast Steam Packet Co
Attwood	1825	1825-?	310	Wood/paddle/steam	Out of service by 1860
Nottingham	1825	1825-1847	42 net	Wood/paddle/steam	Sold
Hylton Jolliffe	1825	1825-?	174	Wood/paddle/steam	
Camilla	1825	1825-1847	173	Wood/paddle/steam	Ex-Mr Molesworth; sold
Prince Frederick	1825	1825-1847	156 net	Wood/paddle/steam	Sold
Duke of York	1826	1826-1830	327	Wood/paddle/steam	Sold to Admiralty
Sir Edward Banks	1826	1826-?	322	Wood/paddle/steam	Out of service by 1876
Harlequin	1826	1826-1856	315	Wood/paddle/steam	Scrapped
Columbine	1826	1826-1855	393	Wood/paddle/steam	Wrecked near Rotterdam
George IV	1826	1826-1830	341 net	Wood/paddle/steam	Ex-Mr Gabriel Britton; sold to Admiralty
William IV	1826	1826-?	327 net	Wood/paddle/steam	
William Jolliffe	1826	1826-?	311	Wood/paddle/steam	Out of service by 1876
Ramona	1828	1829-?	356	Wood/paddle/steam	Out of service by 1860

Name	Built	GSN Service	Gross Tons	Hull/Propulsion/Engine	Comments
Queen of the Netherlands	1824	1830-?	116 net	Wood/paddle/steam	Ex-Wigram & Green
Tourist	1821	1832-?	257	Wood/paddle/steam	Out of service by 1860
London Merchant	1831	1833-?	306 net	Wood/paddle/steam	Out of service by 1860
City of Hamburg	1834	1834-?	518	Wood/paddle/steam	Out of service by 1876
John Bull	1835	1835-1892	591	Wood/paddle/steam	Converted to coal hulk 1876
Britannia	1835	1835-?	219 net	Wood/paddle/steam	Sold to Havre SS Cie, France
Jupiter	1835	1835-1847	288 net	Wood/paddle/steam	Sold
Menai	1830	1836-?	263	Wood/paddle/steam	Out of service by 1860
Kent	1829	1836-?	103	Wood/paddle/steam	
Dart	1825	1836-?	247	Wood/paddle/steam	Out of service 1851/1852
Magnet	1826	1836-1847	296	Wood/paddle/steam	Scrapped
Fame	1834	1836-1865	294	Wood/paddle/steam	Scrapped
Albion	1823	1836-?	166 net	Wood/paddle/steam	Presumed sold
Hero	1821	1836-?	233	Wood/paddle/steam	
Venus	1821	1836-?	185	Wood/paddle/steam	Lost in collision with HMS Firefly
Caledonia	1836	1836-1864	707	Wood/paddle/steam	Ex-London & Edinburgh Steam Packet Co; wrecked off Flamborough Head
James Watt	1821	1836-1853	462	Wood/paddle/steam	Ex-London & Edinburgh Steam Packet Co; scrapped
Clarence	1836	1836-?	760	Wood/paddle/steam	Ex-London & Edinburgh Steam Packet Co; out of service by 1876
Ocean	1836	1836-?	464	Wood/paddle/steam	Ex-London & Edinburgh Steam Packet Co; out of service by 1860
Giraffe	1836	1836-?	410	Wood/paddle/steam	Ex-London & Edinburgh Steam Packet Co; out of service by 1876
Countess of Lonsdale	1836	1836-1869	616	Wood/paddle/steam	Ex-London & Edinburgh Steam Packet Co; sold
Monarch	1833	1836-1846	516 net	Wood/paddle/steam	Ex-London & Edinburgh Steam Packet Co
City of Edinburgh	1821	1836-?	301 net	Wood/paddle/steam	Ex-London & Edinburgh Steam Packet Co
Soho	1823	1836-?	433	Wood/paddle/steam	Out of service by 1860
Neptune	1837	1837-1856	599	Wood/paddle/steam	Sold1846; repurchased 1850; sold
Leith	1837	1837-?	907	Wood/paddle/steam	Out of service by 1860
Rainbow	1837	1837-?	407	Iron/paddle/steam	Out of service by 1870
Sir William Wallace	1829	1839-1847	102 net	Wood/paddle/steam	Ex-Dundee, Perth and London Shipping Co; sold
Princess Royal	1841	1841-?	748	Wood/paddle/steam	Out of service by 1876
Trident	1841	1841-1884	971	Wood/paddle/steam	Converted by coal hulk; sold
Wilberforce	1837	1841-1856	610	Wood/paddle/steam	Ex-Humber Steamship Co; scrapped
Vivid	1835	1841-1855	428	Wood/paddle/steam	Ex-Humber Steamship Co; scrapped
Waterwitch	1835	1842-1865	481	Wood/paddle/steam	Ex-Humber Steamship Co; scrapped
Venezuela	1840	1842-?	308	Wood/paddle/steam	Out of service by 1860
Magician	1843	1842-1878	175	Iron/paddle/steam	Sold
Mercury	1843	1845-?	252	Wood/paddle/steam	Ex-Star Steam Packet Co; out of service by 1860
Triton	1845	1845-1875	357	Iron/paddle/steam	Scrapped
Star	1834	1846-?	231	Wood/paddle/steam	Ex-Star Steam Packet Co; out of service by 1860
Chevy Chase	1847	1847-1864	810	Iron/paddle/steam	Bought from builders; aground in Elbe February 1864; scrapped as lay 1866
Royal William	1849	1849-1875	325	?/paddle/steam	Ex-Margate Steam Packet Co; sold
Seine	1849	1849-1889	391	Iron/paddle/steam	Scrapped
Rhine	1849	1849-1887	547	Iron/paddle/steam	Scrapped (struck and sank the Tongue Light Vessel 1877)

Name	Built	GSN Service	Gross Tons	Hull/Propulsion/Engine	Comments
Tiger	1838	1850-1870	604	Wood/paddle/steam hulked	Ex-James Hartley, London (built originally for Saint George Steam Packet Co);
Monarch	1850	1850-1875	872	?/paddle/steam	Sold
Panther	1851	1850-1885	425	Iron/paddle/steam	Scrapped
Concordia	1851	1851-1887	467	Iron/paddle/steam	Scrapped
Ravensbourne	1851	1851-1857	606	Iron/paddle/steam	Lost in collision off Flushing
Moselle	1852	1852-1886	574	Iron/paddle/steam	Scrapped following a fire at Custom House Quay, London
Belgium	1848	1853-1877	457	Wood/paddle/steam	Ex-*Großherzog von Oldenburg*, Germanic Confederation Navy; hulked
Hanover	1842	1853-1868	519	Wood/paddle/steam	Ex-*Bremen*, Germanic Confederation Navy; sold
Holland	1848	1853-1860	383	Wood/paddle/steam	Ex-*Frankfurt*, Germanic Confederation Navy; sold
Denmark	1841	1853-1859	501	Wood/paddle/steam	Ex-*Hamburg*, Germanic Confederation Navy; sold
Edinburgh	1853	1853-1855	741	Wood/paddle/steam	Ex-*Der Königliche Ernst August*, Germanic Confederation Navy; lost in fog whilst on charter in the Black Sea
Newcastle	1844	1853-1854	447	Iron/paddle/steam	Ex-*Lubec*, Germanic Confederation Navy; sold
Topaz	1837	1853-?	141	Wood/paddle/steam	Ex-Diamond Steam Packet Co; out of service by 1860
Ruby	1836	1853-?	243	Wood/paddle/steam	Ex-Diamond Steam Packet Co; out of service by 1876
Sapphire	1835	1853-?	238	Iron/paddle/steam	Ex-Diamond Steam Packet Co; out of service by 1876
Dragon	1854	1854-1880	475	Iron/paddle/steam	Sunk in collision with *Adamson* off Owers on voyage to Charente
Pioneer	1854	1854-1878	413	Iron/paddle/steam	Scrapped
Pilot	1854	1854-1880	522	Iron/paddle/steam	Sunk in collision with Robinson's *Sumatra* on the Thames
Diamond	1835	1854-?	137	Wood/paddle/steam	Ex-Diamond Steam Packet; out of service by 1860
Dolphin	1855	1855-1885	626	Iron/paddle/steam	Sunk in collision off Kingsgate in the Downs
Germania	1856	1856-1880	630	Iron/screw/steam	Coal hulk from 1876; scrapped
Leo	1847	1856-1880	569	Iron/paddle/steam	Ex-*Quadalquiver*, scrapped following collision damage at Blackwall Reach on the Thames
Bruiser	1853	1857-1888	506	Iron/screw/steam	Sold
Wansbeck	1857	1857-1886	597	Iron/screw/steam	Scrapped
Cologne	1858	1858-1890	435	Iron/paddle/steam	Scrapped
Cosmopolitan	1852	1859-1881	502	Iron/screw/steam	Wrecked in the Scheldte
Metropolitan	1853	1859-1881	521	Iron/screw/steam	Sunk in collision with Hamburg & London Co's *Gemma* off Woolwich on the Thames, raised and scrapped
Harburg	1856	1860 only	?	?	Ex-Harburg Engineering and Navigation Co; wrecked off Texel Island, Holland
Saxonia	1855	1860-1877	358	Iron/screw/steam	Sold to Russia
Leopard	1855	1860-1885	374	Iron/screw/steam	Ex-Harburg Engineering & Navigation Co; reduced to hulk
Boreas	1856	1860-1885	412	Iron/screw/steam	Ex-Harburg Engineering & Navigation Co; scrapped
Berlin	1857	1860-1875	740	Iron/paddle/steam	Ex-*Princess Royal*; scrapped
Perth	1834	1861-1864	595	Wood/paddle/steam	Ex-Dundee Perth & London Steamship Co; destroyed by fire
Arno	1851	1861-1866	485	Iron/screw/steam	Ex-Liverpool & Mediterranean Steamship Co; sunk in collision with brig *Medina* off Whitby
Waterloo	1854	1861-1879	514	Iron/paddle/steam	Ex-Belfast Steamship Co; sunk in collision
Elba	1855	1861-1874	566	Iron/screw/steam	Lost at sea - missing
Chevy Chase	1860	1862-1864	810	Iron/paddle/steam	Sunk in the Elbe and scrapped

Name	Built	GSN Service	Gross Tons	Hull/Propulsion/Engine	Comments
Velocity	1857	1862-1877	259	Iron/pscrew/steam	Ex-East England Steamship Co; scrapped
Vigilant	1857	1862-1878	257	Iron/screw/steam	Ex-East England Steamship Co; scrapped
Forth	1855	1863-1875	401	Iron/screw/steam	Wrecked entering the Maas in bad weather
Earl of Aberdeen	1847	1863-1879	820	Iron/paddle/steam	Scrapped
Hamburg	1857	1863-1886	439	Iron/screw/steam	Ex-Dundee, Perth & London Steamship Co; scrapped
Mermaid	1864	1864-1873	745	Iron/screw/steam	Sunk Gravesend Reach, raised and scrapped
Heron	1860	1864-1888	624	Iron/screw/steam	Scrapped
Maas	1864	1864-1888	692	Iron/paddle/steam	Scrapped
Stork	1864	1864-1897	843	Iron/screw/steam	Sold to J Power & Co
Orion	1865	1865-1890	777	Iron/paddle/steam	Scrapped
Alford	1863	1865-1891	771	Iron/screw/steam	Scrapped
Benbow	1865	1866-1912	894	Iron/screw/steam	Scrapped
Ostrich	1860	1866-1887	624	Iron/screw/steam	Scrapped
Eider	1866	1866-1889	722	Iron/paddle/steam	Scrapped
Taurus	1866	1866-1892	838	Iron/paddle/steam	Sold to Corporation of the City of London
Florence	1864	1867-1881	660	Iron/paddle/steam	Scrapped, last voyage 1877
Granton	1867	1867-1910	1,162	Iron/screw/steam	Scrapped
Scorpio	1869	1869-1875	885	Iron/screw/steam	Missing in storm
Libra	1869	1869-1889	1,030	Iron/screw/steam	Sunk in collision
Virgo	1870	1870-1920	1,016	Iron/screw/steam	Scrapped
Rainbow	1872	1872-1902	1,083	Iron/screw/steam	Sold to McDowell & Barbour
Iris	1872	1872-1914	1,033	Iron/screw/steam	Seized at Hamburg, sunk in 1917 Gulf of Pernan
Capulet	1874	1874-1903	336	Iron/screw/steam	Sunk in collision with sailing ship *Torrens* off Blyth, raised and scrapped
Nautilus	1874	1874-1923	718	Iron/screw/steam	Sunk in collision with *Australia* in the Scheldte
Atlas	1875	1875-1900	46	Iron/paddle/steam	Scrapped
Curlew	1875	1875-1896	630	Iron/screw/steam	Wrecked off Brest
Martin	1875	1875-1899	959	Iron/screw/steam	Sold to Spanish owners
Swallow	1875	1875-1901	625	Iron/paddle/steam	Scrapped
Swift	1875	1875-1901	627	Iron/paddle/steam	Sold to J Power & Co
Condor	1875	1875-1906	682	Iron/screw/steam	Scrapped
Merlin	1875	1875-1911	643	Iron/screw/steam	Wrecked on passage to Charente
Plover	1875	1875-1929	949	Iron/screw/steam	Scrapped
Tern	1875	1875-1931	959	Iron/screw/steam	Sunk in collision with *City of Malines* in the Humber
Lion	1847	1876-1884	667	Iron/paddle/steam	Ex-Malcomson Brothers, Waterford; scrapped
Nora	1861	1876-1879	432	Iron/screw/steam	Ex-Malcomson Brothers, Waterford; wrecked off Banjaard Bank, Netherlands
Era	1861	1876-1895	560	Iron/screw/steam	Ex-William Malcomson, Liverpool; hulked 1889; scrapped
Hollandia	1867	1876-1887	820	Iron/paddle/steam	Ex-William Malcomson, Waterford; chartered to Waterford Steam Ship Co 1878; scrapped following collision with *Ancona* off Blyth
Penguin	1876	1876-1890	906	Iron/screw/steam	On fire in North Sea and sank
Hawk	1876	1876-1897	648	Iron/screw/steam	Scrapped following collision with *Chelsea* at Erith on the Thames
Widgeon	1876	1876-1911	725	Iron/screw/steam	Scrapped after collision damage with *Barking* in Thames; raised and scrapped
Petrel	1876	1876-1912	841	Iron/screw/steam	Sunk in collision with *Tuborg* 10 miles off Amsterdam

Name	Built	GSN Service	Gross Tons	Hull/Propulsion/Engine	Comments
Teal	1876	1876-1916	830	Iron/screw/steam	Torpedoed off Seaham
Falcon	1876	1876-1926	649	Iron/screw/steam	Destroyed by fire off Dover
Osprey	1877	1877-1904	1,095	Iron/screw/steam	Beached at Winterton after collision with *Dunston* and scrapped
Kestrel	1878	1878-1893	960	Iron/screw/steam	Sunk in collision with *Regalia* on the River Elbe
Bittern	1878	1878-1900	948	Iron/screw/steam	Sold to Cia. Transmedoterranea, Spain
Lapwing	1879	1879-1911	1,215	Iron/screw/steam	Sold to Aziz Izazzet, Cairo
Gannet	1879	1879-1916	1,246	Iron/screw/steam	Sunk and raised in 1902 and converted to cargo vessel; mined near Shipwash Lighthouse
Redstart	1880	1880-1931	1,192	Iron/screw/steam	Sold to Messrs Van der Ebb, Antwerp
Deak	1880	1882-1904	1,231	Steel/screw/steam	Renamed *Swan* 1882, sold to Russian owners
Cormorant	1882	1882-1926	927	Iron/screw/steam	Scrapped
Mallard	1882	1882-1926	1,250	Iron/screw/steam	Sold to Palgrave Murphy, Dublin
Cygnet	1883	1883-1903	1,156	Steel/screw/steam	Sank off Vigo following explosion
Egret	1883	1883-1902	723	Iron/screw/steam	Sold C Hannevig, Norway
Raven	1883	1883-1913	1,648	Iron/screw/steam	Scrapped after falling athwart London Bridge
Albatross	1884	1884-1923	1,450	Steel/screw/steam	Sold to Italian owners
Starling	1887	1887-1918	791	Steel/screw/steam	Lost in collision off Tréport
Grebe	1887	1887-1925	814	Steel/screw/steam	Sold to Italian owners
Seamew	1888	1888-1914	1,505	Steel/screw/steam	Sold to Greek owners
Heron	1889	1889-1917	879	Iron/screw/steam	Torpedoed off Ushant
Hirondelle	1890	1890-1917	1,607	Steel/screw/steam	Torpedoed near Belle Isle, Biscay
Peregrine	1891	1891 only	1,664	Steel/screw/steam	Sold Howard Smith & Co; Australia
Ptarmigan	1891	1891-1915	780	Iron-steel/screw/steam	Torpedoed off North Shields
Sparrow	1892	1892-1894	395	Steel/screw/steam	Sold to African Steamship Co
Linnet	1890	1892-1901	1,728	Steel/screw/steam	Ex-*Dieppos*, R de la Rue, Dieppe; abandoned after fire, towed to Santander; sold to Uruguayan owners
Peregrine	1892	1892-1917	1,664	Iron/screw/steam	Wrecked near Sunk Lightship
Adjutant	1893	1893-1912	2,392	Steel/screw/steam	Sunk off Deal in collision with Prince Line's *Ocean Prince*
Guillemot	1894	1894-1911	1,771	Steel/screw/steam	Foundered in Bay of Biscay
Tetuan	1896	1898-1900	1,394	Iron/screw/steam	Ex-Mersey Steamship Co; sold to Swedish owners
Sheldrake	1894	1898-1916	2,697	Steel/screw/steam	Ex-*Kelvingrove*, Glasgow Steamship Co; shelled and sunk off Marittimo Island
Ardanbhan	1880	1899-1900	1,132	Iron/screw/steam	Ex-McLaren Crum; ashore at Port Sunderland, total loss
Preston	1885	1899-1906	2,099	Iron/screw/steam	Ex-Ropner Shipping Co; wrecked near Camarinas
Auk	1877	1899-1915	1,163	Iron/screw/steam	Ex-*Tintern Abbey*, Pyman Watson & Co; sunk at Hamburg
Vesuvio	1879	1900-1916	1,391	Iron/screw/steam	Ex-*Czar*, Mossgiel Steamship Co Glasgow; mined near Owers Lightship
Balgownie	1880	1900-1916	1,061	Iron/screw/steam	Ex-Grampian Steamship Co.; mined near Sunk Head Bay
Alouette	1894	1901-1924	570	Steel/screw/steam	Ex-*Calvados*, London, Brighton & South Coast Railway; scrapped
Pearl	1901	1901-1927	191	Steel/screw/steam	Sold to C V Hardy, Hull
Swift	1884	1901-1911	667	Iron/screw/steam	Ex-Hull & Netherlands Steamship Co; sold to Greek owners
Merannio	1881	1901-1930	939	Iron/screw/steam	Ex-Maclay & McIntyre, Glasgow; sold to Palgrave, Murphy., Dublin
Groningen	1902	1902-1915	988	Steel/screw/steam	Sunk after collision in Thames 1910, raised and put back in service; mined off Sunk Head Buoy

Name	Built	GSN Service	Gross Tons	Hull/Propulsion/Engine	Comments
Ortolan	1902	1902-1917	1,717	Steel/screw/steam	Torpedoed in Atlantic
Bullfinch	1903	1903-1927	246	Steel/screw/steam	Sold, renamed *Archmor*
Leeuwarden	1903	1903-1915	990	Steel/screw/steam	Shelled and sunk near Maas Lightship
Goldfinch	1903	1903-1928	246	Steel/screw/steam	Sold to Lena Fielding, Liverpool
Crane	1904	1904-1930	2,033	Steel/screw/steam	Sold to Yugoslavian owners
Stork	1904	1904-1936	2,029	Steel/screw/steam	Sold to Queen Line, London
Grive	1905	1905-1917	2,037	Steel/screw/steam	Sunk by torpedo off Lerwick serving as an ABV
Kelvinside	1893	1906-1923	219	Steel/screw/steam	Ex-J Crisp & Son, Great Yarmouth; sold to Captain A Dempsey, London
Woodcock	1906	1906-1926	1,673	Steel/screw/steam	Sold to Societa di Navigazione Vapore Puglia, Bari
Drake	1908	1908-1917	2,267	Steel/screw/steam	Renamed *Wildrake* 1914; shelled and sunk by submarine
Laverock	1909	1909-1938	1,199	Steel/screw/steam aft	Sold to Verano Steamship Co (Fred Verano Andlaw), Gibraltar
Corncrake	1910	1910-1937	1,171	Steel/screw/steam aft	Transferred to Moss Hutchison Line and renamed *Chloris*
Lapwing	1911	1911-1917	1,192	Steel/screw/steam	Mined off Southwold
Swift	1911	1911-1929	1,141	Steel/screw/steam	Renamed *Dean Swift* 1914; renamed *Swift* 1919; sold to Aberdeen Steam Navigation Co, Aberdeen
Fauvette	1912	1912-1916	2,644	Steel/screw/steam	Requisitioned by Admiralty; mined in 1916
Mavis	1912	1912-1913	1,200	Steel/screw/steam	Sunk after collision off Maassluis
Kingfisher	1913	1913-1932	289	Steel/screw/steam	Scrapped following collision
Oriole	1914	1914-1915	1,489	Steel/screw/steam	Torpedoed in English Channel
Raven	1914	1914-1930	1,337	Steel/screw/steam	Sunk in collision off Borkum
Halcyon	1915	1915-1916	1,319	Steel/screw/steam	Mined off Folkestone
Seamew	1915	1915-1938	1,332	Steel/screw/steam	Sold to Verano Steam Ship Co (Fred Verano Andlaw), Gibraltar
Philomel	1917	1917-1918	2,429	Steel/screw/steam	Torpedoed off Glenan Island
Ystroom	1898	1918 only	1,027	Steel/screw/steam	Government war prize; sold
Chow Thi	1896	1918-1919	1,811	Steel/screw/steam	Government war prize; sold
Starling	1920	1920-1930	1,303	Steel/screw/steam	Sold to United Baltic Corporation, London
Heron	1920	1920-1935	1,314	Steel/screw/steam	Sold to United Baltic Corporation, London
Lapwing	1920	1920-1941	1,449	Steel/screw/steam aft	Torpedoed in Atlantic
Petrel	1920	1920-1941	1,457	Steel/screw/steam aft	Torpedoed in North Atlantic
Halcyon	1921	1921-1934	1,566	Steel/screw/steam	Sold to Khedivial Mail Line, Alexandria, and renamed *Zamalek*; sold on to UK Ministry of Transport and converted to Convoy Rescue Ship under GSNC Management
Iris	1921	1921-1927	415	Steel/screw/steam	Ex-*Kinnaird Head*, Henry & MacGregor; sold to James Fisher & Sons, Barrow
Mavis	1919	1921-1929	500	Steel/screw/steam	Ex-*War Avon*, completed as *Independance* for Neptunus Soc. d'Armement, Antwerp; sold to James Fisher & Sons, Barrow
Philomel	1921	1921-1934	1,563	Steel/screw/steam	Sold to Khedivial Mail Line, Alexandria and renamed *Zaafaran*; sold on to UK Ministry of Transport and converted to Convoy Rescue Ship under GSNC Management
Blackcock	1921	1921-1937	492	Steel/screw/steam	Sold to Comben Longstaff, London
Ptarmigan	1920	1921-1938	499	Steel/screw/steam	Ex-*Glanton Firth*, Cheviot Coasters (G T Gillie & Blair, Newcastle, managers); sold to Gordonia Freighters Ltd, London, (Harrison Thornton & Co)

Name	Built	GSN Service	Gross Tons	Hull/Propulsion/Engine	Comments
Oriole	1921	1921-1938	488	Steel/screw/steam	Sold to Henry & MacGregor, Leith
Teal	1921	1921-1939	1,444	Steel/screw/steam	Sold to Cie. Navitaise des Chargeurs de l'Ouest, Nantes, but returned to GSNC management between 1940 and 1945 as the **Penestin**
Auk	1921	1921-1944	1,445	Steel/screw/steam	Mined in the Adriatic off Ancona
Gannet	1921	1921-1953	1,443	Steel/screw/steam aft	Scrapped
Guillemot	1900	1922-1929	1,909	Steel/screw/steam	Ex-**Chao Chow Fu**, UK Controller of Shipping; scrapped
Drake	1922	1922-1934	1,592	Steel/screw/steam	Sold to Zanzibar Government
Sheldrake	1920	1922-1937	462	Steel/screw/steam	Ex-**Glanmor**, Shipping Co, Llanelli; sold to Stanhope Shipping Co
Picardy	1920	1923-1931	320	Steel/screw/steam	Ex-R & J Park Ltd, London; transferred to Great Yarmouth Shipping Co.; sold to Barlow & Co., Dundee, 1953
Peronne	1917	1923-1931	207	Steel/screw/steam	Ex-R & J Park Ltd, London; transferred to Great Yarmouth Shipping Co.; sold to Tay Sand Co, 1946
Ortolan	1920	1923-1950	489	Steel/screw/steam aft	Ex-**Beauly Firth**, Ferrum Steamship Co (G T Gillie & Blair, Newcastle, managers); sold to Thorn Line (S William Coe), Liverpool
Fauvette	1874	1924-1925		Steel/screw/steam	Ex-French Government **Crysalis**; sold to Turkish owners
Alouette	1919	1924-1936	638	Steel/screw/steam aft	Ex-**Pentland Firth**, Border Shipping Co (G T Gillie & Blair, Newcastle, managers); sold to Henry & MacGregor, Leith
Peregrine	1921	1924-1938	933	Steel./screw/steam	Ex-**Arbonne**, Thos. Steven, Leith; sold to Navigation Transmarine SA, Antwerp
Albatross	1924	1924-1938	1,942	Steel/screw/steam	Sold to Atlantic & Mediterranean Trading Co (Alfred John Pope)
Adjutant	1921	1924-1949	890	Steel/screw/steam	Ex-**Myrtlepark**, Denhom Shipping Co; sold to Comben Longstaff, London
Fauvette	1925	1925-1934	1,088	Steel/screw/steam	Lost in collision with **Penelope** in North Sea 15 miles off Hinder Light Vessel
Merel	1925	1925-1939	1,014	Steel/screw/steam	Mined off Ramsgate
Roek	1925	1925-1940	893	Steel/screw/steam	Mined in the North Sea off Rotterdam
Hirondelle	1925	1925-1948		Steel/screw/steam	Transferred to Moss Hutchison Line and renamed **Landes**; sold to Italian owners 1953
Grebe	1926	1926-1937	880	Steel/screw/steam	Transferred to Moss Hutchison line and renamed **Philitos**; lost in collision near St Goven's Light 1940
Nero	1907	1927-1927	640	Steel/screw/steam	Ex-Ellerman's Wilson Line; resold to Ellerman's Wilson Line (United Shippping Co)
Hero	1895	1927-1933	640	Steel/screw/steam	Ex-Wilson's & North Eastern Railway; chartered to Ellerman Line; scrapped
Woodcock	1927	1927-1939	1,926	Steel/screw/steam	Transferred to Moss Hutchison Line and renamed **Lormont**; sunk in collision in the Humber
Cormorant	1927	1927-1957	1,220	Steel/screw/steam	Scrapped
Falcon	1927	1927-1957	1,316	Steel/screw/steam	Scrapped
Robin	1928	1927-1931	217	Steel/screw/steam	Renamed **Yellowhammer** 1929; transferred to Great Yarmouth Shipping Co, sold 1948
Silverthorn	1908	1928-1937	436	Steel/screw/steam	Ex-**Deux Frères**, Bennett Steamship Co.; sold to S William Coe, Liverpool
Woodlark	1928	1928-1954	1,501	Steel/screw/steam	Sold to Campania de Navegacion Punta Corna SA, Cyprus
Groningen	1928	1928-1961	1,205	Steel/screw/steam	Renamed **Philomel** 1958; scrapped
Goldfinch	1927	1929-1931	327	Steel/screw/steam	Ex-**Vivonia** Leetham & Sons; transferred to Great Yarmouth Shipping Co and renamed **Lynn Trader**, sold to A Tucker, Cardiff, 1950

Name	Built	GSN Service	Gross Tons	Hull/Propulsion/Engine	Comments
Leeuwarden	1929	1929-1946	1,209	Steel/screw/steam	Mined off Dieppe
Mavis	1930	1930-1940	935	Steel/screw/steam	Bombed off Calais
Swift	1930	1930-1948	936	Steel/screw/steam	Transferred to Moss Hutchison Line and renamed *Lormont*; sold to Cypriot owners 1953
Starling	1930	1930-1960	1,320	Steel/screw/steam	Scrapped
Conifer	1920	1932-1939	453	Steel/screw/steam	Ex-London & Dunkirk Shipping Co; sunk following collision with *Montsante* off the Sandettie Light Vessel
Volga	1881	1932-1937	281	Steel/screw/steam	Ex-Bennett Steamship Co; scrapped
Tern	1932	1932-1949	213	Steel/screw/motor aft	Sold to J Lisle Hindmarsh, Cardiff
Fauvette	1935	1935-1963	614	Steel/twin screw/motor aft	Sold to W J Sumarah, Halifax, Nova Scotia
Mallard	1936	1936-1940	352	Steel/screw/motor	Torpedoed off Portland
Philomel	1936	1936-1957	2,115	Steel/screw/steam	Sold to Italo Groce Spa, Italy
Plover	1936	1936-1961	352	Steel/screw/motor aft	Transferred to Great Yarmouth Shipping Co; scrapped 1961 after collision
Bullfinch	1936	1936-1963	432	Steel/screw/motor aft	Sold to Commodore Shipping Co, Guernsey
Crane	1937	1937-1964	785	Steel/screw/motor	Sold to Fatis Georgopoulis & Partners, Piraeus
Stork	1937	1937-1941	787	Steel/screw/motor	Torpedoed off Spanish coast
Heron	1937	1937-1956	2,373	Steel/screw/motor	Transferred to Moss Hutchison Line and renamed *Kufra*; sold to Lebanese owners 1957
Goldfinch	1937	1937-1962	454	Steel/screw/motor aft	Sold to Allen Shipping, Alderney
Kingfisher	1938	1938-1940	276	Steel/screw/motor	Torpedoed off Beachy Head
Alouette	1938	1938-1966	276	Steel/screw/motor	Sold to M Cugilinas-Kalkasinas, Thessalonika
Drake	1938	1938-1966	531	Steel/screw/motor	Sold to Emmanuel Mashichiade, Piraeus
Oriole	1939	1939-1962	489	Steel/screw/motor aft	Sold to L Gagne, Matane, Canada
West Coaster / Mallard	1938	1943-1964	361	Steel/screw/motor aft	Ex-British Isles Coasters Ltd; renamed *Mallard* 1950; sold to ARC Marine, London
Mallard	1944	1944-1948	377	Steel/screw/motor	Transferred to Great Yarmouth Shipping Co and renamed *Norwich Trader*; sold to Greek owners in 1965
Kingfisher	1944	1944-1961	493	Steel/screw/motor aft	Sold to Puddister & Bennett Shipping, St John's, Newfoundland
Lapwing	1944	1944-1967	921	Steel/screw/motor aft	Scrapped after collision in the Thames
Petrel	1945	1945-1967	921	Steel/screw/motor aft	Sold to Thor. Jensen, Oslo
Stork	1945	1945-1966	493	Steel/screw/motor aft	Sold to M Cugilinas-Kalkasinas, Thessalonika
Peregrine	1941	1946-1961	890	Steel/screw/motor aft	Ex-F Class standard dry cargo coaster, *Empire Spinney*; transferred to Great Yarmouth Shipping Co; sold to D Vassilates, Greece, 1965
Greenfinch	1940	1946-1966	398	Steel/screw/motor aft	Ex-*Caribe II*, S G Hallstrom, Amsterdam, 1940; ex-*Empire Daffodil*; sold to G M Moundreas & Bros, Greece
Mavis	1946	1946-1966	381	Steel/screw/motor aft	Sold to Greek owners
Corncrake	1946	1946-1967	629	Steel/screw/motor aft	Sold to Canadian owners
Redstart	1946	1946-1967	629	Steel/screw/motor aft	Sold to Dimitrios Apesakis, Greece
Ringdove	1912	1947-1950	958	Steel/twin screw/steam	Confiscated German tonnage, ex-*Titania*, A Kirsten, ex-*Empire Conexe*; scrapped
Woodwren	1912	1947-1953	973	Steel/twin screw/steam	Confiscated German tonnage, ex-*Timandra*, A Kirsten, ex-*Empire Confal*; converted to coal hulk *Artemis* on sale to Sandfords
Albatross	1943	1947-1958	1,925	Steel/screw/steam	Confiscated German tonnage seized at Kiel, ex-*Weserstrom*, North German Lloyd, ex-*Empire Galena*; sold to National Shipping Lines of South Africa

Name	Built	GSN Service	Gross Tons	Hull/Propulsion/Engine	Comments
Sheldrake	1944	1947-1958	1,925	Steel/screw/steam	Confiscated German tonnage seized at Flensburg, Ex-Njong 1945, Ex-Empire Garland; sold to Johal Navigation Ltd, Costa Rica, Liberian flag
Teal	1947	1947-1963	1,148	Steel/screw/motor aft	Sold to D Frampton & Co., St John's, Newfoundland
Laverock	1947	1947-1965	1,209	Steel/twin screw/motor	Sold to Greek owners
Seamew	1947	1947-1966	1,220	Steel/twin screw/motor	Sold to Adamantios Bonsses & Co, Piraeus
Ptarmigan	1948	1948-1963	959	Steel/screw/motor	Sold to Anglo-Yugoslav Shipping Co
Woodcock	1948	1948-1964	959	Steel/screw/motor	Sold to Anglo-Yugoslav Shipping Co
Grebe	1948	1948-1967	933	Steel/screw/motor	Scrapped
Robin Redbreast	1930	1949-?	157	Steel/screw/motor	Ex-Constance H, J Harker Ltd, Knottingley
Auk	1949	1949-1965	1,238	Steel/twin screw/motor	Sold to Southern Steamships (London), Greek flag
Hirondelle	1950	1950-1966	757	Steel/twin screw/motor	Sold to Lake Shipping Co, St John's, Newfoundland
Swift	1950	1950-1966	757	Steel/screw/motor aft	Sold to Losinjska Plovidba, Yugoslavia
Ortolan	1945	1951-1958	522	Steel/screw/motor aft	Ex-Empire Seabright, Empire 'F' Type Far East wartime standard ship, 1945, ex-Helen Seabright, Overseas Fish Import Co, Great Yarmouth; transferred to Great Yarmouth Shipping Co; sold 1958 to Cia de Navegacion de Jorge SA, Panama
Tern	1953	1953-1964	1,028	Steel/screw/motor aft	Sold to Demosthenes Navegacion SA, Panama
Whitewing	1953	1953-1965	1,102	Steel/screw/motor	Sold to Anglo-Yugoslav Shipping Co
Adjutant	1954	1954-1966	1,366	Steel/screw/motor	Sold to Yugoslavian owners
Ringdove	1954	1954-1967	1,102	Steel/screw/motor	Sold to Cove Shipping Co., Bahamas
Gannet	1956	1956-1968	923	Steel/screw/motor	Sold to H B Clyde-Lake, St John's, Newfoundland
Woodwren	1954	1956-1969	968	Steel/screw/motor aft	Ex-Eddystone Clyde Shipping Co; sold to Losinjska Plovidba, Yugoslavia
Woodlark	1956	1956-1969	933	Steel/screw/motor	Sold to MoD, London
Sandpiper	1957	1957-1966	916	Steel/screw/motor	based at Marchwood as static vessel for stevedore training
Heron	1957	1957-1969	920	Steel/screw/motor	Sold to Paturel Frères, St Pierre and Miquelon, Canada
Swallow	1947	1961-1967	1,413	Steel/screw/motor	Sold to Reliable Caterers Ltd, Torquay
Philomel	1956	1961-1968	1,661	Steel/screw/motor aft	Ex-Texelstroom, Hollandsche Stoomboot Maatschappij NV; sold to Greek owners
Sheldrake	1956	1963-1968	1,661	Steel/screw/motor aft	Ex-Manchester Venture, Manchester Liners; sold to Mediterranean Lines, Haifa
Oriole	1963	1963-1977	430	Steel/screw/motor aft	Ex-Manchester Vanguard, Manchester Liners; sold to Mediterranean Lines, Haifa
Ortolan	1964	1964-1978	430	Steel/screw/motor aft	Sold to Boston Offshore Maintenance Co
Plover	1965	1965-1971	486	Steel/screw/motor aft	Sold to Boston Offshore Maintenance Co
Albatross	1965	1965-1976	654	Steel/screw/motor aft	Sold to Ramsey Steamship Co, Isle of Man
Avocet	1965	1965-1976	653	Steel/screw/motor aft	Sold to Downlands Shipping Inc, Monrovia
Petrel	1965	1965-1978	450	Steel/screw/motor aft	Sold to Cypriot owners
Marsworth	1952	1965-1969	628	Steel/screw/motor aft	Sold to De Groot & Veenstra, Panama
Blisworth	1957	1965-1970	1,031	Steel/screw/motor aft	Ex-Briar Rose, Hughes Holden Shipping, 1954; transferred from Great Yarmouth Shipping Co; sold to Yugoslavian owners
Dorset Coast	1959	1973-1978	1,225	Steel/screw/motor aft	Sold
					Ex-Coast Lines 1971, ex-Coast Lines (Services); transferred to P&O Ferries (General European) and sold to Egyptian owners in 1979

General Steam Navigation Company - Excursion Steamers

Name	Built	GSN Service	Gross Tons	Hull/Propulsion/Engine	Comments
Little Western	1841	1843-1876	431	iron/paddle/steam	Sunk in collision off Gravesend following conversion to coal hulk
Albion	1848	1848-1887	338	iron/paddle/steam	Scrapped
Prince of Wales	1843	1849-1880	246	iron/paddle/steam	Ex-Margate Steam Packet Co; scrapped
Eagle	1853	1856-1888	325	iron/paddle/steam	Scrapped
Sir Walter Raleigh	1858	1862-1891	239	iron/paddle/steam	Scrapped
Hilda	1862	1869-1889	428	iron/paddle/steam	Ex-*Cornubia*; hulked 1887; scrapped
Hoboken	1873	1877-1897	413	iron/paddle/steam	Ex-Adler Line 1875; Ex-HAPAG; sold
Halcyon	1887	1887-1906	553	steel/paddle/steam	Sold to South of England Steamboat Co 1905; repossessed and resold to Hamburg Stade Atlander Linie
Mavis	1888	1888-1909	537	steel/paddle/steam	Sold to Pockett's Bristol Channel Steam Packet Co
Oriole	1888	1888-1912	484	steel/paddle/steam	Sold to Dutch owners as a hulk
Laverock	1889	1889-1908	470	steel/paddle/steam	Sold to Compagnie Maritime Bordeaux-Ocean, Bordeaux
Philomel	1889	1889-1908	564	steel/paddle/steam	Sold to Furness Railway Co
Eagle	1898	1898-1929	647	steel/paddle/steam	Scrapped
Kingfisher	1906	1906-1912	982	steel/screw/steam turbine	Sold to owners at Trieste and renamed *Venezia*, sold on to Hong Kong owners within the year
Golden Eagle	1909	1909-1951	793	steel/paddle/steam	Scrapped
Crested Eagle	1925	1925-1940	1,110	steel/paddle/steam	Bombed at Dunkirk
Royal Sovereign	1893	1929-1930	727	steel/paddle/steam	Ex-Royal Sovereign Steamship Co; scrapped
Royal Eagle	1932	1932-1950	1,539	steel/paddle/steam	Laid up; scrapped 1954
Isle of Arran	1892	1933-1936	313	steel/paddle/steam	Ex- Williamson-Buchanan Steamers; scrapped
Laguna Belle	1896	1935-1939	617	steel/paddle/steam	Ex-Belle steamers *Southend Belle*, ex-East Anglian Hotels; requisitioned
Royal Daffodil	1939	1939-1967	2,060	steel/twin screw/motor	Scrapped
Crested Eagle	1938	1947-1957	245	steel/twin screw/motor	Ex-*Royal Lady*, sold to Magro & Zammit, Malta
Royal Sovereign	1948	1948-1967	1,850	steel/twin screw/motor	Sold to Townsend Thoresen
Queen of the Channel	1949	1949-1968	1,472	steel/twin screw/motor	Originally registered as owned by New Medway Steam Packet Co; sold to Greek owners

New Medway Steam Packet Company

(Also owned the passenger launches *HRH Princess May*, *New Medway*, and *Rochester City Belle* as well as tugs and barges)

Name	Built	NMSP Service	Gross Tons	Hull/Propulsion/Engine	Comments
Princess of Wales	1896	1919-1928	163	paddle/steam	Ex-Medway Steam Packet Co; on charter to Stanley-Butler Steamship Co 1925; scrapped
City of Rochester	1904	1919-1941	235	paddle/steam	Ex-Medway Steam Packet Co; scrapped
Audrey	1897	1922-1929	203	paddle/steam	Ex-Tyne General Ferry Co 1910; ex-City of Cork Steam Packet Co 1913; ex-Cork, Blackrock & Passage Railway 1914; ex-Captain S J Shippick 1922; scrapped
Medway Queen	1924	1924-1963	318	paddle/steam	Sold to Messrs Forté

Name	Built	GSN Service	Gross Tons	Hull/Propulsion/Engine	Comments
Queen of the South	1891	1924-1932	298	paddle/steam	Ex-Belle Steamers *Woolwich Belle* 1922; ex-Channel Excursion Steamers; scrapped
Essex Queen	1897	1925-1946	465	paddle/steam	Ex-Belle Steamers 1921; ex-PSM Syndicate 1923; ex-RSS Co *Walton Belle*; sold to South Western Steam Navigation Co, Totnes.
Queen of Thanet	1916	1927-1948	792	paddle/steam	Ex-HMS *Melton* 1927; sold to Southampton, Isle of Wight & South of England Steam Packet Co
Queen of Kent	1916	1927-1948	798	paddle/steam	Ex-HMS *Atherstone* 1927; sold to Southampton, Isle of Wight & South of England Steam Packet Co
Queen of Southend / Thames Queen	1898	1928-1947	522	paddle/steam	Ex-Belle Steamers 1921; ex-PSM Syndicate 1923; ex-RSS Co 1926; ex-*Yarmouth Belle* East Anglian Steamship Co 1928; Renamed *Thames Queen* 1938; scrapped
Rochester Queen	1906	1932-1933	255	screw/steam	Ex-*Gertrude* London, Midland & Scottish Railway; sold to H Bland & Co., Gibraltar
Clacton Queen	1897	1933-1935	399	paddle/steam	Ex-*Duchess of Kent*, Southern Railway; sold to Mersey & Blackpool Shipping Co
Royal Daffodil	1905	1934-1938	465	screw/steam	Ex-*Daffodil* 1919, Borough of Wallasey; scrapped
Queen of the Channel	1935	1935-1940	1,030	screw/motor	Bombed at Dunkirk
Royal Sovereign	1937	1937-1940	1,527	screw/motor	Mined in Bristol Channel
Rochester Queen	1944	1948-1955	345	screw/motor	Ex-*LCG(M) 181* 1948; sold to German owners

Moss Hutchison Line

Name	Built	MH Service	Gross Tons	Hull/Propulsion/Engine	Comments
Endymion	1909	1934-1935	887	steam reciprocating	Built for J & P Hutchison; sold
Memphis/Smerdis	1917	1934-1938	1,033	steam reciprocating	Built for J & P Hutchison; renamed *Smerdis* 1935; sold to Moroccan owners
Assiout	1918	1934-1935	4,215	steam reciprocating	Built for Moss Steamship Co; sold
Philotis	1918	1934-1935	1,037	steam reciprocating (aft)	Built for J & P Hutchison; sold to British & Continental Steamship Co., Liverpool
Amarna	1919	1934-1935	4,195	steam reciprocating	Built for Moss Steamship Co; sold
Esneh	1919	1934-1948	1,931	steam reciprocating	Ex-*Western Coast*, Coast Lines; bought by Moss Steamship Co1922; sold
Etrib	1919	1934-1942	1,943	steam reciprocating	Ex-*War Shannon*, completed as *British Coast*, Coast Lines; bought by Moss Steamship Co 1922; torpedoed in homeward Gibraltar convoy
Ardenza	1920	1934-1946	933	steam reciprocating	Built for J & P Hutchison; sold to Wm Cory & Son
Landes	1920	1934-1935	1,276	steam reciprocating	Built for Moss Steamship Co; sold
Lormont	1920	1934-1935	1,276	steam reciprocating	Built for Moss Steamship Co; sold

Name	Built	GSN Service	Gross Tons	Hull/Propulsion/Engine	Commentss
Chloris	1921	1934-1935	1,197	steam reciprocating (aft)	Built for J & P Hutchison; sold
Hatasu	1921	1934-1941	3,198	steam reciprocating	Built for Moss Steamship Co; torpedoed in Atlantic
Procris	1924	1934-1950	1,320	steam reciprocating	Built for J & P Hutchison; scrapped
Fendris	1925	1934-1950	1,309	steam reciprocating	Built for J & P Hutchison; sold to German owners
Kantara	1925	1934-1941	3,273	steam reciprocating	Built for Moss Steamship Co; sunk by gunfire west Atlantic
Kheti	1927	1934-1951	2,650	motor ship	Built for Moss Steamship Co; sold to Mossgiel Steamship Co, Glasgow (John H Bruce & Co, managers)
Sardis	1928	1934-1954	970	steam reciprocating	Built for J & P Hutchison; sold
Busiris	1929	1934-1948	943	steam reciprocating (aft)	Built for J & P Hutchison; sold to Kyle Shipping Co
Kana	1929	1934-1952	2,743	steam reciprocating	Built for Moss Steamship Co; sold
Kavak	1929	1934-1940	2,743	steam reciprocating	Built for Moss Steamship Co; torpedoed in Atlantic
Kufra	1929	1934-1940	2,608	motor ship	Built for Moss Steamship Co; sunk in collision in Gibraltar convoy
Kyrenia	1925	1935-1937	2,486	steam reciprocating	Ex-*Nigerian*, United Africa Co; sold to Bristol City Line of Steamers
Meroe	1928	1935-1950	3,832	steam reciprocating	Ex-*Lafian*, United Africa Co; sold to German owners
Chloris	1910	1937-1945	1,180	steam reciprocating (aft)	Ex-*Corncrake*, GSNC.; caught fire and sank off Italy, later raised and refurbished as the Italian *Sarga*
Philotis	1926	1937-1940	880	steam reciprocating	Ex-*Grebe*, GSNC; sunk in collision
Lormont	1927	1939-1940	1,561	steam reciprocating	Ex-*Woodcock*, GSNC; sunk in collision off Humber
Memphis	1947	1947-1972	3,575	motor ship	Transferred to P&O General Cargo Division in 1971; sold to Sifonar Shipping Co SA, Panama (Greek flag)
Kantara	1947	1947-1971	3,213	motor ship	Sold to Cypriot owners
Karnak	1948	1948-1971	3,198	motor ship	Sold
Landes	1925	1948-1953	893	steam reciprocating	Ex-*Hirondelle*, GSNC; sold to the Torem Co, of Genoa
Lormont	1930	1948-1953	936	steam reciprocating	Ex-*Swift*, GSNC; sold to Cyprus Merchants Shipping Co
Amarna	1949	1949-1975	3,422	motor ship	Temporarily named *Assyria* on charter to Cunard 1967; transferred to P&O General Cargo Division in 1971; sold to Greek owners
Assiout	1949	1949-1973	3,422	motor ship	Sold to Greek owners
Kypros	1950	1950-1976	3,499	motor ship	Temporarily named *Aurania* on charter to Cunard 1967; transferred to P&O General Cargo Division in 1971; re-registered under ownership of P&O Steam Navigation Co, April 1976; sold August 1976
Tabor	1952	1952-1978	3,694	motor ship	Transferred to P&O General Cargo Division in 1971; reregistered under ownership of P&O Steam Navigation Co, 1971; sold to Greek owners
Kufra	1936	1956-1959	2,409	motor ship	Ex-*Heron*, GSNC; sold
Busiris	1961	1961-1962	24,268	steam turbine	Management transferred to Trident Tankers (P&O),
Melita	1971	1971-1979	2,686	motor ship (engines aft)	Transferred to P&O General Cargo Division 1971; registered under ownership of P&O Steam Navigation Co 1973; sold to Panamanian owners
Makaria	1972	1971-1979	2,686	motor ship (engines aft)	Transferred to P&O General Cargo Division 1971; registered under ownership of P&O Steam Navigation Co 1973; sold to Panamanian owners

Great Yarmouth Shipping Company

(also numerous smaller vessels and wherries – see footnote page 55)

Name	Built	GYSC Service	Gross Tons	Hull/Propulsion/Engine	Comments
Picardy	1920	1931-1953	320	steam reciprocating	Ex-R & J Park Ltd, London, 1923; transferred from GSNC; sold 1953 Barlow & Co, Dundee
Peronne	1917	1931-1946	207	steam reciprocating	Ex-R & J Park Ltd, London, 1923, transferred from GSNC; sold to Tay Sand Co
Yellowhammer	1928	1931-1948	217	steam reciprocating	Ex-Robin, 1929; transferred from GSNC, sold 1948
Norwich Trader	1908	1934-1942	217	steam reciprocating	Ex-Elemore, ex-Esparanto; mined off North Foreland
Goldfinch / Lynn Trader	1927	1931-1936	327	steam reciprocating	Ex-Vivoni, Leetham & Sons, 1929; transferred GSNC and renamed Lynn Trader; sold to A Tucker, Cardiff
Yarmouth Trader	1920	1934-1946	321	steam reciprocating	Ex-Ashdene, ex-Stertpoint; sold to Ramsey Steamship Co, Isle of Man
Lowestoft Trader	1934	1934-1962	311	motor ship (engines aft)	Sold
Boston Trader	1936	1936-1962	371	motor ship (engines aft)	Sold
Norwich Trader	1944	1948-1965	377	motor ship (engines aft)	Ex-Mallard, transferred from GSNC; sold to Greek owners in 1965
Yarmouth Trader	1946	1950-1959	945	motor ship (engines aft)	Ex-Friargate, Hull Gates Shipping Co; sold to Greek owners
Lynn Trader	1945	1951-1960	404	motor ship (engines aft)	Ex-Helen Fairplay, Empire 'F' Type wartime standard ship 1949, ex-Helen Fairplay, Overseas Fish Import Co, Great Yarmouth; sold to Fouad Hassan Hamza, Egypt
Norfolk Trader	1954	1956-1970	457	motor ship (engines aft)	Ex-Arbon, Dutch; sold
Ortolan	1945	1957-1958	522	motor ship (engines aft)	Ex-Empire Seabright,Empire 'S' Type Far East wartime standard ship, 1945; ex Helen Seabright, Overseas Fish Import Co, Great Yarmouth, 1951; transferred from GSNC; sold to Panamanian flag owners, 1958
Plover	1936	1960-1961	352	motor ship (engines aft)	Transferred from GSNC; scrapped 1961 after collision
Peregrine	1941	1961-1965	890	motor ship (engines aft)	Ex-Empire Spinney, 'F' class standard dry cargo coaster, 1946; transferred from GSNC; sold to D Vassilates, Greece

Grand Union (Shipping) Company

Name	Built	GU(S)C Service	Gross Tons	Hull/Propulsion/Engine	Comments
Marsworth	1925	1937-1949	368	steam reciprocating (engines aft)	Ex-Koningsdiep 1925, ex-Merwede; sold
Blisworth	1902	1940-1950	738	steam reciprocating (engines aft)	Ex-Kathleen; sold to Holderness Steamship Co, London
Eskwood / Kilworth	1911	1943-1950	791	steam reciprocating (engines aft)	Ex-Eskwood, Constantine Shipping Co 1943; renamed in 1946; sold to Fenchurch Shipping Co (Geo A Tom & Co, managers), London
Bosworth	1946	1946-1965	865	motor ship (engines aft)	Wrecked on voyage from Sydney, Nova Scotia, to Bonavista
Knebworth	1946	1946-1964	857	motor ship (engines aft)	Sold to Limerick Steamship Co, Ireland
Marsworth	1947	1949-1953	519	motor ship (engines aft)	Ex-Somersetbrook, Comben Longstaff, London; sunk in collision of Winterton, Norfolk
Marsworth	1952	1954-1965	628	motor ship (engines aft)	Ex-Briar Rose, Hughes Holden Shipping; transferred to GSNC
Blisworth	1957	1957-1965	1,031	motor ship (engines aft)	Transferred to GSNC

SHIP NAME INDEX

Abukir (1920) 78
Adjutant (1893) 29, 39, 41, 44, 121
Adjutant (1922) 49, 53, 59, 95, 123
Adjutant (1954) 73, 97-99, 101, 125
Adler (1938) 84
Aiglon HMS (1898) 43
Al Said (1922) 58
Albatross (1884) 23, 34, 51, 121
Albatross (1924) 53, 49, 59, 123
Albatross (1943) 84, 85, 124
Albatross (1965) 104, 113, 125
Albion (1823) 16, 118, 126
Alcantara (1927) 69
Alford (1863) 120
Alouette (1894) 19, 32, 42, 43, 46, 48, 121
Alouette (1920) 40, 53, 123
Alouette (1938) 63, 103, 124
Amarna (1919) 68, 70, 127
Amarna (1949) 72, 73, 128
Amsterdam (1950) 90
Antares (1967) 110
Araxes (1855) 67
Arbonne (1921) 49, 53
Ardanbhan (1880) 121
Ardenza (1920) 69, 127
Arno (1851) 119
Assiout (1918) 68, 70, 127
Assiout (1949) 72, 73, 128
Assyria (1949) 73
Asturias (1926) 69

Newcastle (1844)	119
Newhaven (1847)	14
nf Panther (1971)	114
nf Tiger (1972)	114
Nigerian (1925)	70
Nile (1849)	67
Niparound (1952)	95
Njong (1944)	84
Nora (1861)	20, 120
Norbank (1962)	110, 113
Norbrae (1962)	109, 110
Norcape (1979)	113
Norfolk Trader (1954)	97, 108, 129
Norland (1974)	113, 114
Norsea (1987)	114
Norstar (1974)	113, 114
Norsun (1987)	114
North Star (1930)	87
Norwave (1965)	106, 107, 113, 114
Norwich Trader (1908)	79, 129
Norwich Trader (1944)	79, 95, 129
Norwind (1966)	106, 107, 113, 114
Nottingham (1825)	7, 117
Nyroca (1918)	70
Ocean (1836)	9, 16, 118
Orcades (1948)	96
Oriole (1888)	25, 36, 126
Oriole (1914)	38, 41, 42, 44, 122
Oriole (1921)	47, 123
Oriole (1939)	63, 80, 124
Oriole (1963)	103, 106, 113, 125
Orion (1865)	120
Orontes (1849)	67
Orphis (1919)	71
Ortolan (1902)	34, 37, 42, 44, 45, 122
Ortolan (1920)	53, 80, 95, 123
Ortolan (1945)	95, 96, 125, 129
Ortolan (1964)	103, 113, 125
Osprey (1877)	23, 25, 39, 121
Ostrich (1860)	18, 20, 120
Panther (1851)	119
Patroclus (1854)	67
Pearl (1901)	121
Penestin (1921)	77
Penguin (1876)	18, 120
Pentland Firth (1920)	53
Peregrine (1891)	26, 27, 34, 21
Peregrine (1892)	27, 41, 42, 44, 45, 57, 121
Peregrine (1921)	49, 53, 123
Peregrine (1941)	84, 85, 101, 108, 124, 129
Peronne (1917)	53, 55, 87, 123, 129
Perth (1834)	119
Peter Pan (1965)	111, 116
Petrel (1876)	27, 39, 120
Petrel (1920)	47, 78, 79, 122
Petrel (1945)	80, 124
Petrel (1965)	104, 110, 111, 113, 125
Philomel (1889)	25, 30, 36, 126
Philomel (1916)	42, 44, 46, 122
Philomel (1921)	46, 48, 58, 59, 65, 78, 122
Philomel (1936)	59, 60, 64, 73, 87, 98, 124
Philomel (1956)	102, 108, 125
Philotis (1918)	69, 70, 127
Philotis (1926)	70, 71, 128
Picardy (1920)	53, 55, 123, 129
Pilot (1854)	17, 20, 119
Pinto (1928)	78
Pioneer (1854)	17, 119
Plover (1875)	120

Plover (1936)	101, 124, 129
Plover (1965)	104, 110, 125
Preston (1885)	29, 39, 121
Pretoria Castle (1948)	96
Pride of Hull (2001)	114
Pride of Rotterdam (2001)	114
Prince Albert (1937)	82
Prince Arthur (1896)	32
Prince Baudouin (1934)	79, 82
Prince Charles (1930)	82
Prince David (1930)	87
Prince Frederick (1825)	117
Prince Henry (1930)	87
Prince Leopold (1930)	82
Prince of Wales (1843)	16, 126
Prince Philippe (1939)	82
Prince Robert (1930)	87
Princess Alice (1865)	24
Princess Marie-José (1922)	82
Princess Maud (1933)	77
Princess of Wales (1896)	126
Princess Royal (1841)	16, 118
Prinses Astrid (1930)	82
Prinses Josephine Charlotte (1931)	82
Procris (1924)	69, 71, 128
Ptarmigan (1821)	53, 122
Ptarmigan (1891)	41, 44, 121
Ptarmigan (1948)	88, 125
Queen of Kent (1916)	61, 66, 78, 86, 94, 127
Queen of Southend (1898)	66, 87, 127
Queen of Thanet (1916)	61, 66, 76, 78, 86, 94, 127
Queen of the Channel (1935)	61, 66, 76, 77, 127
Queen of the Channel (1949)	94, 107, 108, 126
Queen of the Netherlands (1824)	7, 118
Queen of the South (1891)	127
Quickthorn (1967)	108
Rainbow (1837)	15, 16, 118
Rainbow (1872)	25, 27, 120
Rajaburi (1900)	53
Ramona (1828)	16, 117
Rapid (1820)	6, 7, 12, 117
Rathlin (1936)	79
Raven (1883)	27, 28, 121
Raven (1914)	38, 57, 122
Ravensbourne (1851)	119
Redstart (1880)	22, 43, 121
Redstart (1946)	84, 108, 124
Rhine (1849)	118
Richmond (1814)	5, 6
Ringdove (1912)	85, 95, 124
Ringdove (1954)	73, 98, 125
Rob Roy (1821)	30
Robin (1928)	55, 123
Robin Redbreast (1930)	125
Rochester Queen (1906)	127
Rochester Queen (1944)	87, 94, 99, 127
Roe Deer (1962)	109, 110, 113
Roek (1925)	49, 50, 76, 123
Rora Head (1921)	47
Royal Adelaide (1830)	9
Royal Daffodil (1905)	64, 66, 127
Royal Daffodil (1939)	63, 64, 77, 78, 86, 94, 107, 108, 126
Royal Eagle (1932)	4, 55, 56, 66, 126, 76-78, 86, 94
Royal Fusilier (1924)	52
Royal George (1830)	9
Royal Scot (1910)	52
Royal Scot HMS (1932)	78
Royal Sovereign (1822)	5-7, 12, 117
Royal Sovereign (1893)	36, 126

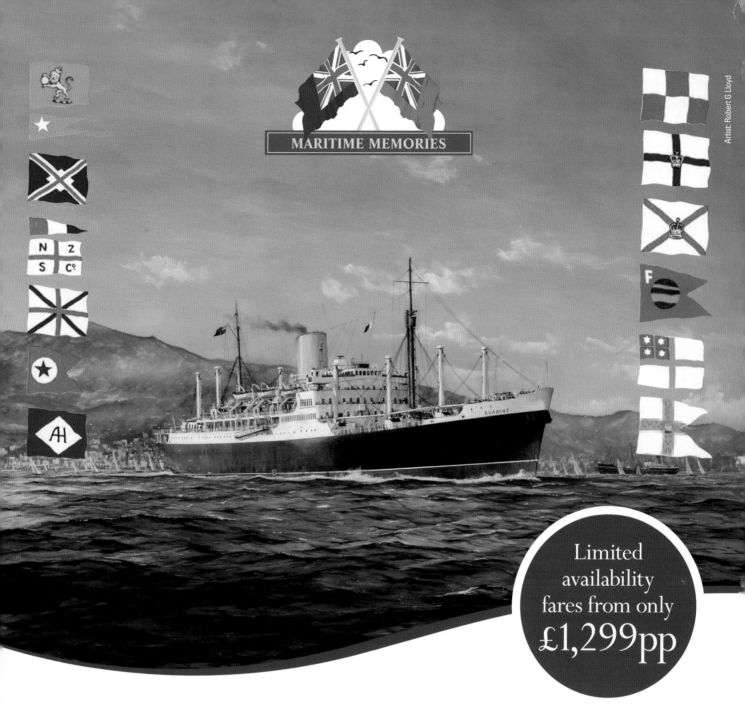

MARITIME MEMORIES

Artist: Robert G Lloyd

Limited availability fares from only £1,299pp

The world is full of extraordinary experiences. And Discovery is certainly one of them.

Take a Maritime Memories voyage to Europe, the Caribbean or South America. And return richer for the experience.

In association with

Voyages of Discovery

There are a lot of ships out there.
But there's only one Discovery.

The key to a cruise on *Discovery* is simplicity itself – see more, do more. So, you'll discover some of the great cities and monuments from the ancient and modern worlds. And along the way, you'll also share the stories and insights not everyone gets to see. Our renowned guest speakers unlock the secrets, whilst *Discovery* is the perfect way to get to any destination. It will be a voyage you won't forget.

A SHIP LIKE NO OTHER AND AN EXPERIENCE TO MATCH

Small enough to reach out-of-the-way ports, yet large enough to make light work of crossing the great oceans, *Discovery* avoids the excesses of today's mega-liners. Instead, she has been expressly conceived for our special brand of 'discovery cruising' to create an atmosphere on board that is friendly and relaxed. There are all the facilities you would expect on a ship of this size, including three restaurants, a choice of bars and lounges, two pools, a well-stocked library, lecture theatre/cinema and internet centre.

FAR FROM THE MADDENING CROWD

During your voyage, you will be accompanied by around 650 like-minded passengers and a highly-acclaimed team of guest speakers who will ensure that your time on board is as memorable as your time ashore. Complementing the talks given by our own lecturers, who will preview the destinations ahead, the programme features historians, explorers, naturalists and diplomats, who will share their expertise, anecdotes and interests with you.

IT'S WHAT WE DON'T HAVE THAT MAKES A REAL DIFFERENCE:

- Smaller ship – 650 passengers not 5000
- Not a casino in sight
- We don't just visit the main ports, we also visit the smaller 'off the beaten track' destinations
- We stay in a destination longer. So you see more and have more time to explore
- No hidden extras. All gratuities and service charges included

Voyages
of Discovery